In Search of the Rainbow's End

Colin Caffell is a sculptor and ceramicist who, in 1985, lost his ex-wife Sheila and their twin sons to the Whitehouse Farm Murders. He wrote *In Search of the Rainbow's End* in the wake of the press scrutiny that followed. Caffell later became a counsellor and workshop facilitator, specialising in the field of trauma and loss.

He now lives in the far west of Cornwall with his wife and their daughter, where they run their own art gallery. He is also an elected member of the Penwith Society of Arts in Cornwall.

In Search of the Rainbow's End

A Father's Story

COLIN CAFFELL

HODDER

First published in Great Britain in 1994 by Hodder & Stoughton
An Hachette UK company

First published in paperback in 1995
This new paperback edition published in 2020

3

A CIP catalogue record for this title is available from the British Library

Paperback ISBN 978 1 529 30916 4
eBook ISBN 978 1 529 30917 1

Typeset in Bembo by Hewer Text UK Ltd, Edinburgh
Printed and bound in Great Britain by Clays Ltd, Elcograf S.p.A.

Hodder & Stoughton policy is to use papers that are natural, renewable
and recyclable products and made from wood grown in sustainable
forests. The logging and manufacturing processes are expected to
conform to the environmental regulations of the country of origin.

Hodder & Stoughton Ltd
Carmelite House
50 Victoria Embankment
London EC4Y 0DZ

www.hodder.co.uk

To the two Hs
Heather and Herbie
– without whose love and selfless caring I may
never have survived the early days.

To Christine
– who has been too far away to share our
comforting embraces. Without her, we would
never have known my crazy, wonderful family
– Bambs, Daniel and Nicholas.

But my special thanks must go to Jill
– for sticking through the rest of it with me.

In portraits [of men] we must pierce without pity the innermost crannies of their souls, must strip them of disguise, lay bare the intemperate, even vicious passions that surge in them daily . . . But a portrait of a woman is another thing, their nature is not ours, we are far from grasping it, we must therefore be respectful and discreet. We must be circumspect in unveiling their tender and delicate mystery. Even with them, always the truth, but not always all the truth.

Sometimes we may, just a little, drop the veil.

Auguste Rodin, sculptor

Contents

Foreword to original 1994 edition

'CONGRATULATIONS! WHAT A *wonderful* opportunity you have been given.'

This somewhat surprising statement from a virtual stranger – a visitor to my home – followed my disclosure that seven years earlier, in the summer of 1985, my life had been completely devastated when my six-year-old twin sons, my ex-wife and both her parents had been killed during a short holiday at the parents' remote farmhouse home. Deaths were caused by numerous gunshot wounds.

Had somebody made such a remark when it first happened, I myself might have been drawn to commit murder but now, after what seems like a lifetime yet no time at all, I could accept and appreciate what this curious man was saying. I had been on a journey, a long painful journey of self-discovery, which eventually led me to doing therapeutic work in prisons with, amongst others, murderers and sex offenders; a journey that first took me back in time, inwards, to the shadowy realms of my own past; maybe even on what mythologist Joseph Campbell describes as 'the hero's journey'.

It certainly felt like an initiation – and one that is not yet over, because when it is finally complete, I will most likely not be here to tell the story; I will have drawn my very last breath and be resting with my sons in a quiet plot in London's Highgate Cemetery. But I feel it is time now to describe the adventure so far – a first episode.

When the shootings first happened, it was thought that my ex-wife, Sheila Caffell (Bambs) – an ex-model with a history of mental illness – had carried out the killings and then committed suicide. Within two months, however, following the evaluation of further evidence, her only brother, Jeremy Bamber, was arrested and eventually convicted of murder on all five counts – but not before his sister's reputation had been wrongfully, and disgracefully, dragged through the mud.

In an attempt to clear her name and put the record straight, I tried to publish my own observation of the events, but it was incomplete and premature; I hadn't even begun to comprehend what I myself was there to learn, or even that I had lessons, let alone begun what turned out to be the even more difficult and hazardous journey back to normality. But I also knew then that I was on the right track; the typical response to the earlier manuscript had been: 'Too personal, too sensitive, too harrowing' – exactly the qualities I had intended for a book which brought the very real possibility of murder and murderers into the fabric of any family – regardless of class or station. The story is still like that, if not more so, but with the addition of a more caring and understanding perspective.

Initially disappointed by the refusals, I eventually began to realise that, as an observer, I was still judging and blaming, still very much attached to those judgements and, most important of all, not owning my own part in the tragedy. This was understandable, in many respects, but I also had to accept some of the blame myself; still pointing a finger 'out there', at others, I had a long way to go. In retrospect, I don't think I was strong enough then to accept that responsibility, so, for the time being, I continued – a little wiser and holier, perhaps, but still with the old thought patterns intact.

Much has changed since then. If nothing else, my original script was still a success because it provided a container in which I could begin to explore all the pain, grief and fear I had experienced. By the same token, what I am writing now will provide the container in which to consolidate all I have learned and establish some meaning to everything that has happened. As one who has suffered very deep emotional wounding, I have learned a great deal about those wounds and scars that cannot be seen with the eyes.

Even though much of it revolves around the events of a mass murder, this is not a murder story. Nor is it another book on how to heal your life in five painless lessons. As an account of my own healing journey, it is written from a purely personal perspective, illustrating what worked for me; my own truth. Even though many of the problems and challenges I faced are universal, there are no hard and fast recipes for success, short of absolute self-honesty and a real will-ingness to try almost anything. Each of us is totally unique. For my part, I am not a psychologist, mythologist or philosopher, but simply an individual with a personal experience of life, a story. We all have our own stories – our own myths – and every one of them is worth sharing. This is mine.

Like many adventures or initiations, it didn't begin out of choice, with a willing step forward, but with a push and a terrifying fall into the abyss. It was only when I found myself in that deep dark place that the choices really began: whether to stay where I was, crying 'Poor me'; to climb back out to where I came from as quickly as possible; or to begin a homeward journey that initially took me onwards and deeper. Some of the book is, therefore, taken from the original manu-script and stands in its rawness. I couldn't even write that part now; it is peacefully buried in the past.

The real journey begins with the choices; some of them conscious, many unconscious and others, I later realised, had long been taken – but that is really moving too far ahead. What is most important is that even though aspects of the book move into the realms of psychology, it mustn't get lost in the kind of jargon that confused and almost scared *me* away when I first began trying to understand. Many of those concepts, free of such blinding encumbrances, are really quite simple and need not be so intimidating.

One thing I did begin to learn very quickly – and it's a premise that runs right through the story – is that the only thing one can really be sure of on such an excursion is that relevant events and encounters *will* happen. They may not be what we want but they will, without exception, be exactly what we need. The only attitude I had to acquire and maintain was that of expectancy. This is very different from having expectations; *they* tend to bring us in touch with all our 'unfinished business' (grief, frustration, disappointment, anger, etc.) quicker than anything – as I was to learn from repeated painful experience.

I also began to learn that all these experiences – including the deaths of my loved ones – were gifts, in that they helped me redis-cover and heal parts of myself that had been lost, stolen or simply hidden away earlier in life. It was only when I finally found the courage to step into the arena myself, as part of the drama, that the jigsaw puzzle really began to make sense. Many of the missing pieces were attached to my own fear and denial. In this sense this is very much a 'living manuscript', because I don't know, with any certainty, the final outcome. I only know where I am now, as I begin.

June 1992

Foreword to 2020 edition

> Home is where one starts from. As we grow older
> The world becomes stranger, the pattern more complicated
> Of dead and living. Not the intense moment
> Isolated, with no before and after,
> But a lifetime burning in every moment
> And not the lifetime of one man only
> But of old stones that cannot be deciphered.
>
> T.S. Eliot, from 'East Coker', *Four Quartets*

WHEN THIS BOOK was first published in 1994, there was, for me, a slight sense that even with the conviction of Jeremy Bamber on all five counts of murder, it was still in some way premature, that there was still more of the story to unfold. Nonetheless, the original had to be published when it was, in order to achieve its stated aim: to repair the reputation of a young mother, who was horribly wronged by a clumsy police investigation and a national press hungry to print any kind of story that they perceived as salacious.

Apart from a string of appeal attempts that were soon to follow, the rebuilding of my life was not as straightforward as I imagined. There were people in my life upon whom this story has also had a significant impact, who were not even on my horizon at that time and now need to be acknowledged: my second wife, and our daughter in particular, who have had to live with all the tensions that Jeremy's appeals threw up. They have also been a driving force in my determination to fully move on and draw a line under the whole episode.

Over the years, I have been approached by numerous authors and producers planning to make 'true crime' renditions about the shootings, but their motives never felt right to me. The approach by New

Pictures was very different. It was sensitive and respectful. They felt there was still an important story to tell, but knew that if they were truly going to get to the psychological truth – to understand why this tragedy happened in this family and get rid of any public doubts once and for all – my book and personal insights would be invaluable. While they were intent on making the series for ITV regardless of my involvement, I have been greatly encouraged by their determination to get it right. With this in mind, and the full support of a wonderful wife and daughter, I am now able to pick up the threads of the original book and finish the broader story.

It is very strange for me to revisit this almost a quarter of a century later, but I have wanted to do something to complete the story for a while now. With the TV production in progress, it feels like the time is right. Many might find it impossible to imagine how one can turn one's life around after such an event, so to relate my full journey now might once again begin to provide help and inspiration in its re-telling.

Colin Caffell
West Cornwall, 2018

Prologue

I HAVE OFTEN WONDERED, since everything happened, whether we are specifically prepared for the major, sometimes traumatic, events of our lives – or is it more a matter that, in times of emergency, we each have an inbuilt ability to draw upon those resources and experiences that make up our past, in order to survive? On the face of it, looking at my own childhood and upbringing, I wouldn't have thought either. I am reminded, however, that throughout both history and fairy tales, some of the most heroic characters were spawned in the least likely places. With that thought, I should perhaps say something about who I am. Or rather, who I was when the story began, where I came from and how my life had been shaped prior to the shootings.

I have very little recollection of that first home (a run-down terraced house near Regent's Park in London) except, perhaps, for the image of a small back garden in which there was an old butler sink that housed a pet frog called Billy. I also remember the day we set him free on Hampstead Heath. One minute he was there, in the box we had carried him in, and then he was gone – lost in the long grass. I didn't even see him go, nor did I understand why he had to go. It was as if, suddenly, he had never existed – that was how I saw it. I suppose that must have been my first experience of bereavement. It was certainly my first conscious memory; I also seem to remember that nothing more was said about it. Questions about sad or unpleasant things were rarely encouraged in our home but met, instead, with silence or awkwardness. I must have been about three years old then, because shortly after that we moved into a nearby block of council flats.

Like many people, most of my early memories of childhood are vague and lacking any sequence, yet punctuated with many significant events: like the time I pushed my sister, Diane, into Hampstead's Whitestone Pond. Apart from that day, and the inevitable scolding I received, the general colour was happy.

My parents, Doris and Reg, were a quiet, ordinary couple, rooted in the working class. My father, a television engineer in the days when televisions were still an innovation, was – and still is – a good-looking man, physically strong with a very dry sense of humour, so dry, in fact, one often couldn't tell when he was joking. Personal fitness and body-building, rather than team sports, were very much part of his youth. As the youngest of four brothers, he came along very late in his parents' lives, so, as he often remarked, he always saw them as 'old people'. My father also harboured a belief about himself, which he still carries, that he was both stupid and lazy. Having realised that I had taken on similar beliefs about myself, and also realising that I am neither, I can no longer accept this.

His father, William Caffell, a small 'hard' man, who was always quick to hit anybody who offended him, did whatever work provided an income and, as a result, travelled a lot. On one trip to South Africa, he worked as an overseer, or slave driver, at a diamond mine. He also wore a glass eye, having lost the real one working on the horse-drawn buses in London, when his horse kicked him in the face.

Grandad's main teaching to his sons, as I remember Dad relating to me, was 'never trust small men and queers', which I thought rather odd considering he was a small man himself. Unless of course he was making a statement of his own untrustworthiness; in psychological terms, he might have been projecting his own 'Shadow' (the inferior, unconscious parts of our own nature that we try to pretend don't exist) on others. I don't think my father, an honest and sensitive man, was very fond of him. Grandad died at the age of seventy-three, when I was only a year and a half old, so I have no conscious memory of him. My paternal grandmother, however, I remember well, because she lived with us until she was moved to an old people's home when I was about seven.

My memories of Nanny Caffell, a devout Methodist, are overwhelmed by an all-pervading smell of lavender. Not very mobile, she would always sit in her chintzy, cluttered little room – where Frank, her oldest son, visited her regularly – or in a large red armchair in the corner of our living-room. Her origins were more from the middle class, and hence an element of snobbishness also existed in the family. I had wondered how it got there. When my father first introduced Mum to her, as his intended, she had said, 'So you're the girl who will be looking after me in my old age.'

Needless to say, their marriage was fated from the start; they never had any real privacy. Nanny was the eyes and ears of our home. When she died at the age of eighty-six (when I was eight years old), I began to hear that Uncle Frank had announced that he had a different father to the rest of his brothers. Grandad had, apparently, taken my grandmother in, with her five-year-old, and, as they said in those days, 'made her respectable'. We never saw Frank again.

My mother, for the most part, worked as a cleaner, either in wealthy people's homes – most notably that of the Tory politician John Profumo and his movie-star wife, Valerie Hobson – or in offices. It had seemed as though she was the hardest working of my parents and brought in all the extra cash that was needed to pay for our little luxuries. So, whenever we were out shopping or on holiday, it always appeared to be Mum's purse that was opened.

Though a lifelong socialist, Mum also had a rather incongruous admiration for people like the Profumos and encouraged Diane and me to improve; for example, to speak well. I suppose that in itself stands as the first paradox of my childhood memory: I was always made to feel really special, but somewhere deep inside I felt the Profumos' children, and others like them, would always be more special. It was also inevitable – as a result of many years of wearing the expensive hand-me-downs of Mrs Profumo's son by her first marriage (many of my clothes bore the label 'Mark Havelock-Allan') and consuming the leftovers of lavish royal dinner parties that Mum often brought home – that I would begin to develop a taste for the finer things. I wanted some of that charmed life myself and felt special enough to expect it.

It is also somewhat ironical, bearing in mind my grandfather's time as an overseer in South Africa, that Caffell, our family name, had its origins in slavery. Apparently, an ancestor some seven generations back was part of the human livestock of one Sir Colin Campbell. This 'made-up' name was given to that ancestor along with his freedom around the turn of the eighteenth century. Knowledge of this was passed down through the women who married into the family – to my grandmother from Grandad's mother to my mother. The documentation, which Nanny Caffell had seen, went off down another branch of the family and is now lost to us.

It was later pointed out to me that the name itself was probably derived from the word 'coffle', a chain of neck manacles with which they used to shackle slaves together. Freedom had been given in one sense but, as I realised much later, the chain was never, psychically, removed from the neck. Here we still were, in the servants' quarters, with a mentality that both resented and yearned for those chattels that make up a 'boss'.

My own arrival into this world took place at home and, from what I gather, I was in such a hurry to get here, I didn't even wait for the midwife to come, so my father had to help with the delivery. This was my first real blessing and has always meant a great deal to me. Unlike many born in the postwar age, I was bonded to both my parents, not to technology – as those who are born in a hospital tend to be. I have also been told that, from a very early age, I possessed the devil of a temper, giving my mother a black eye long before I could even walk! It was also not an isolated incident and it took me almost forty years to work out why I was like that.

Apart from these occasional outbursts, I was basically very happy as a child, but showed little interest in the rough and tumble of boyish games like cowboys and Indians or football. I could tyrannise my family but not other boys. I was far too afraid of getting hurt. 'Doctors and nurses' with the girls always held a much greater appeal to me. Having said that, I also loved to go rowing with Dad on the lake at Regent's Park on a Sunday morning, while Mum cooked the dinner. Once he had taught me how to scull properly, we would hire the only two racing skiffs at the boathouse and have competitions to see who could get to the other end of the lake first.

Diane and I were in fact very lucky, because Dad always had time for us, supporting our interests and taking us on all kinds of excursions. Another thing he introduced us to that must have had a profound effect on my own interests and imagination, and my own sense of wonder, was the Walt Disney film *Fantasia*. Whenever it was showing anywhere, Dad always took us to see it. I must have seen that film at least a dozen times before I reached my teens and never tired of it.

At school, I was far from academic, but at the same time wanted to know everything there was to know about anything which took my interest – to be aware of all the beautiful things of nature around me. My hobbies were numerous and changed frequently as I accumulated collections of sea shells, crystals, butterflies, cacti and so on. I loved visiting old ruined castles and reading the myths of ancient Greece and Rome. Whatever the fascination, I had a remarkable memory for all the names and details. In fact, the only thing these hobbies had in common was that, in some way, they had a visual or tactile appeal, which served to fuel a creative imagination.

Like Parsifal in the Grail legend, I had been taught never to ask questions but simply to accept and respect, which is why I became such an accumulator of 'things'. Wisdom, I realise now, only comes in the light of understanding, *not* through acquisition. I have, for example, spent much of my life trying to understand women, through observation and acquisition, but was always afraid to ask questions; that has now changed.

In the main, I lived in my own little world of fantasy, totally unaware of what other people around me were doing. I certainly wasn't aware, as my sister was, that there were problems in my parents' marriage or even that we were fairly poor. I was always protected from anything of an unpleasant or traumatic nature. But that also had its downside in that I never learned how to stick up for myself and always relied on Mum or Diane to rescue me. I didn't really want to test my father on that, because something in me, even then, didn't feel he would be able to stand up to the threatened fight with another kid's father, in the 'my dad's tougher than your dad' stand-off. He was big enough and probably could but I didn't 'know' it, as other boys did.

I was seen by most people as a 'nice boy' – and still am, fundamentally, a good person – but if the truth be known, I simply felt ashamed if I drew any unfavourable attention. I also have to admit that I was spoilt rotten, because I was rarely made to do anything I didn't want to, like get a Saturday job. Whatever I did well was praised and encouraged. I received generous pocket money by most children's standards – which is how I learned to be good – and my earlier tantrums were quietly refined into the art of manipulative sulking. But I wasn't conscious of it in those terms then. I was, however, conscious of the fact that I had become a prime target for bullying – so I stayed indoors a lot.

At the age of eleven, I went to a comprehensive school in St John's Wood, where I continued to avoid academic life and spent as much time as possible in the art room. I was really very fond of school, as an institution, but somehow totally resistant to any formal academic work like mathematics and writing essays. The bullying continued.

At fifteen, like many teenage boys of my generation, I decorated my bedroom with dark paint, psychedelic posters and numerous pin-ups of naked women. It became a place my mother was loath to enter for fear of what she might find next. The Beatles had released *Sgt. Pepper*, Flower Power began to grow and open-air pop festivals sprang up everywhere. I took to wearing beads, bells and crushed velvet trousers, and my mother, seeing me 'dressed like that', would no longer walk down the street with me. I also had my first serious relationship, with a girl called Jill.

At this point, my O levels, along with all reason, went right out the window. I wanted to marry her – as I did with most of my subsequent girlfriends (to my conditioned adolescent mind, sex was only meant to happen inside a loving, married relationship; the body believed otherwise). After nearly two years, Jill walked out of my world – but not for ever. Broken-hearted, I took up a new hobby: scuba-diving, and for the first time in my life – eager to make the most of every foray into the deep – I even learned to control my breathing. Looking back, everything about me was controlled.

I finally left school shortly before my nineteenth birthday, with very few school certificates – which didn't surprise me or my teachers in the least – but by some extraordinary fluke and a lot of pushing from another girlfriend, Sandra, I got a place on the Foundation Year at Camberwell School of Art, where I went on to take an Honours Degree in Ceramics and Three-Dimensional Design. I had originally planned to study painting, but when I tried my hand at making pottery, sinking my hands in clay for the first time in years, I discovered a natural affinity with the medium and set off in yet another new direction.

It seems that providing I could see an application of my own (or the activity itself gave me pleasure), I could also nearly always master a subject to the level of my needs. Without such a focus, any attempt to teach me was futile. Both at school and art college, I had great trouble writing essays, because I really couldn't see the point in writing about something I would much rather be doing myself.

During my second year at art school, Mum and Dad separated, shattering my illusion that marriage, especially their marriage, was an invulnerable and sacred institution. My own engagement, to Sandra, was also soon called off; I was suddenly scared of where my life was going and had to re-evaluate what I thought were the very foundations of my existence. Little did I know then that this was just scratching at the surface.

In an attempt to maintain something of our family ritual, and ease both mine and my father's confusion, I learned to cook; especially the Sunday roast and apple pie that were the most loved of my mother's specialities.

Mum had met and moved in with Bernie, the office manager of a firm of solicitors at which she worked, and when I first saw them together, I realised she had found a happiness I had never seen in her before. Very soon they had set up a business collecting, buying and selling antiques – a hobby Mum had never really honoured at home. Six months later I met Bambs.

For me, it was love at first sight. In that enchanted moment, across a smoke-filled Hampstead pub, I had found my fairy-tale princess. Had it not been for the presence of Chris Precious, an old friend of less inhibition, I may never have even spoken to her, but out of his carnal desire for her companion, we were brought together. Bambs was not only a stunning beauty – with the biggest grey-blue eyes I'd ever seen – she seemed totally unaware of the fact, which made her all the more attractive. I was now twenty-one years old. She was seventeen and a student at St Godrick's Secretarial College, a very expensive local finishing school.

I found Bambs surprisingly easy to talk to considering my horrible self-consciousness in such situations. I had always believed that the Venuses of this world – and Bambs was one of them – would never bother to speak to mere mortals like myself, but here I was finding another of my illusions crumbling. She was, to me, more beautiful than *all* the girls in my wildest dreams and fantasies – some of which I was having at that very moment. The thought of dating her seemed little more than such a fantasy.

Two days later, on the most wonderful Tuesday lunch-time of my life, Bambs and I sat outside a café laughing, joking and generally getting to know each other. I was completely captivated by her lively, bubbly character. Unlike the dumb-blonde stereotype, she was brunette, but my early impressions were of a girl who loved to talk even if, half the time, she didn't understand what she or anybody else was talking about. With the playful innocence of a child and a delicious naïvety enhanced by sheer enthusiasm, she liked to share her experiences with everyone she met.

Every coin, however, has two sides, and because of this guileless and trusting nature, I began to feel she also had little concept of right and wrong, which appeared to include a limited capacity to learn from her mistakes. Even on our first date, she told me of several episodes in which she had found herself in situations with people who might well have taken advantage, totally unaware of the danger in which she had placed herself. But it was her exasperating innocence in telling the following story that really caused me to shudder.

When she was about sixteen and at boarding school, she would often 'bunk' out of dormitory after lights out and go into Norwich with some of her classmates. On one occasion, when she was on her own, she decided to save her bus fare and hitch a lift back to school some miles out of town. It wasn't long before she was picked up by a man who, during the drive, started to tell her how she shouldn't be out alone after dark and so on. Halfway back to the school he turned down a side road, stopped the car and proved to be the very kind of man he had warned her about.

She, to her credit, kicked up a good fight and called him a dirty old man who ought to know better than to try it on with a girl young enough to be his daughter. On this occasion she was extremely lucky. The man restarted his car and drove the rest of the way back. What really amazed me was that she was more angry than frightened by this incident. It never occurred to her that she might well have come unstuck.

Even on that Tuesday lunch-time in 1974, I felt Bambs was a girl who would always need looking after and I, for my part, believed I could do it – a naïve assumption in one who hadn't yet learned to look after himself properly. But that's the way of youth. It's strange, we hadn't even held each other or kissed at that point, but I somehow knew that our lives and future were already deeply entwined. Our second date was everything I dreamed it would be. A world of fragrant and sensual delights blossomed as we discovered that wonderful, almost frightening, intensity of new love; where just a touch or idle caress would fire up a desperate search for somewhere to be alone. Without a doubt, we were hooked!

So that was the beginning of our relationship; our life together was an endless run of intense passions and stormy differences – pathos, pain and wonder. A second pregnancy (the first having been terminated six months into our relationship while I was still a student) led to our wedding. With my encouragement, Bambs had by then become a model and I, with hers, an advertisement sales executive. Art school had fulfilled my need for a qualification and training, but couldn't support the expense of a wife and child – well, that was *my* excuse. I, basically, didn't have the courage or strength of character to make a go of it as an artist.

Sadly, within weeks of our marriage, Bambs miscarried. Desperate to put it behind her, she accepted two months of gruelling work in Tokyo, which further crippled her emotionally. After much trauma and another miscarriage, she finally fell pregnant with the twins. By then, unfortunately, our relationship had deteriorated to the level of mutual abuse and accusations. We no longer saw each other in the form of radiant supernatural beings, but as ogre and witch. We were reduced to screaming at each other and eventually parted a few months after the boys were born. I still loved Bambs dearly, but found it impossible to live with her any longer. There were even times we could have killed each other; violence was just below the surface.

It may appear that I have skipped rather rapidly through our life together, but that is only because I will be returning to relevant episodes later on. Without a doubt, I came off the better after our separation, because I had met and fallen in love with Jan Flowers, another model and only daughter of a well-known bass player. In fact, meeting Jan made it easier to leave Bambs, who, on the other hand, struggled – no matter how much help she was given. Her whole life had been an endless battle against domestic expectations, family responsibilities and moral constriction. In my failure to face my own share of these, I dumped the whole lot back in her lap.

Our two boys, Daniel and Nicholas, came off best, because they gained, in Jan's family, an extra set of grandparents, a very nurturing surrogate mother and an uncle who played the drums. In the eyes of many, one couldn't have met a more likeable and well-balanced pair of children; they lived every moment of their lives to the full and brought a light into my existence that has been hard to let go of or surpass.

Jan and I stayed together for the next four and a half years and, with a lot of help from her father, Herbie, I returned to making pottery. These were some of the happiest years of my life, the conclusion of which was really heralded by Bambs's first breakdown. For Jan, it was the straw that broke the camel's back and we moved rapidly towards our own separation. She had endured Bambs's constant telephone calls and domestic problems for several years and now, only months before beginning a new career, training as a nurse, there was the likelihood of Nicholas and Daniel moving in permanently. At the age of twenty-two, Jan suddenly saw her career, youth and freedom flying out the window and had to make a break. It was now my turn to feel devastated.

Bambs had never been an easy person to live with, but now her emotional condition had become increasingly erratic. Away from Jan,

I began to spend more time with Bambs, developing a supportive friendship in the hope of helping her heal. But it seemed a losing battle. No matter how much all the medication brought about improvement, her condition always deteriorated rapidly on visiting Whitehouse Farm, or after contact with her direct family – especially her mother.

A second breakdown, in March 1985, precipitated the boys coming to live with me full time. Having said all that, Bambs had a marvellous relationship with them and was always very caring in the most instinctive way. A close friend of hers once described her as more like 'a lioness with her cubs – playful'. Her greatest pressures were not from motherhood itself, but from those *outside* that sacred bond with her sons.

It has troubled me for some time that certain aspects of what I need to say about the Bambers might distress those who knew them. I have come to the conclusion, however, that the very nature of Bambs's humiliation in print, through the inordinate defence of their reputation, has left me little alternative. If, in addition to this, anything can be learned from this tragedy to help prevent even one other family from suffering what we all went through, then it has been a most worthwhile project. My intention is no longer to blame or judge, but to try and understand.

So what was going on, who were the family and why did they have such an effect on Bambs's illness? Naturally, I can only offer – both here and in the rest of the book – my own subjective impressions.

I made my first visit to Whitehouse Farm – the family home in the small Essex village of Tolleshunt D'Arcy – a few weeks after Bambs and I met. She had already told me that her parents, June and Nevill Bamber, were comfortably wealthy, well-respected country folk, who liked to enjoy the image of a local squire and his wife. I must admit, I was quite nervous of meeting them at first, because Bambs had painted such a formal picture of them. I also wasn't sure how they'd react to me – a long-haired art student from a north London council estate.

I was pleasantly surprised, however, by their warmth and hospitality. I could see what Bambs meant about them, but I was immediately made to feel welcome and at ease in their home. I didn't meet her brother Jeremy then, because he was away at boarding school in Norfolk at the time. I also didn't know, at this stage, that both children were adopted.

My first impressions of Nevill Bamber were ones I maintain to this day. He was the kind of man for whom one had instant respect and affection. At six foot, four inches, he was a big man in every sense of the word – almost aristocratic. His sun-tanned skin, fine stature and physical presence told you he was a man of the land; yet his deep-set, clear blue eyes reflected not only his background and 'breeding', but also a rich sense of humour and wisdom, which made him instantly approachable. In addition to farming, he also held the added responsibilities of Justice of the Peace (and, more recently, Chairman of the Juvenile Panel), parish councillor and church warden.

Mrs Bamber, on the other hand, was a quiet, nice-looking lady with a pleasant disposition; a woman who, although very active within the community, preferred to take a back seat role to her 'husband's' (June never referred to him as Nevill) activities.

Most of the family on June's side were of farming stock but Nevill, Bambs believed, was from a far more upper-class background and, as far as I know, was the only member of his family to join the farming community. His father was a Pay Commander in the Royal Navy, of whom Bambs knew very little; however, she had a lot to say about his mother.

As an elegant Edwardian society lady, Granny Bamber had a strict and formal attitude to her grandchildren and always scared the life out of Bambs, who remarked that when her father was a child, he virtually had to make an appointment to speak to his parents. Nevill was absolutely devoted to the old lady and made regular weekly visits to her home, on the other side of London, in Surrey.

Born in June 1924 in Cranleigh, Surrey, he was christened Ralph Nevill Bamber; Nevill being his mother's maiden name. His childhood days – apart from those spent as a boarder at Christ's Hospital School in West Sussex – were filled growing up in a large townhouse in the grounds of Guildford Castle. He had two older sisters, Diana and Audrey, of whom he was very fond. In addition to the house in Guildford, the family had a large apartment in London's Bayswater, where Nevill and his sisters spent much of their youth – especially after their father died. Staying in London after that made life much easier for their mother, as she not only had to bring up three children alone, but also ran Asters, an exclusive clothes shop in Beauchamp Place, in Knightsbridge.

In September 1941, at the age of seventeen, Nevill joined the Royal Air Force. Like many who served, he talked very little of his experiences during that great ordeal. He was a fighter pilot for practically all of his service career. His record card shows him as T/Sergeant Pilot IID, flying with Nos. 13 and 55 Squadrons, both of which were used for army support. As the only outward memento of this period, Nevill still displayed the emblem of No. 13 Squadron on his office wall.

The only thing Bambs ever remembered him saying about his war experience was that he fought in North Africa, flying Hurricanes, and had been shot down late in the confrontation, leaving him hospitalised for about two years with serious back injuries. Apparently the only reason he shared this information with his children was to proudly account for his remarkable skills in knitting; something he learned as an occupational therapy during his long stay in hospital.

Apart from the loss of many friends during the war years, tragedy was to hit Nevill several times during his life. His sister Audrey, who married an RAF Squadron Leader, Reginald Pargeter, died of meningitis in January of 1949, leaving two small children, Anthony and Jackie. Their father, a geologist in peace time, travelled a great deal, so Nevill became a surrogate father to the Pargeter children.

Nevill's other sister, Diana, who looked remarkably like Bambs, carved a successful career as an international public relations consultant to British Airways, then BOAC, and made quite a name for herself promoting safaris and big-game parks in East Africa for them. She also helped organise the East African Safari Rally. Sadly, this is also where life was to end for this stunningly photogenic woman; on 12 March 1968, she was being driven round the course, carrying out a final inspection, when they were caught in a heavy rainstorm and the car hit a stationary lorry. She died instantly.

On 4 September 1947, almost six years after joining the Air Force, Nevill was demobbed and went straight to the Royal Agricultural

College at Cirencester, from where we finally begin to hear more of this very gregarious, sporty young man. His leisure hours were usually spent playing practical jokes, tennis and inventing games involving large quantities of gin and tonic. Apart from this, it goes without saying that he also worked extremely hard. It was his nature. Just to prove his wartime injuries didn't trouble him, he was often seen to lift loads as heavy as any other man on the farm.

June was also born in the summer of 1924, on the 3rd of June, only five days before Nevill. Her parents, Mabel and Leslie Speakman, lived at Vaulty Manor Farm, near Goldhanger in Essex, and were of a long line of Speakmans who farmed in the area. Like her mother, June was also born at Vaulty Manor and grew up there with her older sister Pam.

It would be safe to say that they had a comfortable, rural upbringing, typical of the farming community at that time. Brought up with traditional Christian standards, they were taken to Goldhanger Church every Sunday with their parents. June had a good voice and loved singing so much that, when the war started, she eventually joined the choir. Church was always followed by an 'excellent Sunday lunch' of roast beef, Yorkshire pudding, roast potatoes and Brussels sprouts. Their mother was considered an extremely good cook. And so she had to be; it was not uncommon for Mabel to cater for anything between twenty-two and twenty-eight people at lunch on Christmas Day – a skill both daughters were expected to master.

As a child, June was a wonderful dancer, starting classes when she was about three years old. At five, she went to a local private school, followed by Maldon Grammar, a few miles away, at eleven. Both girls were taught to play tennis and hockey from the age of about ten and, as her sister Pam once pointed out, 'Our parents found time to teach us and play with us. They taught us a wonderful sense of sport; "Enjoy the game, play for the fun of it" .' All in all, Pam remembered with some affection, 'We had a wonderful childhood,' and remarked on the values they grew up with.

'Kindness – honesty – truth were especially impressed on us by Mother and Father,' said Pam. 'We always knew Mother and Father loved us and never knew what it was to be jealous. We were always encouraged to go to them for advice if we were worried or uncertain about anything. Such a lot of love and caring went into our family life; each one of us loved and cared for each other.'

On leaving school, June took a job at the War Office as a secretary, then joined the First Aid Nursing Yeomanry, better known as 'the Fannies'. During this time, she went to India. After the war, life in Essex soon got back to normal; tennis and beach parties resumed, and Pam, now married to a farmer called Robert Boutflour, was expecting their first child. It was on one of these weekends that June and Nevill met for the first time. It wasn't long before love blossomed and their engagement was announced. They were married on 3 September 1949 at St Peter's Church in Goldhanger – after Nevill had graduated from college. The reception was held in a marquee on the lawn at Vaulty Manor Farm; they were the 'perfect couple'. But things began to go wrong.

Having failed to produce any children during the first eight years of their marriage, June and Nevill approached the Church of England Children's Society, from where they first adopted Bambs (christened Sheila Jean) in 1957, and then Jeremy in 1961.

If the Bambers had expectations of those children, both Bambs's and Jeremy's lifestyles as young adults caused them great concern. Rather than marrying someone in the professions or the farming community – as Pam and Bobby's children, David and Ann, did – Bambs fell in love with a penniless art student and began a career as a photographic model. Jeremy, in his turn, did everything he could to avoid a life on the farm. Having picked up poor O level grades at school and technical college, he took to travelling the Far East and working as a cocktail barman – his natural good looks and breeding only exacerbating a taste for the playboy lifestyle. Almost simultaneously, Mrs Bamber turned increasingly towards the Church for guidance. Finally, in 1979, very shortly after the twins were born, she was hospitalised and treated for major depression.

To be fair to June, this also happened to coincide with Nevill bringing his very elderly mother to be cared for at Whitehouse Farm. June was, by that time, already making daily trips to Vaulty to look after her own equally elderly mother. Rather than complain or attempt to spread the workload, she allowed it all to become part of the cross *she* had to bear. But others suffered the consequences: although many would not consider it excessive, over the years June had begun to preach her committed beliefs to all and sundry – especially to her own family.

In time, however, this became a bone of contention for many of those involved, including myself, and, I suspect, was a major contributing factor in not only Bambs's tragic illness, but her own earlier breakdown. Like my own family, anger and feelings were never openly expressed by Nevill and June, with the inevitable result that the children were like a box of firecrackers waiting to explode at the slightest provocation.

Apart from the obvious disparity in social background, how then are we any different – if at all – and why have my own family not suffered a similar psychological collapse? Or have we?

Many of the answers I discovered, some years later, in the writings and workshops of Elisabeth Kübler-Ross MD – one of the world's leading authorities on grief and loss (with whom I went on to do the prison workshops) – others in the writings of C.G. Jung and Alice Miller. But these were only guidelines. The most significant answers, for me, came from inside; from that part we all have within that seems to know everything.

In sentencing Jeremy Bamber, the judge described him as 'evil almost beyond belief'; but what, I have to ask myself, made him become that person? Can someone be born truly evil or are there other factors to bear in mind? Bambs's illness had been used as a cover to hide Jeremy's tracks, but why was she ill in the first place, and had Jeremy been equally disturbed by the same circumstances? Adopted quite separately, they were not natural brother and sister, so the convenient excuse of a congenital illness is out of the question. So what was it that caused a young man to turn a gun on his entire family, and could I myself be driven to doing something just as terrible? I cannot believe the answer to the first part of my question is quite as simple as it was made out to be at the trial. There was, in my opinion, far more than greed involved.

At the bottom line, this is very much a story about feelings, because I believe the tragedy of the Bamber murders is all about them – or rather, about their repression and inadequate expression. It was the awful climax of events brought about by families – including my own – divorced from and refusing to acknowledge or respect the emotional side of their lives, of which I carry my part. The world is full of people refusing to acknowledge their feelings, full of tragedies caused by the alienation of feelings. This book is, in many different ways, about facing and honouring them.

PART ONE

The Fall

CHAPTER ONE

There is a pain – so utter –
It swallows substance up –
Then covers the Abyss with Trance –
So Memory can step
Around – across – upon it –
As one within a Swoon –
Goes safely – where an open eye –
Would drop Him – Bone by Bone.
                                    Emily Dickinson

IT WAS JUST after midday on Wednesday, 7 August 1985, that I went to answer an unexpected ring on the doorbell – I was about to make lunch for myself. At the front door were two young policewomen.

'Mr Colin Caffell?'

'Yes.'

'Do you know Sheila Caffell?'

'Yes, she's my ex-wife. What's wrong?'

'I'm afraid we have to tell you that she's dead.'

Those words caught me completely off guard.

'Oh no, then she finally did it!' I said, almost thinking out loud.

With Bambs's recent history of mental illness, the possibility of suicide rang horribly true, but I didn't have a chance to think or ask questions. The policewoman went on:

'Are you the father of Nicholas and Daniel Caffell?'

'Yes,' I said, feeling a terrible panic rising inside me. I didn't want them to say anything else.

'I think we had better go into your flat, where it's more private.'

I then noticed that my neighbours had opened their door a chink. Once inside, we went to my living-room, and the dark-haired police-woman vanished into the kitchen.

'Mr Caffell, I'm afraid I have to tell you that both your sons, Daniel and Nicholas, are also dead. There has been a shooting at a farmhouse in Essex; there are also two other adults dead . . .'

That sickening moment will remain in my memory for ever. It was like a great, heavy blanket had been thrown over me . . . dragging me down. Suffocating. Sounds became thick and muffled. I had been thrust through a doorway into an airless place where time seemed to stand still . . . For the first time in my life I screamed out 'God help me!' – and meant it.

But I don't know if I screamed in this world . . . I really can't remember. If I did, it was somehow lost in an unbearable emptiness of eternity. A huge part of me died that lunch-time – was burnt away to nothing – vaporised. C.S. Lewis spoke of 'vanishing like an ant in the mouth of a furnace'. Only a person who has been there really knows how it feels.

I had never felt so alone.

As I looked up at the bookshelf, at the school photograph of Daniel and Nicholas together, everything blurred as tears filled my eyes.

Only minutes earlier, I had been sitting in my kitchen quietly working on design ideas, thinking about our coming holiday (a visit to my sister in Norway), totally unaware that my whole world was about to collapse around me.

I couldn't believe it was all happening. My entire being spun into a fast-forward, slow-motion blur, shock and anguish rushed at me from every direction. All concepts of time and reality ceased to function as normal, yet I can remember it all with such remarkable clarity. A thousand futile questions flooded my mind. How did it happen? Did Bambs do it? Could she have done it? Why? What could have pushed her to do such a thing?

At first it seemed most obvious that it was her, but when they said about the twins, something didn't quite make sense. My beautiful sons, did they know what was happening? God, what has happened? Who were the other adults? Was it her parents, June and Nevill, or was it her brother, Jeremy, and his girlfriend, or somebody else altogether? I was confused.

'I'm sorry,' said the policewoman, 'but we don't have any more information.' The other one came back in and gave me a mug of very sweet hot tea. They also offered me a cigarette, which I refused. The woman I had been talking to put her arm around me, as I just stared blankly through the tears. She asked if there was anybody that I would like them to call, to come with me, because they would have to take me to Essex. The person I most wanted to be with me was my girlfriend, Heather, so I gave them her number.

I couldn't believe what I had just been told, it was so unreal. I don't know about your own life flashing before your eyes, the twins' lives flashed before mine. All the fun and happiness, all the laughs and giggles, the tears. The bony cuddles, the tempers, and bedtime stories that went on for hours – some really wonderful things.

And my poor Bambs. I felt so sad for her. What did she go through? So gentle, such an innocent child herself.

'Can't you tell me any more at all?' I said. 'What about the children, can't you tell me any more about them? Did they know anything about it, were they aware of what was happening or were they asleep?' I had this horrific picture in my mind of the boys standing shivering with fear, watching the bloodshed, having to watch each other die. 'Did they know what happened? It can't be true what happened.'

The women in uniform didn't know. The only information they had was that there were five people dead, three of whom appeared to be Bambs and the boys. Their only instructions were to bring me to Essex. 'They will need you to identify the bodies.'

'NO! No, I can't! I don't want to see them like that. I want to remember them as they were!'

Quickly changing the subject, they asked if I had the boys' birth certificates. I had, so I went downstairs to find them. One of them followed me. I was completely numb – lost – the world I had known had changed, but it didn't look any different. When I returned, the school photograph had gone from the bookshelf. They had taken it.

For the next ten, twenty or maybe even thirty minutes, everything was a haze – dark-blue uniforms came and went. A squad-car driver called Rocky introduced himself and told me he would be driving me part of the way to Essex – I was still talking to him when Heather arrived. The moment she saw my face, her worst fears were confirmed and she took me in her arms and held me very, very tight . . .

'I heard it on the radio as I was driving over here.'

'What, already!' I said. What had she heard? I wanted to know who the other adults were. Heather then told me that the news bulletin had reported a farmhouse shooting in Essex involving a magistrate, his wife, daughter and two grandsons; no names were given. The report added that the police saw it as four murders and a suicide. She said she couldn't believe that it was Nicholas and Daniel at first, but in the circumstances had a horrible feeling it had to be.

If it had been on the radio, I realised, it wouldn't be long before my parents heard. At this, I finally came to my senses and asked if they could send someone round to break the news to my father when he got home from work; and could we please stop by my mother's near London Bridge, so that I could at least break it to her in person. 'I can't tell them over the telephone,' I said, 'and I certainly can't risk them finding out from the news on television, or anything like that.'

The nightmare got worse . . .

'I'm very sorry,' said Rocky, 'but we've had orders to take you straight to Essex, and London Bridge is out of our way. It would take far too long.' He could, however, put out a call for someone to go and speak to my father. As I gave him the address, I stressed that whatever happened, my father had to be told properly, by a police officer as I had been. Being on his own, Dad would need a lot of support. My pleas for them to take me to my mother's first were met with their full sympathy, but they 'had their orders'.

It didn't seem to matter what I asked, they couldn't tell me what I needed. All my requests were ignored and it felt like I was screaming at a brick wall. I really couldn't see what difference it would make where we went first, it was all too late; everybody was dead and no amount of hurrying was going to bring them back.

It was suggested that Heather and I pack a bag each, just in case we had to stay overnight. But I had no intention of staying over – my only thought was to get back to what was left of my family, that evening! I couldn't believe how we were being pushed around, and consequently became far more distressed than was necessary. As if it wasn't bad enough being broken such terrible news, to also have my liberty threatened was more than I could bear.

All of a sudden, Heather snapped into gear and I saw a forceful side to her I had never seen before. We had known each other about a year, during which time she played a major part in helping my under-standing of Bambs's condition. Having seen her own mother consumed by similar problems, her knowledge of psychology and family dynamics often made me feel very uncomfortable. Although outwardly soft and gentle, her quiet conviction that Bambs might just drown in a sea of other people's beliefs about her, including my own, was definitely not what I wanted to hear. She could also see me strug-gling with thoughts of pulling Bambs back into the comparative safety of my own somewhat water-logged environment. In my endeavours to sort all this out, both women had become invisible.

Right then, however, Heather was far from invisible. She told the police that it was all very well them being in such a hurry to get us to Essex, but what about getting us home again? 'We're not going anywhere until we've been given a firm guarantee that we will also be driven back to London, this evening.'

Minutes later we were given the assurance and went to the car.

That drive was terrifying; we raced out of London at what seemed like ninety miles per hour, siren screaming and blue light flashing, jumping red lights and forcing other vehicles out of the way. Anyone would have thought they were rushing to prevent a bank robbery. The only time they slowed down and switched off the siren was, ironically, when we got stuck behind a funeral procession going through some roadworks. We were in some kind of a race. They even had a clock set to time the drive as we hurtled along the M25 to meet a car from Essex Police.

It was hot in the back seat of the car. My throat was dry and I felt I couldn't breathe. Heather said I was delirious. I began saying all sorts of mundane things in a futile attempt to pretend none of it was happening; only to be dragged back to the truth and thoughts of poor Jeremy who had lost everyone – his whole family: mum, dad, sister, nephews – everything. In that state of mind, my thoughts drifted back to the previous weekend and the last time I had seen them all alive . . .

* * *

After the success of their sixth birthday party, in late June, the twins and I thought it would be great fun to have another one, for all of us – a kind of summer house-warming. Entertaining was something all three of us loved, plus Daniel and Nicholas had a lot of 'grown-up' friends they hadn't seen for some time. We also thought it would be nice to invite Bambs, because she had not yet met any of the people we often talked about; it would also be a chance for her to see a few of the old faces. The boys had been living with me since her second breakdown, five months earlier.

Bambs was delighted when we invited her, so I then asked if she would like to invite her brother and his girlfriend. I hadn't seen much of Jeremy since our separation and thought I might be able to get him to help me convince his parents that their money might be better spent on Bambs having a different kind of psychiatric treatment to that she'd been receiving. Apart from her feeling almost constantly sick, because of the heavy tranquillisers she had been prescribed, Bambs had been generally very unhappy with the doctor her parents had found for her.

For some strange reason, Bambs didn't seem very keen to speak to her brother when she telephoned him. In fact, rather than talk to Jeremy herself, she handed the receiver straight over to me when he answered. This came as a bit of a surprise, because, only months earlier, she had said how pleased she was that Jeremy had finally found a nice steady girlfriend and was settling down a bit. I could only put this strange reaction down to her monthly injection. But it still worried me none the less; Bambs was beginning to display those familiar long periods of becoming distant and vague again. In fact, it was one of the main reasons for inviting her along; I thought it might do her good to get out of her normal surroundings.

Bambs had asked if she could help us with the preparations, so, on the day of the party, Daniel, Nicholas and I set off fairly early to collect her. It was lovely with just the four of us there, getting things ready, as a family. It was almost the first time this had ever happened.

While Bambs and I prepared the food and cleaned up, Daniel and Nicholas were busy tidying their room and putting the finishing touches to their 'museum and art gallery'. They had planned to charge guests a small entrance fee to their room, then sell them badges and pictures they had made on the way out. It was really Daniel's idea to try and make some money so that he could catch up with younger brother Nicholas, who was far better at saving. Daniel was always losing his pocket money or giving it to his mum because he thought she needed it more.

While we were waiting for people to arrive, Bambs told me that she had spoken to her parents about not being happy with her treatment, but their attitude had still been that they knew best and that they had absolute faith in her existing psychiatrist.

'That's preposterous!' I said, getting really angry about it, adding something to the effect of: 'You're the one being treated and if you can't relate to your doctor – and don't feel safe with him – then he's no good for you. You really mustn't let them keep pushing you around like this. It's about time they stopped treating you like a child and giving you that "we know best" attitude; it doesn't do you any good. [She was now twenty-eight years old.] You must try and stand up to them, because it's almost as if they've broken your spirit!' I then suggested that I would speak to her father when I next saw him. Hopefully I would get a chance when I dropped her and the boys off at the farm the following day.

Little did I realise then – nor would I have accepted such an observation had it been pointed out to me – that I was also doing exactly what I had been accusing June and Nevill of. This was a lesson I was to have thrust upon me time and time again in the future, until I finally understood it; that we often get angriest or most upset at those injustices or hurts we ourselves are most guilty of inflicting. Or, transversely, that we ourselves have suffered.

When Jeremy arrived, later that evening, his silhouetted figure at my front door sent a cold shudder through me before I switched on the hall light and recognised him. It was one of those spontaneous gut feelings that I hadn't yet learned to take notice of and wish now that I had. In all the years I had known Jeremy, it was something I had never experienced on seeing him before. And there *had* been times we were quite close. In many ways, during his early teens, when Bambs and I were first together, I was much like an older brother to him; a relationship in which he took up a number of my own hobbies and interests: growing cacti, for example. We even used to visit the Royal Botanical Gardens at Kew together, to collect any cuttings that might have fallen off the plants, given a little help. Scuba-diving was another thing he later took up.

In those early years, prior to his travels, I had always remembered Jeremy as a brash and arrogant youth, abrasive and full of his own self-importance in his juvenile attempts to emulate his father's natural air of authority. He also teased his parents relentlessly, especially June; dyeing his well-groomed hair all sorts of colours, just to wind them up. The more they reacted, the more he did it. On this occasion, he had dyed his hair and eyebrows black (his natural colour being brown), but his dark demeanour had the effect of being theatrically sinister, rather than making him look like someone who was trying to keep up with fashion trends. It also somehow added to my uneasiness.

During the party, Bambs had very little, if anything, to do with him or his girlfriend, Julie, and sat talking quietly to some of her old friends and new people like Jan's father, Herbie, who had turned up unexpectedly after a long visit to Australia. The boys were over the moon at him being there and, as usual, were having a whale of a time talking to everyone and eating all the goodies – obviously planning on a very late night.

Shortly before midnight, Bambs came up to me and said she was very tired and wanted me to see about getting her home. The fact that I had been drinking meant that I couldn't drive her myself, and I was about to call a cab when I thought her brother might be willing, having not yet drunk much. Bambs's reaction, again, was strange – almost unbelievable between a brother and sister. She seemed really nervous of Jeremy, even frightened, and asked me to ask him for her.

Anyway, Jeremy drove Bambs home and on his return we got into conversation about her illness. As we talked, however, I realised that he seemed to know much less than I thought he might, as he pressed me for further information. So I told him all about how I had been looking into alternative forms of treatment for her, specifically Jungian psychotherapy, and explained how his parents had said they couldn't afford any more. Jeremy's response was that this was absolutely ridiculous, his parents were 'loaded' and money was no problem for them. They had recently borrowed a considerable sum from the business to pay for both Bambs's and his mother's treatment and there was plenty more where it came from. Mrs Bamber had begun treatment with the same psychiatrist several years earlier, prior to Bambs.

In Jeremy's opinion, his parents' attitude was all down to the fact that they had very little respect for me or my ideas and 'treated me like dirt', or at least thought of me in that context. I knew that I hadn't come up to their expectations as a son-in-law, but this still came as a bit of a shock. He then went on to suggest that, right from the start, I had always had a raw deal with regards his family. For example, the way in which Bambs and I were 'bludgeoned into marriage' when she became pregnant; his sister being a 'difficult and selfish person'; my having to look after the twins so much because she was 'incapable', and, finally, being left as a full-time single parent. These were all his words.

When Jeremy told me that he saw the boys as a 'millstone' round my neck, I pointed out that this was far from the truth; the twins were not only my sons but my closest friends, and being a full-time parent was my own choice – something I thoroughly enjoyed.

Jeremy just couldn't see it that way and went on to talk about how his parents had been trying to push him and Julie into marriage using similar methods of financial coercion as they had on us.

When Bambs and I got married (she was then pregnant for the second time), it wasn't because we felt we had to – we were already living together in stylish squalor and planned to have our baby that way – but June and Nevill, in fear of what people might think, offered to buy us a flat, wherever we liked in London, on condition that we got married and as quickly as possible.

'We're not doing it for you,' they said, 'we're doing it for the child.'

Apart from responding to the obvious guilt trip, the offer became very appealing and we eventually turned our backs on our instincts and found a small garden flat in Hampstead. It was probably one of the biggest mistakes we ever made; by accepting this tempting carrot, we seemed to lose control of our destiny; we had sold our souls, as it were. Although we were very grateful for their gift, I began to feel resentful and belittled by it – as Bambs was aware – because I hadn't worked for it myself. The flat was never really like our own, because there were always those strings attached.

Having reluctantly agreed to get married, Bambs was then denied her dream of the full traditional white wedding in the local church – as all her cousins had enjoyed – with the reception in a marquee on her parents' lawn. June's immediate reaction had been, 'Not in *my* church, you don't!' Bambs and I stared in disbelief at these words; Nevill shuffled uncomfortably but didn't intervene. Having offered to buy us somewhere to live, they probably couldn't afford both, but to Bambs it was another rejection, another judgement that she wasn't 'good enough', that she wasn't really one of them.

Our wedding was held, instead, at Chelmsford Registry Office, to which she was driven in her father's car – rather than a limousine, which would have been far more suitable for a full wedding dress; the reception was held at a motel, some miles from the village, and her dress, which was cream, was another judgement and public state- ment; her mother had refused to pay for a white one. Added to that, my own mother didn't even come; she had to look after Bernie, my stepfather, who wasn't well.

According to his own account, for Jeremy and Julie things hadn't changed much, except it was now the Bambers' own son that was being emotionally castrated.

Daniel, who said he was feeling a little tired, had, by this time, gone for a short lie-down and was in fact fast asleep. Nicholas, however, insisted on having a bedtime story, which Julie offered to do. He was very fond of Julie and really pleased when she said she would make one up especially for him. Daniel didn't wake up for it. Not long after that, Jeremy and Julie left.

Looking back at that party, I could only remember it as a lovely happy night, yet sad because it was the last evening Daniel, Nicholas and I ever spent together; one of the few times I hadn't told them a bedtime story myself. It was such a special time; an evening of meet- ings, reunions and partings – an unconscious farewell to Bambs and the boys.

At about four o'clock on the following afternoon, we picked up Bambs at her flat in Maida Vale and drove to Essex. As on the previous evening, she was very quiet. In fact, Bambs said very little during the entire journey. The boys were still talking excitedly about the party, but Daniel was also beginning to worry about their visit.

It had been planned some months earlier for the twins to visit the farm for a week before we went to Norway. June and Nevill had been pressing for them to come down for a holiday with their mother. I wasn't completely happy about this, but without more concrete reasons, I couldn't really refuse. I'd had this nagging fear about the visit – a gut feeling that they shouldn't go – but I put it all down to June's religious excesses and the fact that Bambs's own mental condition always deteriorated when she spent time with her mother – nothing else. It was only because I had been assured that the whole family would be there that I finally agreed to it. As it was, the boys wanted me to come with them, to have a word with June about the proselytising and her shouting at them if they didn't eat their meat.

Apart from the fact that since they had been living with me Daniel had decided to become a vegetarian, I'd had serious cause to confront June about her forcing the twins to kneel and say prayers at every opportunity. She didn't take kindly to my correction.

'You will remember to have a word with Granny about the prayers and everything, won't you, Daddy?' shouted Daniel from the back seat of our very noisy Volkswagen Camper.

'Yes, of course I will. Now don't worry about it.'

'Do you promise?'

'Yes, I promise. And besides, Mummy will be there with you to make sure, once I've said something, won't you, Bambs?'

She was absolutely miles away and, if she was listening at all, certainly didn't follow or take in anything I had said. I was beginning to wonder if I was doing the right thing by allowing this holiday. But then what harm could come to them? The whole family would be around most of the time and, once I'd had a word with June and Nevill, things should be OK. So what was troubling me, why didn't I want them to go? For some reason, which I couldn't fathom out, it was still against my basic instincts to leave them there. But what could I do? We were on our way now.

When we got to Whitehouse, Daniel and Nicholas, who were both refusing to leave my side, reminded me once again about my promise. So I explained to June and Nevill how the twins were feeling about everything – especially about being forced to say prayers all the time. They listened but I could see that June was having a very hard time not retaliating. Daniel cringed when Nevill started making a joke about him being a vegetarian.

'You don't eat meat!' said Nevill, laughing. 'You've got to eat some meat, boy, or you'll never grow up big and strong like your grandpa. You'll never be a farmer if you don't eat your meat.'

Poor Daniel, he didn't know what to say. In desperation he looked at me for support. I assured them he was quite serious about it and that they must respect his wishes – I had been the same at his age. Nothing more was said.

After supper, they asked me if I wanted to stay the night, but I told them I needed to get going because I was expected elsewhere. Bambs, who had said very little since our arrival, looked very disappointed. I had, once again, chickened out of talking to them on her behalf. I avoided her eyes.

When I went to leave, the twins' feeling of insecurity was so strong, it would be difficult to express how tightly they hugged me to say goodbye. They had never acted like this before. It was the most desperately strong embrace I can ever remember them giving me. They threw themselves into my arms with such force, wrapping their arms and legs around me so tightly, I could hardly breathe. I found it so hard to leave them, they were almost crying as they buried their faces in my neck. I didn't want to go.

It was almost as if they knew it would be the last time we would ever see each other and didn't want that moment to end.

CHAPTER TWO

ALMOST EXACTLY HALF an hour after leaving Kilburn in north-west London, a drive which would normally have taken me an hour, we arrived at the change-over point. Rocky handed over my documents and left us with the policeman from Essex. The second part of the drive was much slower, even unhurried. When I asked our new driver exactly where we were going, he said he was taking us to a house in Head Street, Goldhanger.

'That sounds like Jeremy's place,' I told Heather.

When we arrived, Jeremy came out to meet us, his face pale and grief-stricken. I hugged him and with tears in my eyes said, 'Don't worry, Jem, you've still got me as your family. I'll be a brother to you from now on.'

He quickly confirmed my suspicions about Bambs by starting to tell me all about an argument at his parents' house the previous evening. Before Jeremy had finished, someone ushered us into the house saying something about the press hanging around in the neighbourhood. Inside we were greeted by two of Jeremy's cousins, David Boutflour and his sister, Ann Eaton. They were very sympathetic, but obviously most uncomfortable and upset themselves. David left almost immediately and Ann started to make herself busy in the kitchen.

In the living-room we met Jeremy's girlfriend, Julie, and a young detective constable, Michael Clark, who had been in the middle of taking Jeremy's statement. While Ann made the tea, Jeremy asked if we would like something stronger and got us each a glass of whisky. I don't normally drink the stuff, but at that moment it tasted very good and helped to ease the pain and turmoil in my head.

I was desperate to know why *they* thought Bambs had done it and asked Jeremy to tell me everything he knew about it all. Sitting on the sofa, he told me that the family conference after supper the previous evening had been about Bambs's abilities as a mother; that his mother and father had told her they didn't think she was capable of looking after the twins any more – especially in her current mental state. They had said they were going to make arrangements to take custody of the children from her and place them with a young Christian family as foster-parents, in a nearby village. By doing that, it would also enable them to see a lot more of the boys themselves.

'That's ludicrous!' I said. Although I wouldn't put it past them to try. They wouldn't have been able to do it! Didn't they know that Bambs and I had joint custody of the twins and, in the present circumstances, they would have had to take custody of them from me. Even then, I could more than prove myself a competent father. Jeremy reminded me of our conversation at the party, when he had told me that his parents had never had a lot of respect for me.

'The bloody fools!' I said. 'It's only because of your mother's religious mania frightening the twins so much that I had to restrict their visits lately.' If June and Nevill had said something like that to Bambs in the condition she was in, I could almost understand her doing something desperate; just to protect her children, to save them from what would have appeared to her as a fate worse than death. 'Bambs could see as well as I what sort of religious monster your mother was. Oh, what a bloody mess!'

Jeremy agreed, adding that things got pretty heated before he left them to it, but Bambs had just sat there, not saying anything, staring into space.

'Before you go any further,' I said, desperate to put my mind at rest, 'does anybody know if the twins were aware of what was happening? Nobody has been able to tell me so far.'

'Perhaps I can answer that,' said the young detective, speaking up for the first time. 'I was one of the first to go into the house. We found the old gentleman in the kitchen and then went upstairs where we found your wife and her mother. I looked in the other bedrooms and saw your two little boys in bed. They looked like they were asleep. In fact, one of them still had his thumb in his mouth. I actually thought they were asleep.'

'That would have been Daniel with his thumb in his mouth,' I said eagerly, hoping he was going to say that they were all right after all. The detective went on and said that he thought he would leave the boys to sleep a bit longer, so that the bodies could be covered up before waking them. It was only when he went in a little later and looked more closely that he realised they too had been shot. He then assured me that from the way they were lying, it looked as though they would have been asleep when they died. There was no doubt in his mind that they knew nothing that had happened. Heather and I were both crying again, but this time with some relief; we thanked him for telling us.

When I asked Jeremy to continue his story, he went on to tell us that after the row blew up he left the house and went straight home for the rest of the evening. At about 3.30 a.m., he received a telephone call from his father, who had 'blurted out' quite clearly, 'Sheila's gone berserk and she's got a gun!' Then the line went dead. At this point, Jeremy turned to the detective and said, so that everyone could hear, 'I still feel that my father was already wounded at this point; I really feel that.' He then went on to say something like, 'He sounded very distressed, as if he had already been shot.'

When we asked Jeremy what happened next, he told us that he rang the police straight away and drove to Whitehouse as fast as he could. The police had told him not to try and enter the house, but to sit tight and wait. When he got there, the police had already arrived. They didn't know whether it was a siege situation or if anybody was still alive, so they had to be cautious and wait. At one point, somebody (Jeremy, I think) thought they saw a movement at a window, so a firearms squad was also called.

They then waited for another three hours until about 7.30 a.m. before the police were, finally, satisfied it was safe to go in, Jeremy being told to wait where he was. I felt terribly sorry for him, having to wait outside all that time – not knowing. I couldn't imagine what it must have been like and was thankful I had been told when it was all over.

'I feel like I am partly responsible,' said Jeremy. 'I had been out shooting rabbits yesterday afternoon and when I came in for supper I didn't put my gun away. I left it out on the side. So through my neglect, Sheila must have seen it as a sign or something and used the gun.'

I had sat and accepted everything I was being told so far, but this was one thing I just couldn't make sense of at all. I know for a fact that Nevill was a very cautious and safety-conscious man. He would never have allowed any gun to be left lying around with children in the house, and it wouldn't have escaped his attention for more than a few minutes. Refusing to accept this point without question, I put it to Jeremy, who said that this was what he had thought. He then suggested that in the heat of the argument, they had all overlooked it. In retrospect, the row Jeremy had described between his parents and Bambs sounded like a one-way dispute and therefore couldn't have been very heated.

Someone, I don't know if it was the policeman or Jeremy, then started to tell me the details of how everybody had been found, but I stopped them very quickly. At that time, I had no wish to know any of that. My reasons have changed very little since then. Now, of course, I am fully aware of the details but even years later, I still find it extremely distressing. This, however, is the sequence of events based on what was later presented, by police and civilian witnesses, at the trial:

The telephone call from Jeremy to the police had been received by them at 3.26 a.m. on Chelmsford Police Station's direct line, and not through the emergency 999 switchboard. Jeremy said to the officer who took his call, 'You've got to help me. I've just had a call from my father. My sister's gone nutty with a gun.' A number of cars were immediately dispatched to the scene; Jeremy was told to meet them there. Police officers rushing to the scene were puzzled when they later realised they had actually passed his silver Vauxhall Astra on the way. Although he had started before them and had to travel a much shorter distance, Jeremy did not seem to be in any hurry.

On arriving at the farm, he had repeated his earlier story describing his sister as 'a nutter' and that she had gone 'doolally'. He had also explained that there were a number of firearms in the house. At first the police had tried to approach the house accompanied by Jeremy, but, on catching sight of what appeared to be a shadow at one of the windows, they pulled back and called in the firearms squad. While they were waiting, attempts were made through the telephone line to make contact with anybody inside the house who may have been alive. With the help of telephone engineers, they established that the telephone was off the hook and that the line was left open, which enabled them to listen in on the house.

As the siege went on, various officers had spoken to Jeremy, and they had all found him to be 'well dressed for the time of day', 'remarkably calm' and showing 'no outward signs of impatience'. They got him to make a plan of the house as well as list the guns kept on the property. On being questioned about the guns, Jeremy had said that there was a semi-automatic .22 rifle which he had left, with a loaded magazine, on the table in the kitchen the previous evening. He even told one officer that Sheila (Bambs) had often been 'target shooting' with the family and knew how to use all the guns in the house. He also told them that he did not get on too well with Sheila and that she was a psychopath with a history of mental illness. He had suggested that they get in touch with her psychiatrist Dr Ferguson, if they wanted someone to talk to her, or about her. Several officers bore witness to him making suggestions about her having a suicidal or psycho-pathic nature.

Once the decision to go in had been made, the police approached the house and forced an entry with sledge hammers, through the scullery door. Inside the kitchen, Nevill was found, in a crouched position, near to the fireplace. He had been shot eight times in all; four times in the head, jaw and larynx. These last two wounds would have made it difficult, it not impossible, for him to speak. He had also been very badly beaten. The kitchen showed all the signs of a bitter struggle and parts of a broken rifle butt were found on the floor near him. The telephone in the kitchen had its receiver off the hook and, it was later proved, was the one normally kept in the main bedroom, making any call for help from there impossible.

Upstairs in the bedroom occupied by the twins, both boys were found tucked up in their beds apparently asleep, one of them still having his thumb in his mouth. There were no signs of a struggle. Nicholas had three shots to the back of his head and Daniel had been shot five times, also in the back of his head. In the main bedroom, June was found on the floor behind the door. She had been shot several times, including one shot between her eyes and into her brain; blood had run down her legs and on *to the carpet, as if she had walked around the bed and across the room before the final fatal shot. Like her husband, she had been beaten as well as shot.*

Bambs was lying on the floor next to the bed; the rifle lay on her chest with an empty, ten-round ammunition case nearby: her mother's Bible, heavily bloodstained, was on the floor almost next to her. She had two wounds to the neck. A bullet was also found in June's pillow.

Outside the house, after the discovery of the bodies, Jeremy had appeared unwilling to accept what had happened. The police surgeon, Dr Ian Craig, who certified the deaths, had found him sitting in the back of a patrol car in 'a state of shock'. Dr Craig suggested that they go for a walk, at which point Jeremy asked him, 'Why can't my father come too?' After telling him that his father was dead, Jeremy broke down and the doctor gave him a drop of whisky. Jeremy had then wandered off into a field from where he was heard retching. He had also told Dr Craig that the previous evening his parents had been discussing the future of the twins with his sister and had suggested to her that they should be fostered. Jeremy had also alleged that Sheila had physically abused her children.

It was mid-afternoon by this time and I felt I should call my parents without further delay. It was the task I had been most dreading. As I slowly began dialling my mother's number, I desperately tried to work out how I was going to tell her, but realised there was no easy way. I had decided to call her first because, as far as I was aware, the police had already broken the news to my father. I didn't want to tell Mum over the phone, but even with the television news people on strike, I couldn't risk waiting till later to break it to her in person; I had to use the telephone.

When she answered, I asked if Bernie, my stepfather, was in the room with her and told her to sit down. Up till then she had sounded pleased to hear from me, as she normally would, but then her tone changed.

'What's wrong!' she said.

I still can hardly bear to think about those next five minutes on the telephone, but I will never ever forget them. Before I rang off, I told Mum that I would call Dad and make sure he was all right. She suggested that I sent him over to her place until I got back.

I had been told that another officer would soon be coming to take my statement – so I just waited, unaware most of the time that other people were around me. My mind was finding life in the present far too painful, so it kept slipping back into safe little corners of the past, where everything had been so much happier . . .

Those last five months of living with the boys in our own flat had been so idyllic. In a way, I felt a bit like the eccentric inventor Caractacus Potts – the main character in the film *Chitty Chitty Bang Bang* – with his two children. Like them, we didn't have much money to spend but we ate well, had an abundance of love and laughter and, most of all, each other. Living on dreams and fantasy, we were happy; the stereo provided constant musical entertainment and our new garden, after a bit of work, gave full rein to our fertile imaginations . . .

After clearing most of the weeds and nettles (we left some for the butterflies and fairies), we planted nasturtiums, sweet peas and about thirty sunflower seeds. The idea was to create a ten-foot-high, fairy-tale jungle to wander in. Every morning, Daniel and Nicholas would race outdoors to see if anything was happening, and when the sunflower seedlings did eventually appear, I would be woken by the activity outside my window as they measured, watered and fed the plants. They must have been the best-kept sunflowers in our street, because they soon outgrew their gardeners.

Daniel and Nicholas had been measuring the plants against themselves, but they soon had to start using me as a ruler. By the end of July, they were towering way above my head and the first buds were beginning to show. Not wanting to miss them after all that tender loving care, we were praying they would flower before our trip to Norway. The twins had loved their first visit the previous year and couldn't wait to go again.

It was while I was thinking about this period that I remembered a conversation I'd had with Bambs only weeks earlier; a conversation which may have been a clue to her parents wanting to do something as drastic as having the boys fostered. This was, however, something I had previously only thought of as an amusing anecdote.

Bambs had said to me: 'Do you ever smoke pot in front of the boys?'

'I might have done,' I said, 'but it's highly unlikely. I very rarely smoke any more. Why?'

'Well, I wish you wouldn't,' she said, 'because while Mum and Dad were here the other day I couldn't find my cigarettes, so Daniel and Nicholas took the usual opportunity to start telling me off about smoking. At this point, Mum joined in and said, "Yes, Mummy should be like your dad and stop smoking altogether." Then, agreeing with her, Nicholas said, "Yes, but even Daddy smokes sometimes. I've seen him share one with a friend of his."'

'Good old Nicholas,' I said, laughing, 'he always manages to put his foot in it. I bet that upset your parents?'

'It's not funny,' she said. 'Please don't do it again. They were really po-faced after that.'

I told her not to worry, because I certainly didn't make a habit of it. I could only think it must have been when an old friend had recently turned up for tea. This, however, was a harmless mistake which I thought little more about. It could hardly be considered grounds for losing custody of the boys. Smoking dope had ceased to have the appeal it had in my youth and I had virtually stopped anyway. I decided there would be no point in offering this information to the police; it would only confuse things, so I put it out of my mind and continued my reassuring but uneasy reverie . . .

Just then another policeman arrived – a tallish man who introduced himself as Detective Sergeant Stan Jones. I don't know if he offered his sympathy, because I couldn't understand what he was saying half the time, he spoke so fast, but at least he was friendly and that made me feel a little more at ease.

During the next five minutes, he brought Heather and me up to date on the events of the morning. By this time, Jeremy was standing at the door listening and added that he hadn't liked Detective Sergeant Jones at all that morning. Jeremy accused him of being really horrible to him.

'I had to be,' said Jones. 'I had to pull you to your senses and get some information out of you. It's part of my job. There might have been some people still alive in there.' He then quickly dismissed Jeremy by asking if he had finished giving his statement yet, and then pointed out that he needed to interview me and take my statement without him around. Sergeant Jones appeared to have a very casual, light-hearted attitude to his job, like a television detective. Without warning, he then said to me, 'We're going to need you to identify your children's bodies.'

'I can't!' I said. 'I've already told the other officer I'm not going to. I value my memories of Daniel and Nicholas far too much. You'll have to get somebody else.'

'There isn't anybody else who can tell them apart, what with them being twins; you'll have to do it. I know it will be painful, but we have no choice.'

I still refused.

'Would you know which bed each of them slept in on their visits?' said Jones. 'You know – would they have always slept in the same beds?'

'Yes, they almost certainly would have done, but I don't know who slept where, not having stayed at the farm much since the separation; in fact, I think I have only stayed there once since, and that was last Christmas.'

'That doesn't really help us much, does it?' he said. 'I really think you are going to have to see them.'

I then remembered the small scar on Nicholas's cheek and in desperation said, 'If I could give you some positive means of telling them apart, would that let me off going?' He said it would help, so I gave him a description of the scar's location. It had happened when he broke a glass coffee-table as a toddler.

'Does that help?'

'Yes, but we're still going to need you to say that they are in fact your sons, Daniel and Nicholas Caffell.'

I couldn't believe this man, he seemed to be playing games with me. I felt as though I was sitting there bargaining with him, when all I really wanted was to find some way of waking myself from this terrible nightmare. Just then Heather intervened and offered to go on my behalf. She really wanted to see the boys one last time and to say goodbye to them. For some reason, Jones ignored her request and said something really patronising like, 'No, no, we can't have that. Why don't you stick to writing in your notebook and looking after this feller? Eh?'

Ever since we had arrived, Heather had been busy taking notes and making sure she had everybody's name, rank and telephone number, just in case we needed to talk to anyone at any time. The way she started organising everybody, including the police, was absolutely marvellous. I don't know what I would have done without her in those coming weeks.

Sergeant Jones continued to put pressure on me, but finally realised it was hopeless trying to persuade me any longer. I felt completely intimidated by him but I was damned if I was going to let him undermine what little sense of self I had left that day.

He then asked if I thought Bambs had in it her or hated her parents enough to shoot them. I said that as far as I knew, she thought the world of her father and loved him dearly, but I didn't think there was much love lost between Bambs and her mother. If what Jeremy had said about an argument was true, then I could imagine that Bambs, in her psychotic state, might really want to punish her mother for wanting to take the children away – because you can bet your bottom dollar such a scheme would have been June's idea.

'Oh, she suffered all right,' said Jones, 'she really suffered. So did the father.'

I pleaded with him not to tell me any more. I felt sick. When he asked me about Sheila's mental condition, I told him that my mother had spoken to me of her conversation with an emergency doctor who had been called out to treat Bambs at the time of her last breakdown back in March. The doctor had said it was a good thing my mother had called when she did; it was a wonder that Bambs hadn't done any harm to herself already – or anybody else for that matter.

Those words had stuck in my mind, even though Bambs's private psychiatrist, Dr Ferguson, had subsequently assured me, when I told him of this, that she was absolutely no danger to anyone. He had previously explained that Bambs suffered from a mild form of schizophrenia, which manifested itself in much the same religiose way her mother's illness did.

Prior to her first hospitalisation, Bambs had become caught up in a deep inner struggle with the concept of good and evil that eventually overwhelmed her, causing episodes of psychosis in which she believed she was possessed by the devil. At other times, she believed she was Joan of Arc or the Virgin Mary. Occasionally she said she heard voices. During her second hospitalisation, I remember Bambs speaking about conversations with God. But even then, it never seemed like she really quite believed it: by taking this conflict into herself, she was spared the rod of her mother's puritanical beliefs about her; caught up in a barbed-wire cage of her mother's making. Just to think about it still makes my skin crawl.

I remember Sergeant Jones telling me, at some point, that one of the boys, the one without the thumb in his mouth, had been shot through the cheek. I think this came up because I had asked him if the boys' faces had been messed up at all; although, after what the other officer had said, I suspected they hadn't been. (Had I realised then that a semi-automatic rifle, and not a shotgun, had been used, my immediate testimony would have been very different; Bambs wouldn't have had the first idea how to use one, let alone reload it. In fact, I didn't even know the farm had such a gun; it was a very new acquisition.)

'That's another reason why I think you should identify the bodies,' said Sergeant Jones, who hadn't given up after all. For me, the thought of a shotgun wound to my son's face was all the more reason for me not to do it. I had made up my mind and Jones wasn't going to change it. So, in resignation, he suggested we get on with my statement. It's a wonder some people don't go mad faced with such treatment by investigating officers following the murder of a loved one.

Sergeant Jones continued, 'I'll need to know everything you can tell me about your wife and her family, from the day you met her right up to the present time, when you last saw her or spoke to her. There's no point holding anything back, because you can't hurt anybody by what you say, not now they are all dead, can you?'

In retrospect, I wish I hadn't listened to him. So many of the facts were to be twisted in the press due to leaks from what could only be police sources. I was later told that this was probably from the typing pool, where statements are copied up for the records. I must also re-emphasise that although I was in severe shock and in no condition to remember the exact words of my conversations, certain comments have stuck in my mind very clearly indeed. What you have just read are mainly the remembered impressions of them, pieced back together over the ensuing months.

Fortunately, I have been able to double-check nearly everything with Heather, who was present most of the time, except, of course, while I was making my actual statement. During that time, she was sitting in the living-room, a witness to Jeremy concluding his.

CHAPTER THREE

IT WASN'T VERY long after Detective Sergeant Jones had thrown everyone out of the dining-room to interview me that the telephone rang. It was my father.

'Hello, Col', are you all right? What's going on there, has something happened to Bambs?'

'Oh my God! Haven't you been told?'

'Told what?' he said angrily. 'All I've had is a policeman round here telling me that you and Heather had been picked up and taken to Essex! What's happened, has Bambs killed herself or something?'

I then realised that the police had screwed up very badly and suggested he prepare himself for a shock. 'Bambs has been found shot dead,' I said, 'and so have her mother and father.' Then I hesitated and cried, 'And so have Daniel and Nicholas!'

'Oh no,' he screamed, 'not my Daniel!' The line went dead.

I quickly rang back to find only the sound of his tears. My poor father was in such a terrible state. He was all on his own and there was nothing I could do to help him.

After explaining everything I could, I tried to find out what had happened when the police had called, but he was too upset to say anything. It was dreadful listening to him on the other end of the line so I told him to go straight over to Mum's, where she was expecting him. He asked me if the Flowers family knew yet. Not having any idea, I asked him to call Herbie and make sure they did – before the press got to them. I then explained that I was in the middle of giving a statement and would see him at Mum's as soon as we could get away. Before ringing off, Dad volunteered to tell my sister in Norway and muttered, 'It's unbelievable, just unbelievable.'

I put the phone down absolutely furious over the police's careless attitude to informing him and made my feelings very clear to Sergeant Jones. Some weeks later, my father finally told me the full story of what happened that afternoon and, as a result, I was even more enraged than I had been then.

Apparently, just after he got home from work, Dad answered the door to a young constable from his local police station, who said, 'I've been instructed to tell you that your son, Colin, and his girl-friend have been picked up and taken down to Essex, to help with some enquiries.' When my father asked him why, he said he didn't know any more and that the message had originated from a different police station. On hearing Essex mentioned, Dad asked if it was anything to do with his daughter-in-law, but it was no use. The officer left.

In a bit of a panic by this time, Dad called Kentish Town Police and asked *them* what was going on, but they gave him exactly the same story. When he asked them if it was anything to do with Bambs, the officer just said, 'It might be.' The only suggestion he could make was for Dad to call Police Headquarters at Chelmsford in Essex, and gave him the number. This was where he really came up against the brick wall of officialdom and drew a complete blank. Even when he explained his situation, they denied all knowledge of me and said that he must have his information wrong. If the truth be known, the place must have been buzzing with the news by then.

By this time, Dad was getting frantic so, in desperation, he rang Whitehouse Farm in the hope that someone there might know what was going on. To his surprise, there was a strange man's voice on the other end of the line. Dad asked if Nevill was there and the man just said, very bluntly, 'Who are you?' as if he had no right to ask. It was only then he discovered it was a policeman.

'I am only trying to find out what has happened to my son, Colin Caffell, but I'm just being given the runaround,' said my father. The policeman apologised but couldn't tell him anything. 'If you ring this number, there might be somebody there who can help you.' Which is how he finally got through to Jeremy's.

'If I had been given one more telephone number at that point,' said Dad, 'I don't know what I would have done. I was so overwrought and frustrated by the time I talked to you, I was wound up even before you broke the news to me!'

On reflection, I can understand why the police had to be careful in giving information over the phone; they are fully aware of the lies and tricks used by reporters to gain their stories, as we were soon to find out. For this reason alone, they should have done their job properly and informed him as I had requested. It would have saved my father so much unnecessary distress when there was absolutely no reason for him not to be told.

When I was halfway through giving my statement, Jeremy stuck his head round the door and proudly announced that he had finished giving his.

'I've done over twenty-four pages,' he said. 'How many have you done?' I remember thinking at the time that it was a strange way to behave and told him, for what it was worth, about eight pages. 'Ah, well, I suppose I've had much more to cover,' said Jeremy. 'I've had all twenty-seven years of Sheila's life to go over.'

'Are you sure you've covered everything?' asked Jones.

'Yes, everything except the drugs,' said Jeremy. 'I refuse to say anything about them.'

'Drugs?' said Jones.

'Perhaps I can shed some light on that, then,' I said, 'because if Jeremy won't say anything, I most certainly am going to.' I then told Jones of a conversation I'd had with Bambs's psychiatrist concerning a recent relationship. I also told him the rumours I had heard about this man's alleged involvement with drug-trafficking. Knowing the doctor's concern over this friendship, I had informed him of my own worries and asked him to bear it in mind when treating her. I had wanted to help Bambs as much as possible and if there was even the slightest chance she herself had been taking drugs, I felt it might have been something to do with this man's apparent hold over her, which was very strong. When I told all this to Stan Jones, I said that I hadn't spoken to Dr Ferguson since, so I didn't know the results of his tests.

'So there is a possibility that she might have been on cocaine or something?' said Jones. I agreed that it was a possibility, but stressed that it was also highly unlikely.

'It's just that I thought Jeremy was talking about the opium fields,' said Jones.

Opium fields? What was he talking about? Sergeant Jones then explained, as he got on the phone and told them to check Bambs's body for drugs, that Nevill was growing opium under a special government licence for the pharmaceutical industry. If I had known what was going to be said about Bambs in the newspapers on the following day, I might have thought twice about saying anything at all.

As it turned out, tests for illegal narcotics like cocaine proved negative, but instead revealed an unusually high level of haloperidol, the major tranquilliser administered by her doctor to deal with her schizophrenia. This tied up with what I had heard from her GP, who had asked the psychiatrist to reduce the prescribed dose because it was having such a powerful effect on Bambs, making her extremely sluggish and nauseous a lot of the time.

With this in mind, Bambs was even more unlikely to have had the mental co-ordination or the physical motor responses to use a rifle, let alone fire it accurately without any wasted bullets. As it was, she couldn't even make coffee without making a mess everywhere; missing the cup with both the coffee granules and the kettle of hot water. This had not been the case prior to her receiving medication.

When I eventually finished giving my statement, Sergeant Jones organised a car to take Heather and me back to London. While we waited, Jeremy told me that he would be arranging to have Bambs and his parents cremated after a service at the church in Tolleshunt D'Arcy. He said that he would also be willing to make similar arrangements for the twins but if I preferred it, I could make my own arrangements and the estate would cover the costs. He told me the executor had given him full authority to offer this.

It seemed strange to me that he was having them cremated, because I was sure June and Nevill would have much preferred a burial, as I know Bambs would have done. Straight away, I told him I wished to have Daniel and Nicholas buried, and that I also wanted them near me in London, so I would in fact be making my own arrangements for them.

On top of that, I was now convinced that June and Nevill had pushed Bambs to murdering them all by threatening to have the twins fostered to a local Christian family. With June's history in mind, I naturally blamed the Church, and more specifically the local one, for much of the family's mental illness – regardless of the tragedy itself. For that reason alone, I had no intention of allowing my sons' bodies near a funeral service in D'Arcy. My fears were not without foundation.

Before going any further, I should also make it clear that it is not the spiritual values within Christianity that had antagonised me so much, but the infuriating misinterpretation of its teachings and frequent misuse of them to manipulate people's lives. Having said that, I couldn't leave the Church out of Daniel and Nicholas's funeral altogether; I had to respect the fact that they had learned to love and believe in Jesus through their mother and grandparents.

Personally, I don't follow any religion, but keep an open mind on all of them. I was probably an agnostic. What I didn't want for my sons was the traditional Christian funeral with all the inevitable sermons and misery; readings from books, other than the Bible, meant far more to me and were far more suitable for the funeral of two such vibrant children. At the same time, I also wanted Bambs to be there with them, as she had been so much in life, and they with her. What right had I to separate them in death? Even if Bambs had taken their lives, as was thought at the time, it had only been so she could be together with them in a place where nobody could take them away from her again.

Later that week, I asked Jeremy if he would allow me to have Bambs's ashes buried with the twins at their funeral, to which he agreed. I had really wanted to ask if I could bury her body with them but being divorced, I didn't feel I had the right to ask. I also thought he might be loath to pay the added expense in the circumstances.

Before we left and, I felt, almost as if taking a lead from my own sensitivity about not wishing to see the twins, Jeremy told the policemen that he wanted his parents' house thoroughly cleaned up before he would enter it again. As time went on, I began to feel that I was constantly being observed and copied by Jeremy, as if he wasn't aware himself of what was appropriate behaviour and needed to follow my lead. In retrospect, these often overstated displays came over as both clumsy and grandiose but, above all, devoid of any proper feeling; like a ham actor spouting his lines.

'I want all the bloodstained bed-linen and carpets taken out and burnt,' he said, 'and any bloodstains on the walls thoroughly washed down.'

'You're not going to burn that lovely old carpet upstairs, are you?' said Ann Eaton.

'Everything,' said Jeremy.

'Don't worry about that,' said Sergeant Jones, 'it will all be done, once we've finished making all our investigations and tests.'

'Tests?' said Jeremy.

'Yes, it's standard procedure.'

Not long after this, the car arrived to take Heather and me to Witham Police Station, from where an off-duty uniformed sergeant kindly drove us to my mother's. On parting, we told Jeremy and Julie that if everything got too much for them there, they were welcome to come and stay at my place, which they accepted.

On the way back to London, it really began to sink in that the twins were in fact dead, and that I would have to start thinking about their funeral, but I really had no idea where to begin. I couldn't bear the thought of separating them into two little coffins. I had this vivid picture of them always sharing a double bed whenever they stayed with me at my old flat; snuggling under one duvet together, cuddling in their sleep. This was how I now wanted them to be for ever – in the same coffin, wearing their pyjamas and facing each other with their thumbs in their mouths; their 'snuggits' (security rags) in their hands and their favourite toys around their feet.

Whenever I think of the twins, I think of laughter and music, so I began to remember the many songs and tunes they were fond of; nursery rhymes, school songs, tunes they loved from the numerous recording sessions they had attended and especially the music of Sky, the group in which Herbie was then the bass player. It was at this point that I realised there was only one person I could ask to conduct the service; a man who was loved by all who knew him and probably more so by the twins than anyone else.

Patrick Rös, a black priest from Dutch Guyana, who had recorded many of his own beautiful love songs at Herbie's studio, was not only a beautiful human being, generous in spirit, he was the one person in the Church that I respected and trusted; he was also someone who loved the twins dearly and would understand my feelings about their funeral. Herbie once described his laugh as 'like being hit with a bucketful of warm feathers', and I would say the same for his songs, one of which I hoped he might sing as part of the service.

As we touched the outskirts of London, tender memories of the boys' favourite bedtime stories drifted through my mind; especially Enid Blyton's tales of *The Magic Faraway Tree*. Bambs and I had read these books to them over and over again, and were never allowed to put them down without a great deal of fuss. The stories, about three children who discover a magical tree in the forest, take in unusual adventures with its strange inhabitants, in weird and wonderful lands which swirl about its upper branches. Some of these lands, the Land of Dreams, for example, were not as pleasant as their name might suggest, but it was always an adventure to the ears of our eager listeners.

It was then that I knew I had to use my skills as a potter to create my own ceramic memorial – a replica of the tree in all its detail. The only unusual feature might be a small foot vanishing up the ladder at the top – into the clouds. A simple inscription would read, 'And they went up the ladder at the top of the Faraway Tree, with Silky, Moonface and the Old Saucepan Man'.

When I described the idea to Heather, I choked on the words, knowing I would never read those tales to them again. I must admit, I loved those stories as much as the boys did and often carried on reading them secretly after they had gone to bed. The more I thought about it, the more strong and everlasting the idea felt. Good children's stories will live for ever, so long as there are young children to enjoy them and old children to remember them. They are immortal in the minds of all children – we don't ever completely forget them.

When we got to my mother's, Dad was there, grief-stricken and angry. Mum and Bernie were crying, which in turn started Heather and me off, but Dad just couldn't let it out. He had been brought up with the belief that a man must never cry or have tears, so he tortured himself by pushing it all back inside whenever he started to break down. I cried so much for him. He couldn't even let me hug him. Poor Dad, I'll never forget that uncontrolled cry of anguish when I had to break the news to him. I asked him if Diane had been told yet and he said that he had spoken to her some hours earlier. Like him, she had been alone at the time.

Fortunately, a next-door neighbour came in and sat with her until Einer, her husband, came home. My nieces, Lucy and Abbi, were already in England on holiday with their father. I was also glad to hear that Diane would be catching the first available flight in the morning; relieved to know that we would soon be together again as a family; reunited in our hour of need. I knew how much we would need each other in the coming weeks, but I didn't realise quite how large the family was going to get.

In a futile search for the truth, everyone started asking questions, but there was so little Heather and I could tell them. One by one, we each fell into silence as our thoughts drifted away, only to come crowding back seconds later – waves of despair, anger and self-pity. We sat there, stunned, with the ugly truth of their dying screaming in our ears. Looking at each other through tears of reluctant acceptance, we were each alone; sometimes crying, sometimes still. Trying to piece it all together – trying to make some sense of it all. Mum could only walk up and down wringing her hands.

Through the numbness and despair I began to worry about everyone else; the extended family of friends, especially Jan, Ann, Herbie and Nick Flowers. How were they going to find out and how were they going to feel? I didn't want to tell them over the phone, I didn't think it fair, but there was little else I could do. I wanted to give them the same support we were giving each other, because I knew they would be just as devastated. It was when Dad told me about the reporters being on the phone to him that afternoon that I realised it wouldn't take them long to find Herbie's studio and my old pottery workshop, over which Jan and I used to live. Dad then told me he had already rung there and had left a message with Nicky Flowers to call.

I was told to stop worrying about other people. 'You can't protect them all. It's going to be just as horrible for them, no matter how they find out. You're the only one who needs looking after now!' But I really couldn't see it like that and could only think about various friends and how they might react. Eventually I realised it was futile to think I could speak to everyone before they saw the news. I could, however, reassure them that, as far as I knew, the twins would not have been aware of the horrors of the previous night.

I was relieved when Dad suggested we stay with him that night. There was a very strong possibility of the press being outside my place by this time. Expecting me to be in Essex, they might not realise who I was at Dad's. It was also suggested that my flat might prove too harrowing and empty for me in the circumstances. Before we left, we arranged to return to my mother's the next day because, no longer being a Caffell, hers was a safe house where the press wouldn't find us. I also telephoned Herbie to find out how they all were but, as I feared, they already knew the worst by this time.

'Where are you?' said Herbie shakily. 'Are you all right?'

'Yes, I'm OK, I'm at Mum's, but don't worry about me. Are Jan and Ann all right? Have they been told?'

'Yes, they've been told,' said Herbie. 'They're here, we're all here together. I still can't believe it, the boys and Bambs? What happened?' I didn't really want to talk on the phone, so I suggested we meet at my father's. 'All right,' he said, 'we'll see you there at about ten-thirty, but watch out, you might find some reporters on the doorstep when you get there. If you do, don't say a word to them, just pretend they're not there; they don't exist.'

'How do you mean?'

'Oh, we've had some round here, in fact it was a couple of reporters who told us what happened.' He then gave me some further sound advice that I will never forget:

'Don't talk to any of them, they'll distort anything you say. Be very careful, they'll try and goad you into saying anything just to print it as your statement. You might feel like hitting them; well, don't, because that's exactly what they want! Don't hit them, swear at them or say anything, just ignore them! They're not worthy of an answer, you are too far above them and they're the scum of the earth.'

I thanked him for the warning, remembering that he must have had similar trouble as a member of T. Rex when Marc Bolan died. After the call, I passed on his advice to everyone else, especially to my father, who was bottling up his feelings and, I thought, the one most likely to explode in the face of provocation.

When we reached his flat, as predicted, the reporters were waiting for us; two sitting in a black Porsche Carrera. As soon as Dad got out of the car and headed for the downstairs door, they were upon him, firing questions: 'Are you Mr Caffell? Have you seen your son?' I began to fear Dad was actually going to hit one of them, but he managed to control himself and kept his mouth shut. Not knowing what I looked like and probably assuming I was still in Essex, they totally ignored Heather and me. Once inside my father's flat, however, the siege really began.

After following us up the stairs, they started ringing his doorbell and shouting questions through the letter-box:

'What sort of mother was Sheila Caffell?'

'Was she on drugs?'

'Was she normally a violent person?'

'Where is your son and how's he taking it?'

'Will he be identifying the bodies?'

Dad was terribly upset by their hysterical behaviour and started shouting back at them through the door, even though I told him to ignore them. I was really worried about his blood pressure. Just then Heather said that Herbie's car had pulled up outside and told me to stay where I was while she let them in. As I heard the front door open, followed by Jan and Ann's voices, I also heard Herbie shouting at the reporters and an anguished cry as one of them fell down the stairs shouting, 'But the public have a right to know!'

'Bollocks!' said Herbie. 'Your public rights stop at street level, outside this block, and if you step inside these flats once more I'm calling the police! Now that's the law and you know it! If you want to stand in the street and shout, that's up to you, but it won't be long before the police have you for causing a disturbance. Nobody here is going to talk to you, so go home!'

Inside the flat, Jan and I held each other tightly. We hadn't seen each other, or she the twins, since a senseless argument had caused a rift in our remaining friendship some months earlier. It was very difficult for Heather, being witness to our closeness, but she fully understood the depth of our past relationship and the enormous role Jan had played in the twins' lives. Sensing Heather's discomfort, we both put our arms around her and all three of us cried uncontrollably for some time. Past differences now seemed so futile as we huddled together for mutual comfort. When the barriers are down, they really are down and I was so relieved that we could, finally, forget all our foolish pride.

Jan's brother, Nicky, stood to one side, red-eyed and confused; crying quietly as we heard how his normally gentle nature was lost when he grabbed a reporter by the throat and tried to frog-march him out of the mews where my workshop had once been. Jan said she didn't know what came over him – he was like a different person.

I was amazed at Herbie's behaviour outside, especially in the light of the advice he had given me earlier, but he just said, 'I've nothing to lose, they don't know me from Adam.' When I asked about how they had been told, Nick and Herbie said it was about three o'clock when Nicky answered the door to a smartly dressed man and a woman who asked if he was Colin Caffell. Because the man held a small notebook, Nicky thought they were police officers. When he said that I wasn't there, could he help, the woman said, 'Oh! Well, we've come about the shootings.' What shootings? They then told him that Bambs and the boys were dead. Nick was speechless. At that moment Herbie came down. Was he Colin Caffell? 'No, why? Who wants him?' said Herbie, not to be intimidated.

Having done the damage, obviously hoping to break the news to me, they finally owned up to being reporters from one of the better national newspapers. Who were Nick and Herbie to me? 'Never mind that,' said Herbie. 'Why are you here? Put me straight first!' They then gave him the full details as they were known at that time.

Just as Herbie was finishing his story, my father's phone started ringing, but when Dad answered it, he found it to be reporters again. Dad slammed it down but it was no good, they kept on ringing back. If we tried to leave the phone off the hook instead, they were always still there, listening, deliberately jamming the line open – trying to eavesdrop on our grief!

That night as I lay in bed, the anguish and sense of loss really started to drive home and I found myself hiding like a frightened child under the covers. Tender memories and images of horror intermittently flashed in stark contrast through my mind. And that awful question: could I have prevented it? I was exhausted but sleep was impossible. As I stared blankly into the darkness, thoughts of that terrible day strained at every nerve ending . . .

CHAPTER FOUR

I N MANY WAYS, I could accept nearly everything I had been told, but at the same time I couldn't fully understand it. The police seemed to have made up their minds that Bambs had caused the deaths and therefore moulded their investigations accordingly. It was now, apparently, just a matter of them doing their paperwork and I was in no state to question them.

Apart from a few scattered radio and evening newspaper reports that day, the news didn't really break for nearly twenty-four hours. When it did, however, it was on the front page of every national newspaper. The horrific but simple facts of a private family tragedy had justified a report by the media, purely because of the extent of the bloodshed, but no more. Unfortunately, the few known facts were blown out of all proportion and huge banner headlines proclaimed:

TOP MODEL MASSACRES FAMILY
Drugs probe after massacre by mother of twins

MODEL MURDERS 4 OF HER FAMILY
SLAUGHTER AT FARMHOUSE, BERSERK MOTHER BLASTS FAMILY

With heads full of preconceived ideas about the fashion world, of which Bambs was never fully a part, the press began to tear her to pieces with the relish of a pack of starving hyenas. From a simple police statement which said that they 'believed' Bambs's finger had been on the trigger, these so-called journalists feasted themselves on the idea and clung to an image of fast living, clubs, sex, drugs and all-night parties, seemingly to satisfy their own wildest fantasies.

Opening their background coverage, under a second massive head-line – 'HELL RAISER BAMBI' – the *Sun*, for example, said:

> **Crazed killer Sheila Caffell swapped a quiet country life for the jet-set glamour of fashion modelling – but only found heartache and despair.**
>
> **The beautiful redhead, known as Bambi because of her maiden name Bamber and her long shapely legs, spent her last days alive trying to get a job as a cleaner.**
>
> **And friends revealed that she had slid into the twilight world of hard drugs which were freely available to her.**
>
> **One pal even revealed that Sheila took methadone, which addicts use to wean themselves off heroin . . .**

They continued:

> **But the high-living fashion model preferred her ground-floor flat in Maida Vale, West London, to the fields and lanes of East Anglia.**
>
> **By DAY she was a devoted mother to her twin sons Daniel and Nicholas.**
>
> **But by NIGHT she hit the whirlwind circuit of plush London discos and clubs.**

The fact that the children were living with me during the time she was said to have led this double life didn't come into it.

Within hours, Bambs had been submitted to trial by Fleet Street, found guilty and executed. Those of us who knew her well were left reeling by the savagery with which she had been condemned. For me, it was impossible to reconcile the memories of my two laughing children and their loving mother with the grossly distorted images that had been presented. Within another twenty-four hours, the press ruthlessly completed Bambs's character assassination in a way that I can only describe as rape. Having stuck the knife into her corpse, newspapers proceeded to twist it round, desperately trying to outdo each other in mutilating her memory:

CRAZY LIFE OF KILLER MOTHER
Boyfriend in knife terror
GIRL WITH MAD EYES

and

Weird and double life of the beauty
who mowed down her family
— TWO FACES OF BAMBI

This last headline was part of a '*Star* Special' showing photographs of a girl *who wasn't even Bambs* – they were of a girl who really did model under the name of 'Bambi', to whom the *Star* had to print an apology shortly afterwards. It's a pity they never did the same for Bambs.

Finding those closest to her unwilling to submit to their perjury, reporters had begun fabricating their own stories and putting words into the mouths of neighbours, nodding acquaintances and gossips. Questions beginning with 'Would you say she . . .?' or 'Don't you think that . . .?' were guaranteed an answer, even if it was only a nod or a nervous twitch! For a family who never shared their problems with anyone, it seemed that an awful lot of people suddenly had a tremendous insight into the Bambers' affairs. To quote the London *Evening Standard*:

A friend of the family said, 'Sheila got mixed up with a drugs crowd after her marriage broke up three years ago. It caused the family a lot of heartache at the time, but we all thought she had got over her problems.'

Under the words, '**WILD, STARING EYES**', the *Star* said that Bambs's neighbours were 'convinced she was on drugs after she continually created uproar'. They then quoted one of them as saying, 'I often wondered if she was an addict. She had that sort of look in her eyes when you talked to her. People used to say she looked strange.' And in another report, an Essex neighbour said: 'But there's obviously a lot of drugs in London and she got in with the wrong set.' If these were not answers to leading questions, I don't know what else they were.

To make it worse, many reporters, wallowing in a plethora of gruesome details, almost sank to the level of video-nasty scriptwriters. Again the *Sun* excelled with their front page; in their opening paragraphs, they not only claimed Bambs's guilt as a fact, they were even prepared to state the order of death, even though this is still not known to this day:

Newly-divorced Mrs Caffell started the carnage by shooting her boys Nicholas and Daniel as they slept side by side. Then the beautiful redhead, known as Bambi, blasted her wealthy farmer father, Nevill Bamber and Mum, June, both 61. Finally she shot herself in the head . . .

They went on:

The blood-covered twins were in a side bedroom, one of them still had a thumb in his mouth. Mrs Bamber was spread-eagled across the bed in the master bedroom . . .

And the *Express*, who also described Bambs as 'deranged' and 'frenzied', said:

A farming family, affectionately dubbed the Archers, were slaughtered by their crazed daughter in a bloodbath yesterday.

No matter how a person dies, surely their death should be treated with dignity and allowed the privacy it deserves? From what was being said, the press might as well have stripped all the victims, photographed their naked bodies and pasted the results all over their front pages; had it been allowed, I am sure they would have done. The horrible truth of it is, the press can say anything they damn well like about a person once they are dead, whether it's true or not; one cannot libel the dead.

Fortunately, I was spared the violation of reading these early reports for quite some time, but from what I was told they were saying, during the coming days, I was furious and wanted to go outside and put things straight there and then. Friends like Herbie, however, warned me not to: 'Everything you say will be written down or taped, hacked about and edited, added to, rewritten, put into a different context and then printed to look like your "Exclusive" statement, but it would only be exclusive in as much that it would bear little resemblance to what you actually said.'

This was something I discovered to my cost when, several days later, I released, by telex to the Press Association, the following carefully worded statement; that vicious stalemate with which I was faced made me feel so helplessly impotent, paralysed, but I had to say something:

> Although I have been devastated by this tragedy, my heart goes out to Sheila (Bambs). I don't think anyone could imagine the pain and anguish she suffered on that dreadful night. No mother on earth could have loved her children more. Nothing was more precious to her than Nicholas and Daniel, yet she was a naïve and frightened child herself. She had been through a very difficult time recently, the world frightened her. She tried to cover this up and only those closest to her knew how lonely and vulnerable she was. Her parents were lovely, kind people who only wanted the best for her and couldn't understand her illness. I will always remember Sheila as a beautiful and tragic woman, the loving and dedicated mother of my twin sons. Her brother Jeremy and I and all her real friends and caring family love and respect her and hope that now, at last, she is at peace.

Even though reporters were breaking their necks to get an interview with me, very few newspapers actually picked up and used the statement. Their reluctance was almost certainly due to the fact that it didn't, in any way, fit in with the story they were selling to their readers. My attitude didn't fit in with their preconceived idea of how I should feel towards the woman who had, apparently, murdered my children. Of the two papers who did use it, I must thank the *Star* for presenting it almost verbatim and almost in its entirety.

The *Daily Mail*, however, despite assurances from one of their reporters that it was 'not a sensationalist paper', chose to lift words or sentences and place them in a context to fit the story all the others were putting out. They did not, as he went on to say, 'put the terrible tragedy in its correct context'. Under the headline, ' "Anguish" of mother who killed her family', they said, as if I were making it all up, that I 'claimed' Bambs was a 'loving and dedicated mother', leaving much doubt on the rest of my, heavily edited, statement.

I will say one thing for the *Mail*, however: they were the only tabloid that didn't jump on the bandwagon of calling her 'Bambi', or not at least for the first couple of weeks. Very few of her real friends ever called her that; she was always known as Bambs, as she had introduced herself. Personally, I find the name 'Bambi' degrading in the way it has been abused; it makes her sound like a mindless plaything – which she certainly wasn't.

It seems sadly ironical that Bambs had always dreamed of having her picture on the covers of magazines and newspapers, but it took something like this to make it happen – and even sadder that she was not alive to see it.

CHAPTER FIVE

Dreampoem

in a corner of my bedroom
grew a tree
a happy tree
my own tree
its leaves were soft
like flesh
and its birds sang poems for me
then
without warning
two men
with understanding smiles
and axes
made out of forged excuses
came and chopped it down
either   yesterday
or the day before
i think it was the day before
Roger McGough

'I DON'T THINK YOU should look at any of the newspapers today,' said my mother when we spoke early the next morning. 'They've gone completely mad and I don't think there's any point distressing yourself unnecessarily.'

This was to be reiterated many times during the next few days by everybody I spoke to, so I decided to take their advice without further question. It was in fact many months before I had the courage to look at those reports and even when I did, I wasn't sufficiently prepared for what I saw. Had I looked at them then, I don't think I would have been able to find my way through this nightmare as well as I have.

It would have been the same had I viewed the bodies. Even with hindsight, and now considerable experience in the field of grief and loss, I have no doubt that had I seen them all – so many that I loved and cared for – I would have gone irreconcilably nuts, and I am eternally grateful to Julie Mugford, Jeremy's girlfriend, for making the formal identifications. My very strong imagination was doing more than enough without the help of reality.

As it is, I must accept that had Nicholas and Daniel suffered in any way, this would almost certainly have been a different story. I cannot imagine how I would have reacted had they been awake or their death been slow. As for June and Nevill, and to some extent even Bambs, I didn't have grief to spare at that time.

The next two weeks were to be a period of revelation and mixed emotions; a tragic time of grief and humour, when many unexpected things took place. The day after the shootings, although I was relieved to have what was left of my family around me, I also began to feel a little claustrophobic. It had been many years since we had all spent any time together. For this reason, Heather and I decided to get some fresh air and went for a walk on our own after lunch.

Making our way along Borough High Street, towards London Bridge, we couldn't avoid seeing the fly-sheets and banner headlines of tabloid newspapers promoting details of the Essex Farmhouse Massacre. I tried not to look, but I couldn't help being drawn to their foul and horrific words. Even after seeing those few glimpses for myself, I knew the press had it completely wrong. It was crazy, Bambs wasn't like that. Even accepting that she had pulled the trigger, I could only see her as one of the victims.

As I dragged my eyes away, I couldn't help noticing a very familiar photograph on the cover of what I now know to have been the *Daily Express*. 'How the hell did they get hold of that picture?' I said angrily. 'The only copy I know of is in a frame on Bambs's living-room wall!'

Some time later, I asked one of the detectives whether the police had been responsible for giving newspapers access to Bambs's photographs but they denied it. I was told instead that, apparently, two reporters who had been hanging around outside her flat broke the news to a friend who was keeping an eye on the place for her, as he went to let himself in. Then, on the pretence of comforting him, they also gained access. As one of them sat with him in the living-room, the other went to make him a hot drink and have a good look round while the kettle boiled. Using the excuse of not being able to find the coffee, he was asked to show them where it was, but while he was in the kitchen, the first one remained in the living-room with the portrait. I still find it hard to believe just how low the press can stoop for a picture or story.

Whether I thought Heather and I might find some temporary escape from the visual assault of the news-stands or maybe simply because it was there, we wandered into Southwark Cathedral. I suppose I felt drawn to it as a peaceful haven. Almost by chance, I wandered up to the lectern, upon which the Bible couldn't have been open at a more poignant place: *'To everything there is a season, and a time to every purpose under the heaven. A time to be born and a time to die . . .'*

But what really first caught my eye was from Chapter 4 of Ecclesiastes, on the facing page:

'So I returned, and considered all the oppressions that are done under the sun: and behold the tears of such as were oppressed, and they had no comforter; and on the side of their oppressors there was power; but they had no comforter.'

When I turned to show Heather, she had vanished. I looked everywhere for her and eventually found her sitting outside, crying bitterly, determined that the Church was really behind the cause of our grief, and I had to agree.

Heavy in thought, we walked back to my mother's, where I soon realised how much I also needed my friends. The decision to return home that evening was very much my own – I felt lost away from my familiar surroundings. At first, everyone thought it would be far too traumatic for me, going back so soon. They thought the prospect of being faced with all my memories and a home bereft of children would be too much for me, but that was the very reason I had to go back. I needed to be close to my memories and find comfort in the place I felt nearest to Daniel and Nicholas.

When I finally got back home, Telemessages and notes had already begun to arrive and even before I'd finished reading, so had some of those friends I had spoken to that afternoon. It was now time for the larger family to come in from the cold reaches of their grief; to share in our mutual comfort. And so they came, *en masse*, drifting in as dazed, confused and heartbroken as we were; hoping to be of some help, but needing all the love and support we could give each other.

Now I began to learn about every aspect of human behaviour. With the barriers down, I was overwhelmed by the unconditional depth of people's love; where to be hugged by other men as well as women didn't have any of the usual, unnecessary sexual connotations. I shall never forget the arrival of an older, Egyptian friend, who, without inhibition, held me in his arms as if I was his own son and cried his heart out. The fact we were both men didn't matter at all. It was a pure love that we all shared as Bambs, Daniel and Nicholas were remembered and any past differences forgotten. Even those who hardly knew each other were locked in tearful embraces. I had never known anything like it. This was all new to me.

The events of the next couple of weeks did in fact forge the bonds of many new friendships; they certainly changed the course of many people's lives. The one thing that bound us all together was the love Nicholas and Daniel had given to everyone there, the results of which generated such a strong electric atmosphere in my home, it was many months before it faded. (I haven't mentioned Bambs here because most of these friends had never met her before the party at the weekend.)

By eight o'clock, the flat was full – many more had turned up on the off-chance of finding me home. My living-room and kitchen were littered with tearful, red-eyed people, crying and muttering quietly to themselves. All of a sudden, Herbie, in a panic and unable to stand the mournful atmosphere any longer, came into the living-room with a cup of tea in his hand and a smile on his face.

'Well, I know how I'll remember the boys,' he said, taking a sip of his tea. 'I'll never forget the time when Sky were in Number Three studio at Abbey Road, working on one of our albums. The boys must have been about four years old and . . .'

He then went on to tell us how – during a rather heated band meeting – the studio door had crashed open announcing the arrival of the twins, followed by Jan and a confused security man. Breathlessly, both boys, in unison, shouted to Herbie that Jan had got lost because Daddy had given her all the wrong directions to Mummy's house and they didn't know *how* they were going to get back home again. This invasion itself was not an unusual occurrence. What really sent up the whole situation was the fact that Daniel was wearing a Spider-Man outfit and Nicholas was dressed as a nurse – make-up on, the lot.

'It was really funny,' said Herb, 'the look John Williams gave, you know, *absolute* disapproval at first but when they burst in it made everyone laugh so much, it defused a bit of a heavy situation. You could almost say it saved the album – and probably the band as well! It was the same backstage,' he said finally. 'They would always put any celebrities in their place because, as kids, they were the true celebrities.'

When he finished telling his story, we found ourselves laughing unashamedly for the first time. God knows what the neighbours must have thought – but then who was to judge? In a few minutes, Herbie had turned everyone's tears of sorrow into tears of laughter. We had begun to learn that grief has two sides: tears *and* laughter. From then on everyone started remembering those little anecdotes that meant so much to us; we found consolation in our happier memories, because nobody can ever take those away.

The next day, Herbie received a telephone call from John Williams, who, through his own tears, asked Herbie to pass on a very tender and heartfelt message: 'I know nothing I can say or feel is enough. I just hope that playing some beautiful music can express something to be with you in spirit.'

As well as my many friends arriving, the press were also there in force when I got home. Fortunately, they still had no idea what I looked like and, because I had arrived with a number of people, they had no chance of finding out. I had anonymity in a crowd; something that was maintained almost right up to the twins' funeral. Once we were indoors, however, the doorbell never stopped ringing; in fact it was so bad we ended up having to remove the bell part completely. All we then had to suffer was its strangulated rattle. Once again, Herbie went outside to confront them, pointing out where their rights stopped. But the total invasion of our privacy had begun in earnest. The almost constant presence of photographers outside also meant that my living-room curtains could not be opened for many weeks to come and we had to live in virtual darkness.

When Herbie came back in from one such foray, he told us how the press had received a somewhat moist reception at his place earlier that day. 'And another thing they don't like,' he said, showing us his mini tape recorder, 'is if you shove a tape recorder under their nose and tell them you're taping everything. For some reason, they cower in horror at a taste of their own medicine.'

The worst violation that week happened a few days later, when one reporter even tried to physically force his way past Heather into my flat, when she was there on her own for the afternoon. She had, accidentally, opened the door to him, thinking it was me returning. Fortunately for her, as she struggled to close the door against this thug, help arrived just in time and the reporter, chased around the corner, ended up temporarily imprisoned in a refrigerator outside a nearby junk shop. He had been apprehended by the shop owners, thinking he was a runaway thief.

My family had been somewhat taken aback by the crazy onslaught of friends eager to do anything to help. They had virtually been snowploughed out of the way in the rush. I had hoped they would sit back and allow the others to look after them, as I was, but I think they found it all too much to accept. The trouble is, it's absolutely impossible to stop an avalanche once it has started. As a very touching example of this caring, I can remember one person in particular who turned up a few days later but in his sorrow was unable to say anything. Without a word, he walked straight past me into the kitchen, took off his jacket and looked around for something to do. He then proceeded to do the washing-up and clean my cooker, thoroughly, from top to bottom – inside and out! No sooner had he finished, he picked up his jacket again and left with little more than a wave goodbye. When the simplest of chores become almost impossible tasks, it's amazing how such an unselfish gesture can help so much.

On that first afternoon home, Patrick Rös called to say he had found a church where not only could he conduct the boys' service, but we could do our own thing as well. It was just opposite Herbie's studio. He had also fixed up a meeting with Peter Wheatley, the vicar, for the next morning.

Even before I saw Patrick the following day, I seemed to have come to terms with the initial shock and began to feel incredibly calm. Whether this dreamy state was a result of all the love and kindness from the night before, or whether it is the feeling everyone has when in shock, I don't know. I also cannot say whether it was my imagination, but when I walked back into my flat for the first time, it didn't feel at all cold or empty, as some had expected, but actually felt surprisingly warm and welcoming – as if there was something awaiting my return, as if my presence made a completeness of the surroundings.

Almost as soon as we arrived, Jan, Heather and I each felt a strong need to go into the twins' bedroom; although it was incredibly painful at first, seeing the remnants of their little museum, I felt it was the perfect place to sit quietly. Speaking for myself, I felt at one with my children. And when Jan went in, she actually fell into a deep healing sleep for the first time in days on Daniel's bed. Many couldn't face going in at all, but for those who needed it, the room almost became a little sanctuary where one could be guaranteed some solitude.

At first, some people offered to take down and put away all the boys' photographs, toys and drawings, but I wouldn't allow it. I was horrified at the suggestion and actually started hanging more of their drawings on the walls. If their spirits did survive after death, as I was beginning to feel they had, the first places they would go would be where they had felt happiest and safest when they were alive. Imagine their anguish if they returned home to find their memory shut away in cupboards!

Heather didn't really want to wake Dan up when she found him snoring away peacefully, with an empty whisky bottle by his side, but on the dot of 8.30, the doorbell rattled and he woke with a start. As one of my dearest and closest friends, Dan was almost indispensable during that time; one couldn't have a better doorman than a hungover, bad-tempered American who got up and told the first reporters where they could put their notebooks. Then, before we'd even had our first cup of tea, friends and helpers were also arriving again. When the time came for us to go and meet Patrick, Herbie repeated his earlier warning about the press. 'Just walk straight past them and get in the car. The same applies when we get to my place . . .'

Having run the gauntlet outside my home with no problem, we drove to Herbie's only to find several more reporters and photographers waiting outside. Again we walked straight past them into the house as they came running up firing questions. Just as we got inside, Patrick came running in behind us. He was dressed as I had never seen him before – wearing a dog collar. Of course, seeing a clergyman had the immediate effect of starting the cameras clicking. As we were saying hello, Herbie also came running in and grabbed a bucket of water which had been standing inside the door. The last thing I saw, as I turned away in disbelief, was 'the world's greatest bass player' flying horizontally through the air that split second after the water left the bucket and just before it hit the photographer – full in the face!

'What in God's name is he doing?' said Patrick, laughing.

'I don't know,' I said, beginning to smile again. 'He's been behaving like this ever since it all happened. I think he's working a lifelong vendetta out of his system. Somebody at the local police station recommended the water. They said, "By the time they get all the way here, to make a complaint, their clothes will be almost completely dry in this hot weather." Talking about clothes,' I said, 'it's strange to see you dressed like that?'

Heather looked confused by my last remark.

'Oh, well, I thought I had better wear the uniform today, as I'm here on official business,' said Patrick. 'Father Wheatley has never met me before.' Then, ripping his collar off as he went into the studio, he added, 'This damned thing is too hot to wear in here!' Heather's mouth dropped open in stunned amazement; she had never heard a vicar talk like that before – but then she had never met Patrick before either.

'I told you he was special,' I said, winking at her as I introduced them to each other. Just seeing Patrick was making me feel better.

Herbie soon came back in and said, 'I think we've beaten them for the time being. They've just said, "You lot are unbelievable, we've never known such a solid, close-knit family of people. We give in, we're going home." So they've gone. How about a cup of tea, everyone?'

Our meeting with Peter Wheatley was equally encouraging and heralded the beginning of a wave of synchronistic events, which went on for months.

With Patrick's help, I explained my ideas for the service and to my surprise and relief, Peter was in complete sympathy with all my requests. I couldn't believe it when he said, 'This church is yours to do whatever you like in,' because, at that point, there was also the possibility of there being a live group playing! He never once pushed any of his own ideas on me. In retrospect, what most impressed Heather and me about that morning's meeting was the incredible humility of these men. As she said later, 'Those two have restored some of my faith in the clergy.'

Looking back, it seemed that every person involved was so highly attuned to the needs of others, things kept on falling into place – almost miraculously. When I mentioned my choice of readings to Peter, his copy of *The Prophet* was already marked and fell open at the passage I wanted when he fetched it from his study. Jill, the girlfriend from my teenage days, who had bought *The Little Prince* for me a year or so earlier, was already thinking about it when, later that day, I asked her to do a reading from it at the funeral. Then, quite independently, we both thought of exactly the same passage from the many possibilities. Finally, that hauntingly beautiful place, Highgate Cemetery, which I thought was full up, not only turned out to have spaces available, it was one of the only places in north London that would allow me to bury the twins in the same coffin.

Apparently, due to some archaic health law, council-run cemeteries refused to allow this. Likewise, Highgate would also allow me to erect what most would consider a somewhat unconventional monument. I couldn't believe my luck. Had circumstances been less tragic, I might have even said I was pleased with how it was all going.

Later that same evening, Jeremy and Julie arrived in what appeared to be a very heavy and depressed mood. He had telephoned me earlier to say that he was being given a very hard time by his other relatives in Essex and couldn't wait to get away. I told him about the incredible, almost electric atmosphere which had developed and was permeating my home, so I suggested they get to us as soon as possible and take in some of it; they would be able to fully relax and get away from those pressures with us.

When we finally sat down to talk quietly, Jeremy said that he'd had a very busy week, what with sorting things out with the bank and solicitors. This alone had been pretty gruelling, but not as bad as the pressures he said he was getting from his uncles, aunts, cousins and neighbours. He said something like, 'They're all trying to slice up the big cake and take their share already; they're like a load of fucking magpies! They've been in the house trying to sneak out various bits and pieces under their coats saying that this or that had always been promised to them. Auntie Pam even went round and collected up all of Mother's jewellery and we had an argument over who should look after it. She had said, "Oh no, Jeremy, I think I should look after Junie's jewellery. Got to keep it safe, boy!" There was even one person,' he said, 'who started to fence off a piece of land saying my father had promised it to him months before.'

I was horrified by all this apparent greed, but not at all surprised either. I had always had the impression that underneath they were a tough family, who would always put money and business first. Jeremy was no different, but he had just lost his whole family and, as far as I was concerned, they could have had the decency to hold off for a while. This, however, could never compare with what had really upset me during this conversation. While we were discussing the flowers and what to tell people if they asked, Jeremy said to me, 'Some people have been so damning about Sheila; one person even suggested her coffin should be decked with only black flowers!'

I can't describe how disgusted I was by this news and can only add that it drove a wedge of mistrust between myself and Jeremy's relations for quite some time. When I told my family and some of my friends what had been said, their reaction was much the same as my own. In the case of my sister, she said damn the expense. 'We're going to buy Bambs the biggest and best show of flowers we can afford. How dare they say that!'

When I spoke to Jeremy about the more positive attitude of people around me and how he must also remember the happy times, it seemed to me then as if he only needed my permission to lift his depression and let go of his grief. My suggestion that he recall some of the more amusing memories of his family – his father's wicked sense of humour for one – brought him quickly out of it and he started smiling again. Apparently much lighter, Jeremy then told us about how he and Nevill used to amuse themselves by making agricultural sales representatives think they were in for a very large order; ten combines for example, and then, at the last minute – as the man licked his pen and mentally totted up his commission – ask the price of a second-hand one. 'As for my mother,' Jeremy added, 'I don't have any happy memories of her. I don't think she ever made me laugh.'

After this he started talking about his thoughts for the future; about giving up Whitehouse Farm and setting up a wine bar, or buying a smallholding in somewhere like Dorset. This ebullient mood persisted from then on, but I put much of this down to the tranquillisers his doctor had prescribed, and the fact that he was taking and regularly washing them down with large quantities of alcohol. He, therefore, spent most of the weekend asleep and was always conveniently crashed out whenever any of my family were around.

He did, however, get caught out one time when, unbeknown to him, my mother arrived while he was downstairs washing his hair. Jeremy apparently came running upstairs with his soapy hair pulled out into spikes, giggling like a little boy. On seeing my mother, he ran back downstairs in horror. Minutes later, he re-presented himself with the grief-stricken visage that later became so famous in the newspaper photographs of the first funeral. Unfortunately, I didn't know about this till much later.

The only other time he really came to life in our presence was on the Saturday evening, when about ten of us went out for an Indian meal, which he insisted on paying for. All through the evening, he kept on waving a thick wallet of money around saying, 'I'll pay for the meal, I've got all the men's wages here, but I also drew too much from the bank.'

After this, we all went to a local community centre, where some friends had organised a small jazz evening on behalf of Live Aid.

Herbie's new group, The English Jazz Quartet, was top of the bill. It was an intimate evening, where everybody knew each other. I could certainly see no point in missing it, especially when music can be such a great healer. Daniel and Nicholas wouldn't have missed it for the world.

Another special thing about that evening was that four out of the five women who had ever meant anything to me were all there together – Jan, Jill, Heather and Sandra. The only one missing was Bambs; the one who had, supposedly, brought them all together on this occasion. Under normal circumstances, I might have crept away and hidden somewhere – because they were all getting on far too well – but instead, I will always remember that sight with a mixture of joy and sadness.

On Monday morning, Herbie drove Heather and me to Highgate Cemetery, where we met the curate and Bill Herman, the grave-digger, who told us many interesting tales about the place. Walking through the Eastern Cemetery, I was enchanted by the way in which the undergrowth had been allowed to grow wild over the monu-ments, showing only glimpses of long-forgotten sentiment. Nature was winning back in a strange, controlled sort of way. We found a perfect plot in the shade of a big old rosebush.

Little else could be done until we knew exactly when or if the police would be releasing the bodies. They said that it probably wouldn't be till after the inquest on Wednesday, but then there was no guarantee. As it turned out, we were more fortunate than most families of murder victims. Under normal circumstances, bodies can be kept in the mortuary for months, even years, pending further investigations, but because our case was classified as four murders and a suicide, release was as predicted.

When Jeremy said his parents and Bambs's funeral would be on the Friday, it meant that I would have to wait till after the weekend for Nicholas and Daniel's. I was in fact relieved to have it that way, because it would allow time for Bambs's ashes to be processed and brought to London in time for the other service. It meant so much to me that her remains be placed close to the boys, at their heads – which could only really be done at their funeral – rather than added at a later date, yards above them. This wish, however, would entail her ashes being collected from Colchester at nine o'clock on the Monday morning. Some of Bambs's relations offered to collect them on their way to London, but after the 'black flower' story, I no longer felt any trust. I wouldn't have put it past any of them to accidentally spill the container on the roadside during the journey. Instead, Bruce, an Australian friend, to whom I'll always be indebted, offered to guarantee their safe arrival at the service.

A few days later, the undertaker asked us to deliver all the boys' personal effects that were to be buried with them. I didn't want them to get muddled up, so two separate carrier bags were prepared. Their treasured Flower Fairy dolls, Care Bears and favourite cuddly toys were only small things, but extremely important to all of us. I also included Cuthbert, Bambs's own very worn and very loved teddy bear, subsequently adopted by Nicholas. Apart from these, a few small personal gifts from other people were included; a tiny elf pendant on a chain from Nicky Flowers and a letter from Jan.

I still couldn't face seeing them myself, but I had to be sure that all my wishes were fulfilled. I could appreciate the undertaker's advice but I didn't fully trust him; he was almost too keen that nobody should see the bodies 'in the condition they were in'. Once again, Heather told me she would like to see them, to say goodbye in her own way, and offered to go on my behalf; she was prepared for them to be an unpleasant sight.

Satisfied that she wasn't just doing it for me, I gave strict instructions that only Heather be allowed to view the bodies before the coffin was sealed. I have since had many regrets about my decision not to view the bodies, but I am also confirmed in my opinion that it was the right one for me. Unfortunately, through my own fear of viewing the harsh reality, I took away the opportunity for others to complete their own grief process as they might have chosen. At the time, however, I thought I was doing the best for everyone.

Although I have spoken of my 'peaceful' demeanour, this is not to be mistaken for happiness, because I was far from being happy. I spent much of this period shut in my room crying my eyes out, listening to the music we had always enjoyed together, or staring out of the window at the sunflowers waving in the breeze – waiting to bloom.

Sometimes I just sat and read *The Magic Faraway Tree*. This said, I wasn't only crying for Bambs and the boys, I was also crying for myself, knowing I would never ever be able to read to or talk to them again; never be able to enjoy their lively company, their friendship or their bony little cuddles.

I also spent a lot of this time going over everything in my mind. Not only the horrors of the tragedy, but also the premonitions that had plagued me before it all happened. I kept on admonishing myself for ignoring those tiny intuitive voices that had told me things I thought were so improbable. I put my nagging fear of taking the boys to the farm down to Bambs not being strong enough to protect them from June's over-zealous religious assaults.

But this was an acceptable and understandable fear and doesn't compare with some of the other precognitive thoughts which had also flashed through my mind; thoughts which had sent a shiver down my spine before being pushed away into my subconscious; feelings which always occurred when my mind was at its blankest and most open. For example, while walking along a grey London street, I had the premonition that I was going to lose both boys – they were both going to die. But this was so unlikely I immediately dismissed the idea. One child maybe – through an accident or something – but never two!

On another occasion, a thought flashed through my mind that I would be investigated and accused by the police in a murder case. As things turned out, that is exactly how I was to feel, more and more; especially when the investigations were later reopened. Having said this, I wasn't aware of these visions being anything more than unpleasant thoughts in a fertile imagination; until one particular experience which, I feel, was nothing less than strong mental telepathy. I just couldn't stop remembering that terrible fear I'd experienced on the eve of the shootings – completely uncontrolled and unaccountable.

I had been feeling somewhat frustrated by my increasing involvement with Bambs and the fact that our friendship and her illness had been causing a lot of strain between Heather and me – especially having invited Bambs to the party. But this alone was not the cause of my build-up of anxiety that evening. Something else was bothering me. In an attempt to clear the air, I went to see Heather at her flat, where we tried to continue an earlier discussion, but we were still at loggerheads.

Suddenly, for no understandable reason except perhaps frustration, I broke down and cried out, 'All these bloody problems with Bambs, I sometimes wish she was dead!' At that very moment, I began to feel extremely frightened for Daniel and Nicholas. I had no idea why, but I was soon shaking with tears and crying that I missed them terribly.

'I hope they're all right at the farm. I want to see them so much. I want to hold them, I want to talk to them, I'm really frightened for them!'

Heather suggested I telephone, to put my mind at rest, but when I looked at the clock, I saw it was far too late; it was nearly eleven o'clock. They would have all been asleep. And besides, they would probably think I was crazy, waking them up with some hare-brained story that I had been worried about them. After a while I calmed down and began to feel much less anxious, in fact, unbelievably so. My sudden outburst had helped us both to resolve our differences, so I eventually went home to sleep like a log, not realising how much that fateful oath was going to ring in my ears on the following day – and for many weeks to come.

I have also often wondered whether anyone would have answered the telephone that night had I made a call, or whether I had actually picked up, telepathically, the moment of their deaths. I suppose that's something I shall never know.

CHAPTER SIX

Cold,
naked,
alone
in the dark.
They brought us
to the mausoleum.
Cold,
naked
and alone
in the vault.
That's how they left us;
in the dark.
Why?

FOR MOST PEOPLE, funerals invoke images of darkness and gloom; black clothes, pale flowers and lonely solemn moments for the grieving relatives; that last chance to be physically close to those departed; to be alone with one's thoughts and memories; a private time for grief and farewells. As things turned out, neither of the funerals bore any resemblance to the norm. I had already decided Nicholas and Daniel's was going to be far from normal. I wanted it to be a celebration of their lives, short though they were, and not a conventional mournful dirge. Unfortunately, there was little I could do about Bambs's funeral, but I could at least make it up for her at theirs.

To the best of my knowledge, nobody was looking forward to either event with any relish. I also had a strong suspicion that the one in Tolleshunt D'Arcy was going to be little more than a black pantomime organised by the church and, as the day went on, my fears were justified – the whole funeral in respect of Bambs and Nevill was an absolute farce. As for Daniel and Nicholas, they weren't mentioned once during the service – even though they'd shared the same fate. Having said that, the boys didn't go unnoticed and I, think, made their own, very individual contribution to the day. In many ways, what felt like their spiritual presence took some of the sting out of our mood and sent us on our way to Essex in a much lighter frame of mind.

There was loads to do that Friday morning and all seemed straightforward until I tried to start the car. It was as dead as a door-nail. Not even a whine – except from my mouth. Thinking the battery was flat, I called the garage to come and rescue me, but when the mechanic arrived, he told me that the wiring had burnt out during the night.

'This car's not going anywhere today,' he said. 'In fact, you're lucky the whole thing didn't catch fire – that's what usually happens.' He then told me he had a BMW in for service that I could borrow, providing I had it back in time for valeting first thing in the morning. I couldn't believe my luck when he handed over the keys. I felt a little like Cinderella must have done after the transformation of the pumpkin into a carriage fit for a princess. The car, which I nicknamed 'the Sweaty Lemon' – but more because of how I was feeling – was bright yellow, like a sunflower, fast and very sporty.

When I got back home, somebody had been to fetch the equally bright arrangement of yellow roses and lilies I had ordered for Bambs the day before. They were so beautiful, but could barely begin to do justice to her memory. What really amazed me was that they and the car happened to be a perfect match for each other.

Earlier that year, Bambs had met her real mother for the first time, and it was one of the biggest, most important events of her life. Although they had been corresponding for a few years, sadly it was to be the one and only time they ever met, but a very special occasion for both of them. I will never forget the look of sheer joy on Bambs's face when I first saw them together. She was beaming from ear to ear, with a smile I hadn't seen the like of since she gave birth to the twins.

Christine, an elegant woman in her mid-forties, was as beautiful as her daughter, as sexy, and so obviously her real mum. To see them chatting together, one would have thought they were more like sisters – or old school friends comparing notes. There was an instant rapport between them. Bambs later told me that Christine was everything she ever dreamed she would be; that she had this wonderful feeling that she had an identity at last. 'She gave me so many hugs,' said Bambs. Something, she had often remarked in the past, June never did.

There was a great deal of fuss and adverse publicity in the press regarding this meeting. It was claimed by both the journalists and their invited psychiatric experts that this had been a very traumatic experience for Bambs; intensifying and speeding up her mental decline. Having been witness to this reunion, I would say it had exactly the opposite effect. If anything, it had been a great boost for her; the catalyst in her recovery that gave her hope.

I mention all this now because we spent much of that week trying to locate Christine, who now lived in North America, but without much success; the police had not been very helpful in giving us information from Bambs's address book – now in their possession. Fortunately, I received a letter from her brother, Peter, who lives in London, so at the last minute we arranged to give him a lift to the funeral. Bambs had spoken a lot about her new-found and quietly spoken uncle, a poet, but I had never met him before that day. He has since become a good friend.

I was so glad Bambs's natural family would be represented at her funeral. It would have meant so much to her to have known this.

When we reached Goldhanger, most of my friends went to the pub, while I took my family into Jeremy's house to meet Bambs's relations. The atmosphere was, to say the least, strained and tense but also strange; rather like a charade. Apart from two detectives, trying not to look conspicuous, people stood and chatted while Jeremy's friends ran about offering sandwiches and drinks. Although we were all visibly aged by the ordeal, everybody was putting on their usual good face, except Uncle Bobby (Robert Boutflour). He couldn't even come into the house and was standing in the garden, grey-faced and eyes wet with weeping.

One of the most striking things about that day, although not altogether surprising for me, was the fact that, the more I talked to June and Nevill's relations, the more I realised none of them actually knew anything had been seriously wrong with Bambs – not even June's sister Pam. Many of them said that had they known, they would have been more than willing to help and share the burden. Why hadn't I contacted them and told them all about it? I couldn't believe what I was hearing and could only reply by saying that I didn't feel it had been my business to betray the Bambers' confidence. They were very private people whose decisions I had to respect – whether they were right or wrong. These people could have no idea how much I'd needed them as allies to convince June and Nevill of how strongly I felt Bambs's treatment should have been changed.

Their lack of awareness was probably a tremendous blessing, because without a full appreciation of her illness – which, for me, had acted like a smokescreen to the truth – they were absolutely convinced Bambs couldn't have done it and, unbeknown to me then, were already pressing the police into further investigations, albeit with little initial success.

With their intimate first-hand knowledge of the Bambers and their habits, especially with regard to Nevill and his guns – and, for that matter, guns in general – a great deal did not tie up. Remembered conversations and snippets overheard of Jeremy giving his statement further added to their suspicion. But most damning of all, for the police, was their discovery – on being given access to the farmhouse to clear up – of, amongst other things, a bloodstained silencer. This was found standing in a box right at the back of Nevill's gun cupboard, along with the ammunition and telescopic sights which were normally fitted to the gun.

Unfortunately, they didn't tell me any of this for some time. There was, after all, the possibility they suspected me as much as they did Jeremy. Having welcomed him into my home, both prior to the shootings, at my party, and afterwards, when he effectively isolated me from any desire to communicate with his family, it would appear, very easily to them, that we were closer than truth would have it.

* * *

The bright yellow sports car raised many eyebrows when I arrived, and I felt like the twins had somehow fixed it for me to attend that day in style; driving a brightly coloured banner on their behalf. Some thought it rather ostentatious for the occasion, but I didn't think so at all.

'Whose yellow BMW is that outside?' said Jeremy, shortly after I arrived. So I told him the story of our morning. When I had finished, he said he had only asked because one of his friends was crazy about BMWs and would like the opportunity to take it for a spin. Would I mind if this friend drove the rest of the flowers to the church in it, with his girlfriend? 'It would really make his day.'

This was the first time I really thought Jeremy's behaviour a bit unusual, though I was so surprised by the request, I agreed. He seemed to be playing sugar-daddy to all his attendant friends – by pandering to their every whim. Fortunately, this part of the panto-mime soon gave way to our departure, in which Jeremy had put me in the first car with the rest of my own family, Julie and himself.

Everybody else was being organised by Jeremy's friend Brett, a stocky fair-haired New Zealander that Jeremy had met on his earlier travels there. When I asked about him, I was told that he had first arrived in England about a month or so before but went away again, to Greece, until earlier that week. He and Jeremy seemed to be very close but with a definite sense, to me, of Brett being in charge. He brought up the rear of the cortège driving Nevill's blue Citroën.

I was amazed at the enormous number of people outside as we drove in a solemn procession of five limousines to the church in Tolleshunt D'Arcy. The village streets were crammed tight with locals out for an afternoon's sightseeing; some to genuinely pay their last respects; some from morbid curiosity, and many to catch a glimpse of a family's desolation.

When we attempted to enter the church, it was even worse. Apart from the crush of reporters, there were more people standing at the back than most churches could boast in a full congregation on a good Sunday. Every pew, with the exception of the front row on the right-hand side, was full. I don't know where they thought we would all sit. In the end, most of the family had to make do with the choir seating behind the clergymen, where they couldn't see. The overbearing mass of villagers, it seemed, held priority over the real mourners – those close friends and family who had travelled many miles to be there.

Right from the early stages of planning, there had been little consideration for the feelings of relatives who wanted a quiet, private, family funeral. They had very little say in its organisation and were, in fact, told by the vicar, when they said they wanted privacy, that it was, and would be, a public occasion. Much against their wishes it became a church display, a media event with loudspeakers outside for those who couldn't get in; it certainly bore little resemblance to a funeral. Even from the very first day, it appeared to me that the vicar seemed intent on getting his name in the press as often as possible.

On entering the church, I saw the three coffins fanned out in front of the altar as we were led to the front row on the right. As soon as I saw them I knew which one was Bambs. Someone had taken the care to cover her with beautiful pink roses. I was also glad to see that, quite accidentally, Peter, Bambs's only blood relative present, found himself seated at her head. I wish I had been sitting near her myself, but I was led to the other side, next to Jeremy, where Nevill's coffin was placed. June, as most recent church warden, was placed in the centre. There were three clergymen in attendance.

After a short preamble, the service opened with everyone singing Psalm 23: 'The Lord is my Shepherd'. The tune more than the words had the immediate effect of opening my floodgates but it was very short-lived. No sooner had they begun the eulogy, I found myself clenching my teeth in anger – as were many others who came as friends of Bambs or Nevill. It seemed that because of her recent appointment to the post of church warden, the entire service was geared towards singing the praises of June Bamber, and one might have been mistaken for thinking she had been the only one to die. The others were only mentioned in passing – if at all – and in Bambs's case, only in a condemnatory way. Whatever happened to the mercy of the Church?

During the service, mourners were told, 'Sheila found no physical security against distress but eternal security *may* still be hers.' Unfortunately, these clergymen failed to make any attempt to say or ask why she found no physical security. As I listened, I began to remember those passages I had found in Southwark Cathedral a week earlier.

'So I returned, and considered all the oppressions that are done under the sun: and behold the tears of such as were oppressed, and they had no comforter; and on the side of their oppressors there was power; but they had no comforter.'

The congregation was then called upon to show forgiveness to her and told, 'Love does not keep a family record of wrongs.' Just for a moment, I thought I could detect a hint of compassion, but when the elderly canon said, 'We pray for God's mercy for Sheila, sadly and tragically deranged . . . ,' I felt like screaming out at their self-righteousness; they couldn't even recognise the sickness within their own congregation. The only time they came anywhere near mentioning the twins was when the vicar said, 'Sheila was a mother and I understand she knew her gospel.' But that was all that was said of Daniel and Nicholas; their actual names were never mentioned.

All in all, I began to feel very bitter. Not so much for the deaths – for those I just felt very sad – but bitterness towards this pantheon of hypocrisy. Rather than being able to cry, as I desperately wanted and needed to, I was enraged.

To make things worse, there were the reporters and cameramen; a great wall of them waiting for us, both on the way in and on the way out of the church. It wasn't too bad as we entered – because we didn't have to hang about. They were really there to capitalise on our grief after the service.

I don't think I will ever forget that banshee-like whirr of camera motor drives. It has become, for me, one of the most disturbing noises I've ever heard. Whenever I hear them now, they cause me to shudder with the memory of that day; I have instant recollection of that moment coming out of the church and all the cameras screaming into action; blinding flashes, shouted questions and motor drives. It was horrible.

Although we were prepared for it all after the service, we were naturally far more emotional, which is exactly what they wanted. The worst part was that one couldn't escape, I wanted to make a run for the limousine and leave there quickly, but I couldn't. Out of respect for the dead, we had to stand and wait while the coffins were loaded; cameras screaming at us constantly. It was just as we were about to move forward again that Jeremy staged his infamous collapse for the cameras. I was behind him with my arm round my sister; Julie had her arm around Jeremy's waist and was holding his hand with the other as she stared blankly at all the cameras.

Suddenly, I heard a moan or a big sob and Jeremy's knees buckled briefly beneath him, firing off the cameras even more. My sister leapt forward, catching his elbow. My own reaction was equally spontaneous. 'It's all right, Jem,' I said, grasping his shoulder. 'Don't worry, I'm here. I'm right behind you.' I now feel really sick that I was taken in by it, but I couldn't see his face at the time, he had his back to me. In fact, I can't say I really saw his face at all that day; I was too locked up in my own feelings of grief and anger.

By the time we were eventually allowed into the cars and the doors were closed, we all breathed a sigh of relief but, as we followed the three hearses out of the village, with the undertaker walking slowly in front, Jeremy started cracking jokes and laughing. To some extent I could accept it as an understandable release of tension, but his joking became unnecessarily smutty; making all sorts of remarks about what he would like to be doing to Julie later that afternoon. It was in poor taste in any circumstances, but with my family in the car, it was completely out of order. That fifteen-mile drive to the crematorium – coming nearer to that final farewell – was awful. And when we got there, it was over so suddenly. No sooner had we sat down, the curtains were drawn across the coffins.

The thought of cremating Bambs had never felt right to me, but even more so at that moment than any other time. I didn't want it that way and never had. I wanted to scream out, 'No, stop! I don't want her burnt, I want to bury her with the twins, as she is.' I began to feel that, once again, she had been cheated – by both Church and family; cheated in death as she had been in life. I wanted her placed in the ground, together with the sons she loved, as she was, whole. But there was nothing I could say or do; the curtains closed and that was that. Her body and beautiful face were gone for ever.

If that moment in the crematorium hadn't been enough to tear me apart, the press had already added to my pain the day before with some really crass speculations about the twins having a separate funeral; presumptions that caused a lot of very distressful hate-mail to arrive at the pottery. Fortunately, Herbie was censoring my post, so I didn't see any of it, or in fact even hear of it, for some time.

'**Massacre mum won't be buried with sons**', said one of the headlines. 'Twins shot dead by their mother in farm massacre will not be buried with her. Mrs Caffell's ex-husband, Colin, refused to let the boys share their grave.'

'**Killer's twins buried alone**', said another tabloid. 'Twin brothers who were killed by their demented mother will be buried apart from her. Their father has refused to let them share the same resting place.'

The *Sun*, however, made the most emphatic presumption with, 'FINAL SNUB FOR MUM IN MASSACRE'.

Apart from the invasion of our private grief, encouraged by the vicar in Tolleshunt D'Arcy, the real invasion came in the coverage of the funeral itself. Many newspapers took the liberty of quoting my personal messages from wreaths I had left for Bambs from the twins and myself. In the case of the *Sun* newspaper, they went right over the top and even printed photographs of the two cards under the headline:

MASSACRE KID'S DAD FORGIVES HIS BAMBI

Amazing wreath notes . . . Ex-husband of massacre model Sheila 'Bambi' Caffell forgave her yesterday for murdering their children.

The reception at Jeremy's house was fairly brief, as his friends and relatives seemed in a hurry to get back to their homes in time for the television news. They seemed more interested in seeing if they had been filmed than thinking about the day and what had been happening; this didn't make any sense to me at all. It was a great relief going back to London knowing the twins' funeral was going to follow, rather than precede, this one – and be a complete contrast to the whole thing. I said to everybody that afternoon, 'Please don't wear black at the twins' funeral on Monday, it would offend them to see us like that.'

I told them it was not going to be at all like the one we'd just attended; it was going to be a celebration to which I was openly encouraging mourners to wear colourful clothes. After all, Daniel, Nicholas and their mum had been very colourful people. When it actually came to the day, everybody was, in fact, that much brighter; Heather had found a lovely floral dress and I bought myself a light grey suit, turquoise shirt and white tie.

On the Saturday morning, after Heather came back from seeing the boys, I went to order the flowers for their coffin in a much lighter frame of mind. At the florist's, I asked for the brightest, most colourful selection of flowers they could find. 'Use lots of prime colours. I don't care how much they clash, I want them to dazzle and hurt the eyes!' This was another decision I had already made, but after experiencing the first funeral, it made me all the more determined to ensure that Bambs, Daniel and Nicholas were finally sent off in style. It seemed that each knock or blessing I received, as the days went by, both strengthened and sensitised me for the next challenge.

Friday had also confirmed my feelings about making the twins' funeral an occasion of light and progression. I wanted all the sadness and anger to be tempered with the other emotions of joy and serenity. I hoped to raise everybody's heaviness and depression – if only temporarily – so that, perhaps, we could all go part of the way on the journey with them. During their lives, Bambs and the boys shared with us their love and their humour; therefore, they should also be remembered with laughter and humour.

One of the most magical and uncanny things about the day of Nicholas and Daniel's funeral was the fact that the first two sunflowers, which *they* had planted and nurtured in our garden, opened that very morning. These two had somehow accelerated their growth and flowered almost two weeks before the rest of the crop. So I took this as a special gift and cut them to go on the coffin with the rest of the flowers. It was almost as if the boys' faces had blossomed once again for their funeral.

I had planned to walk the half-mile to the church and spend an hour on my own with the boys, rather than arrive in the procession.

I hadn't been anywhere near the twins before that morning and wanted one last opportunity to read to them from *The Magic Faraway Tree*. I also didn't feel like speaking to anybody before the service. It was decided, however, that I might get pestered, so I agreed to be driven. Fortunately, the danger of running into reporters had been minimised, because Herbie had sent those who were foolish enough to ask him for the venue on a wild-goose chase to another church in Richmond. To my relief, Jan volunteered to take me.

Spending that last hour together in private – just the two of us with the boys – was how it was really meant to be that morning. Even after Heather later joined us at the service, Jan stayed by my side for the rest of the day. In my eyes, nothing will change the fact that Daniel and Nicholas will always be her little boys too.

The white, fabric-covered coffin looked so tiny, standing alone in the large red-brick church, but it also glowed with a gentle light from the candles on the altar and the riot of flowers which covered it. The small casket containing Bambs's ashes already stood to one side with a warm posy of autumn-coloured flowers in front of it. As things turned out, it was almost impossible to be completely private because a few strangers, probably reporters, were already standing at the back of the church. With Jan by my side, I managed to sit by the coffin and quietly read out a few pages, but it wasn't very long before the first mourners also started arriving.

I hadn't thought about it beforehand, but it was comforting to be able to greet them as they arrived. There were many I hadn't seen for so long and many more still who I couldn't see through my tears on the way out. By the time the service began, the church was almost full of colourful people wearing colourful clothes.

Right from the start, everything about Patrick's service was so much lighter than the funeral at Tolleshunt D'Arcy. Sharing his own fond memories of the twins, and how he had first met them as 'two naked cherubs' who came running into Herbie's studio having heard, from their bedroom above, his singing for the first time. Patrick told the assembly, 'Everyone is deeply moved by the tragic events which brought us here. The little ones were well loved.' Even never having met Bambs, he still spoke of her with tremendous kindness and respect, adding, 'We must remember that, whatever the circumstances, God is Love.' He also took great care in including June and Nevill in this eulogy; there were no more barriers erected.

Readings and songs followed on much as I'd hoped. Patrick took up his guitar and sang one of his own songs as promised, but when another friend, Mark Duxbury, sang 'It's a Big, Big Beautiful World', one of his own compositions, written just for children, he almost had everyone clapping their hands as we all joined in the chorus. For me, though, the most special part of that service was when Jill and Chris read from *The Little Prince* a short passage with something that seemed very fresh to say about bereavement, especially for those who have lost children.

There was an extra special quality about Jill's voice that day. When she spoke the words of the little prince, it was almost as if there were tiny bells ringing somewhere, like laughter in the eaves. I also couldn't help noticing the effect it had on others as several mourners sat up, moved by her clarity. The passage was taken from very near the end of the book where the little prince, who comes from a very small star, tells his earthbound companion that he will soon be going home and that, when he leaves, it will appear that he has died. But what most touched me about this piece was his talk of the gift he would leave behind; a gift I feel the twins have also left with me:

'In one of the stars I shall be living. In one of them I shall be laughing. And so it will be as if all the stars were laughing, when you look at the sky at night. You – only you – will have stars that can laugh!' And he laughed again.

By the time the service had ended with 'Morning Has Broken', I had almost forgotten we were at a funeral. But the joy was very short-lived. No sooner had we stopped singing, the traditional funeral music began – a signal for the four pall-bearers to step forward. As they lifted the little white coffin on to their shoulders, and the funeral director picked up the casket with Bambs's ashes, it was all too much for me and the racking convulsions of grief once again flooded my body.

Outside, those infernal cameramen were there again, lying in wait with their glassy-eyed instruments of torture! And, again, there was nothing we could do about it: we just stood there, helpless and vulnerable as we watched the coffin being loaded into the hearse; motor drives once again screaming in our ears. But it seemed, to some extent, that Herbie's ploy had worked. On the following day, only three national papers ran a story. The *Daily Express* was the worst, having really gone to town with a centre spread 'Express Picture Special' under the headline:

FATHER'S FAREWELL TO HIS LITTLE ANGELS
A SINGLE little coffin . . . a heartbroken father. These harrowing pictures mark the final sad chapter of the Massacre at Whitehouse Farm.

Almost as if reviewing the première of a new movie rather than a funeral, they went on to describe how I was dressed; they couldn't even get my age right. '**Mr Caffell, 35, who wore a light grey suit and white tie, prayed tearfully over the boys' coffin . . .**'

At Highgate, I was surprised to see that a large number of those at the service had followed the procession. There must have been nearly fifty at the graveside. A short rain-shower had freshened the grass on the way there, but it soon cleared up and the sun came out again on our arrival. At this, the most harrowing moment, when the coffin had been lowered into the ground, two things moved me very deeply.

The first was a very touching act by the grave-digger who, to the annoyance of the undertaker, lowered his ladder into the grave and climbed down so that his assistant could pass him the casket containing Bambs's ashes. Having placed them at Nicholas and Daniel's heads, he took a large red flower from their coffin and tucked it under the sash of their mother's casket. He then climbed out, removed the ladder and bowed his head in respect, then quietly stepped back out of the scene.

After this Patrick blessed the burial, and at the moment I felt most alone, Chantelle, a little six-year-old West Indian girl, came and held my hand. So we both stood and looked into the grave together. Chantelle was one of Nicholas and Daniel's best friends from school; one of the little girls they most liked to bring home for tea – the *only* child at the funeral. For those few minutes, Chantelle made me feel that everything was going to be all right. Thank heavens for little children.

I had hoped there would be a few more there but, in the case of my two nieces, Lucy and Abbi, my family had decided it would be 'better for them' if they didn't come and sent them back to Norway a few days earlier. Their absence really began to make me wonder about all the times I too hadn't been allowed to attend a funeral. But at the same time, this was no different to me not allowing my family to view the bodies; the patterns and messages of childhood, it seemed, were being passed on to yet another generation, and I was colluding with that.

As it turned out, this left Lucy and Abbi with a whole load of unresolved grief, unanswered questions and an unnatural view, possibly even fear, of the inevitable reality. It took Abbi, the youngest, another four years to ask questions about death and about what had happened – and that was only after she had seen me talking about it all on television. When will we finally learn not to perpetuate all the fears that cripple our lives by passing them on to our children? There really is no need!

It took some time before everybody was ready to leave. In fact the only one who seemed to be in any hurry was Jeremy. He went to sit in the car straight away – as he had also done at the crematorium – waiting impatiently for the rest of us, who were happy to stand in the sun and chat for a while. On the way home, Ann Flowers came and squeezed into the first car with my family, telling me later that she had felt really uncomfortable in the other car with Jeremy. He had given her the creeps on the way there, and she didn't know why.

Back at my place, everybody finally relaxed, except for Jeremy, who, after a few choice remarks to Patrick about his entire family being mad, left soon afterwards. It was one of the last times I was to see him as a free man.

To sum up the spirit of that afternoon, one friend, almost a year later, trying to remind Jill of a conversation they'd had that afternoon, made a wonderful *faux pas* when he said: 'Don't you remember, it was at that great party Colin held at his flat last summer?' Jill paused and thought for a moment, and then said, 'Mick, that wasn't a party, that was Nicholas and Daniel's funeral.' Horribly embarrassed, he then said, 'Promise me you'll never tell Colin I said that', but she did; she knew how touched I would be to know it was remembered in such a way.

Another friend sent some very touching words in a letter the day after:

> *I'm still 'tingling' after yesterday; there was such a feeling of togetherness and love and mutual understanding between us all. I keep singing, 'It's a beautiful world'!*
>
> *The events of the last ten days have made us all look at life in a slightly different way. I suppose I now know that it's important to live and enjoy each day as it comes, make the most of it and try to enjoy fond memories of yesterday.*

CHAPTER SEVEN

I HAVE SPOKEN A lot about my own unbelievably peaceful state of mind during the weeks following the shootings; a feeling of being held and supported by unseen hands. Well, I was not the only one to feel like this: Jan and Heather also had, in the ensuing weeks, what they could only describe as very strong, quite separate, 'spiritual' experiences. These were, for both of them, very personal, very moving and quite unexpected. It would also be safe to say that these were not people I would ever describe as prone to fantasy, hysteria or exaggeration.

The morning Herbie drove Heather to the Chapel of Rest (to see the boys before they were sealed up) had been preceded a day or two earlier by a sudden battle of wills between them over whether *anyone* should be allowed to view the bodies. In fact it was Herbie's own fear, along with his very strong personality, that had influenced much of *my* fear and decision-making during that time. But Heather was not so easily put off. She was going to see Daniel and Nicholas regardless. So a truce was eventually called, with Herbie maintaining some face by insisting that he would drive her there.

After they had left – with Heather clutching the small bag of letters and trinkets people had asked to be included – I just sat at home worrying about it; beating myself up because I was letting Heather do something I was too afraid to do myself; wondering, anxiously, what she was having to go through on my behalf, still wishing I'd had the courage to go myself. But I had no need to fear . . . Within what seemed like no time at all they returned: Heather with the biggest smile I had ever seen on her face. Herbie said he couldn't believe her expression when she came out. He was absolutely stunned: 'It was like the sun had come out.'

I couldn't wait to sit down alone with her, after Herbie had gone, so she could tell me what it was that had made her so bright.

Apparently, when Heather went in, she was naturally very nervous, and apprehensive, not knowing quite what to expect. She saw to it that everything was exactly as I had asked – with their thumbs in their mouths and everything – and then became aware of a sort of presence, higher in the room. She said it wasn't anything tangible – it didn't have any sound or shape or colour, but she knew there were definitely two in number.

Without words they said, 'Why are you crying over those two empty shells down there? We're not there any more. We are up here playing and we're happy.' She felt she wanted to talk to them but found she actually couldn't say anything – she felt she wasn't allowed to ask questions. She said, 'They gave me something that was soft and warm and loving. It was a feeling which they gave to my heart to give to you.'

This was indeed a very precious gift and I have had a lot of uncertainty over whether it would really be appropriate to describe or talk about it – to risk demeaning the sacredness of what had happened there. But after a great deal of consideration, I decided that its significance to my own healing, to my change from victim to survivor, cannot leave it unsaid.

Jan's experience came about some three weeks later, while Heather and I were on the last leg of our journey home from Norway – which we finally got to for a couple of weeks after the funeral.

Jan had spent much of that afternoon at Highgate Cemetery, sitting on the grass by the grave with her boyfriend, Martin. While they were there other people turned up, including her mother and my father. Being a warm sunny day they all sat and chatted, affectionately, about the twins for an hour or so. But eventually, they each wandered off to have a look round – leaving Jan to lie in the sun next to the grave. Only minutes later, Martin returned to find her very agitated and almost in a state of shock . . .

While all this was happening, I was driving back to London from Harwich and suddenly got it into my head that I had to get to the cemetery before it closed. I raced the last ten miles so that we arrived just before closing time at five o'clock. We saw Jan's car outside and thought, great, we're still early enough to get in! But we very nearly didn't. 'Sorry, we're closed now,' they said. 'Come back tomorrow.' I pleaded with them to let us through, but it was only when I pointed out that a friend was still at the grave that they eventually allowed us in. 'Please don't run!' they shouted after us when, to their horror, we raced down the hill at full speed.

Much to our surprise we found the grave deserted, so we just stood quietly for a few minutes, getting our breath back and enjoying the flowers and the warm evening sunshine. That special quietness hung in the air; a loud silence which has become very familiar to me. I was so glad we had made it. We then walked quietly back to the gate, where there was still no sign of Jan. The following evening she telephoned to welcome me home and said she had something very important to tell me. She also suggested that we meet at the grave, so we made an arrangement for Monday morning before she went to work – she was now a nurse at the hospital next door to the cemetery.

Monday was another warm, sunny day and we both arrived at the same time. We sat on the grass by the grave and, after exchanging general news, I asked what was so important that she had to tell me.

'I don't know how to say this,' she said, 'but last week, while I was here, I had a very strong spiritual experience.' I asked her what she meant, so she set the scene as I have already described, but added that because everybody had been talking and laughing about the twins and their antics, there had been a lovely atmosphere all around. So when the others wandered off to explore, she was content to lie in the warm sun and reflect on her memories . . .

She couldn't tell if it was seconds or minutes later, but she became aware of an incredible energy which moved right through her body; it was like a vibration which teased and calmed her all at the same time. In the same moment, the light became intensified and the colour of the flowers took on a depth she had never seen before. Like Heather, she couldn't actually see or hear anything in the physical sense, but knew that the two of them were there. She said it was as if the boys just came running out of the bushes, pleased to see her, and playing as they would when they were alive.

She also became aware that they were speaking to her but without words – more in the form of telepathy. They teased her and told her not to be so silly; she mustn't cry about them. They said they weren't with their bodies any more, but out finding new games and places to play. Jan then became aware of a new presence, one which was more serious but still reassuring and warm, and instantly felt this to be Bambs. She said it was as if the boys had run off playing without her and she had come to collect them – to take them back.

Just then her boyfriend returned, so Jan told him what had happened. She was also much too shaken up to drive anywhere, so they found her mother and went for tea in nearby Waterlow Park. 'They were still there when we left,' she said, 'over by the stone piano, watching us go.' When I asked when this had happened, she said, 'Last Friday afternoon,' and I quickly realised why her car had been there. And possibly the reason for my own sudden need to get there fast.

Both of these experiences were totally subjective and quite unquantifiable, which is wonderful because they prove absolutely nothing. Whatever happened, however, was very real, because both women received something which brought about some form of healing and peace of mind. And that, I am beginning to realise, is all that matters. Even if what occurred was simply a product of imagination, and was received from within, we cannot ignore the fact that something beneficial took place. For myself, I didn't know then how much strength knowledge of these events was going to give me in the coming weeks – but I'm so glad they both told me. It was something to see the incredible light in their faces.

PART TWO

Choices

CHAPTER EIGHT

Slowly the Truth Dawns

*To waken, and feel
your heart sink
heavy and dark
and hardening . . .*

*Slowly the sea lifts its billow,
slowly the forest reddens in the gorge,
slowly the flames begin to lick in hell,
slowly the truth dawns.*

Olav H. Hauge
(translation by Robin Fulton)

So THAT WAS the beginning of my fall into the abyss. I say beginning, because I had landed on a ledge where I found some
comforting but temporary respite from the trauma; a place in which
I could take stock of my life – experience Grace – but I was soon to
suffer the sudden collapse of even that safe haven and continued the
descent even further.

The visit to Norway had been very beneficial to Heather and me – a
retreat from the trials of previous weeks and a chance to recuperate.
Although I was horrified by the murders and the loss of my children,
I had also begun to find a greater feeling of peace with it. In my state
of shock I had accepted everything I'd been told and could only feel
a great sense of sadness that various events and a lack of understanding
could lead to such a tragedy. Little else had changed in me since my

childhood: I lived in a world of fantasy and cosy memories – where I could escape the harsh realities of life – and still relied on other people, especially strong women, to look after and protect me. I had also acquired the family trait of 'taking' care of others as another way of avoiding my own pain.

What did seem to be intact, and a real blessing to me, was an intuitive side of my personality, which seemed to include a spiritual 'back-room', where guardian angels must have been working over-time in order to make so much happen in such strange and uncanny ways. What most stumped me, however, was the fact that my rational 'thinking' side only seemed to be working with the aid of that intu-ition; on its own it was absolutely useless.

In my numbness, it seemed, I was slowly changing – like a cater-pillar inside a cocoon. I began to feel that my life, as it had been, with so many people running around after me – looking after my needs and bailing me out of trouble – really had to change. This was not a conscious decision, but an inner knowing that I could no longer ignore. I *had* to begin to take responsibility for myself and ease away from that network of support. In being overwhelmed by it, I realised I had to break free in order to survive. But these choices and changes didn't, and couldn't, happen overnight. It's very hard to change the patterns of a lifetime, especially when the pay-off is so cosy and safe – when staying the same has its many rewards. But I also knew that if I didn't, I might not survive with my soul intact.

In a way, I had no choice. The scariest part was knowing that I would finally have to start facing some of my biggest fears. For example: those people who, for whatever reason, I saw in a position of authority above me – or that had power over me. Part of what made this possible was the decision to live my life, from then on, by Nicholas and Daniel's example; not to be beaten by their deaths, but to live my life to the full. Why I should feel that way was very simple, in that I had no intention of becoming engulfed in bitterness, self-pity or remorse – which seemed to be the other alternatives. Needless to say, that was challenged a great deal as time went on.

It's quite clear that I had a lot of anger inside me, but very little for 'the murderer' herself. In my eyes, Bambs was never anything more than a victim from beginning to end. I was asked how I could feel so much compassion rather than anger towards Bambs, who had taken our children's lives, but I could only ask, in reply, 'How can one feel bitter towards a mother who loved her children so dearly and apparently believed she was saving them from a possible future akin to her own past? They were *her* children and she desperately wanted to be with them again in a place where nobody could take them away.'

My real anger and bitterness, then, was more towards those red-faced vultures known as the press; to the Church, for reasons I have already given; but most of all, towards June and Nevill – regardless of the fact they were also dead. In my opinion, *they* had created the tragedy and brought the whole damned thing to their doorstep, because they had failed to hear or attempt to understand their daughter's desperate cries for help. At the same time, I couldn't even begin to appreciate how they must have felt on that fateful night, when they realised how misguided their decisions must have been, or that they hadn't done enough.

During our stay in Norway, I grew to accept these beliefs fairly easily and found it possible to live, mainly, with a feeling of deep sadness. But this was soon to be shattered by a whole torrent of new emotions: repulsion, nausea and hatred mixed with a tremendous feeling of betrayal and fear.

I had hoped to stay in Norway longer, but chose to return at this time because I was due to meet Bambs's real mother again. Her brother, Peter, had told me she would be passing through Heathrow Airport, on her way to the Middle East, and had arranged a six-hour stopover so that we could meet up.

I had always hoped to meet Christine again, but never imagined it would happen in such tragic circumstances. Even after such a brief meeting earlier in the year, I felt closer to her than I had ever done to June; I was very aware of an instinctive understanding between Bambs and her real mother. Now, six months later, Christine, like all of us, appeared pale and drawn by the recent ordeal.

I found that morning with Christine one of the most moving and tragic of the entire story. I was faced with a tormented and sensitive woman, who had been drawn into the whole catastrophe right at the very last minute. She was almost a stranger, yet so deeply and intrinsically involved.

The previous month had been an absolute nightmare for her. With little sympathy or understanding from her husband, Christine had been unable to speak freely with anyone or find out anything in detail. The press cuttings Peter had sent her had been very misleading, and the few brief telephone conversations with her parents had been extremely restricted, because her other children didn't know about Bambs and might overhear. Desperate for answers, she had a hundred questions in her mind but didn't know where to begin.

Sadly, our meeting was all too brief, but before we parted Christine asked how I now felt about Bambs. She had been feeling so guilty since it all happened. 'I feel like I'm partly responsible,' she said, 'having had her adopted in the first place.' There was little I could say but reaffirm my opinion that, if she was anything like her daughter, she must have had a very difficult time making that decision. When Bambs was pregnant the first time, she really didn't want to make that choice. 'How then could I hate Bambs, knowing how much she loved our two little boys?'

Christine looked very relieved and said how glad she was we had met again.

When I got home, Heather said that Jeremy had been round to see us, in response to a message I had left on his answering machine the day before on our way home. He was no longer at Goldhanger but had moved into Bambs's flat, where we could drop round in the afternoon if we liked. When I asked Heather what his mood had been like, she said that he seemed very cheerful, like a different person.

When we got to the flat, Jeremy let us in and the first thing I noticed was that one of the old paintings from the farm was leaning against the wall in the hallway. It was the one of Granny Bamber as a little girl, painted at the turn of the century. I had always admired it as a beautiful picture, but because it had hung on the stairs, this was the first time I had ever been able to look at it closely. Jeremy then told me he was expecting someone from Sotheby's to come on Monday to give it a valuation.

'Surely you're not going to sell it, are you? It's a family heirloom!' I was astonished.

'Of course I am,' he said, 'I am going to sell everything. I need the money to pay the massive death duties.' He then added that he had already taken all the silver and another of the paintings to Sotheby's. Then I noticed that all the old Chinese plates were gone from the wall of Bambs's living-room.

'You haven't got rid of everything yet, have you?' I asked. I had wanted to ask for certain things myself, or even buy them if necessary.

'Oh, you should have been here yesterday,' he said. 'We had loads from the house spread out all over the floor, but I had an antique dealer friend here who bought all of it for cash.'

'What, everything?'

'Yes, virtually everything, except a load of the glass. He's coming back on Monday to look at that. You're welcome to have a look if you wish to buy any of it. It's all in the dining-room with one of the other paintings.' I couldn't believe what I was hearing and dragged the old portrait into the living-room, where I could have a better look at it.

'You can't sell this, it's beautiful; part of your family heritage!' This didn't seem to worry him. He just said that he had heard it was worth a lot of money, so it had to be worth selling.

'I don't care about any of it,' he said. 'I just want to get rid of it all.'

For the next ten minutes he resumed a denigration of his remaining family, punctuated by endless talk about himself, but I really wasn't interested and had also begun to feel very uncomfortable in his presence. He had changed a lot since we last saw him, almost as if he no longer needed my support or unconscious co-operation, and began to make light of my sadness; that I need not worry, he would make sure I was 'well looked after' when he got the money.

I finally reminded Jeremy that my main reason for coming was to sort out the boys' things and collect all Bambs's photographs and correspondence together. A gut feeling again had told me to get hold of anything relating to Christine's identity – to protect her privacy – but I certainly couldn't tell Jeremy that. My heart sank when he told me that he and Brett, his friend who was staying there with him, had already cleaned the boys' room and put all their clothes and toys into black bags in the hall cupboard.

'Let me show you,' he said, leading the way to their room. It was spotlessly clean; even the drawers had been hoovered out. I felt heart-broken and violated. It had been so important for me that I do it myself. He then led us to the other hall cupboard and said, pointing to the bottom shelf, 'This is where Sheila's photographs are.'

I began to feel that everything I was being shown had been care-fully set up and orchestrated in order to gain an effect. In the cupboard there was a small pile of Bambs's modelling shots, a box of contact sheets and five photograph albums of the kids. There was also a box of slides and some other very personal items. I asked Jeremy about her actual portfolio, but he told me that he had that at his house in Goldhanger; and besides, he wished to keep all the 'famous photo-graphs' for himself. (I didn't know there were any famous ones.)

The albums contained all of her photographs of the twins through the years, carefully labelled with names, dates and ages. The model-ling shots were all her rejects from the portfolio. I opened the container of slides, thinking they might be old ones of my own, and was surprised to find it full of Bambs in the nude; the sort of pictures one might find in a glossy men's magazine.

I couldn't believe it, Bambs had always been very adamant about not doing any glamour work – she must have been really desperate for work. I later discovered that these were just test shots, taken by a friend, and were never published – or ever likely to be. I then realised Jeremy was gloating over my shoulder; eager to tell me there were a few more similar boxes, but even more revealing.

'You see everything right down to the last detail in the others.' He laughed.

I was finding his behaviour extremely distasteful and more like that of an immature schoolboy ogling at his first girly magazine, snigger-ing with his classmates. Not a twenty-five-year-old man looking at photographs of his dead sister.

'There's also another box of nude shots that you took in the fields at Whitehouse; I found *them* in Mum's bureau.'

'I remember those,' I said, 'I took them a long time ago, when we were first together.' When I asked how his mother had got them, he said that she was probably snooping around here when Bambs was in hospital and decided to take them home. I asked what he thought his mother wanted them for and he told me she probably kept them so that she could bring them out if she ever wanted to shame Sheila, or use them to make her toe the line in future.

'They kept all sorts of things in Dad's safe, which they could use to make various people behave or do as they're told,' said Jeremy. 'There was even a lump of hash that had been confiscated from someone who was staying at the farm a long time ago. It was still in the safe with the accompanying letter.' (I remembered Bambs telling me about that and always found it amusing that her father had kept it for so long.)

I wasn't at all happy about the nude photographs being left around and asked him to let me have *all* of them, so that I could destroy them. I said that it wouldn't be very nice if they got into the wrong hands. I also asked where the rest of her photographs were, the ones before the twins were born, for example. I didn't feel it was a good idea to be more specific about them. I didn't want to draw his attention to the fact that Bambs kept a small collection of photographs of her real mother and family, including pictures of them together with the twins during their meeting in the spring. Unfortunately, he denied all knowledge of there being any other photographs and said that these were all the photos she had kept, both here and at the farm.

I felt distinctly uneasy, his mood and attitude had upset me, so I decided to take just the photos and return the next day to collect the rest of the things. He said he wouldn't be there in the morning, so he gave me the key to let myself in. Before we left, I reminded him to leave the rest of the slides with the other things and quickly said goodbye.

The following morning, Heather and I were up really early, so after breakfast we left again for the flat. Before going, however, Heather telephoned just to make sure we weren't in fact barging in. A minute or so later she came back and said that a man describing himself as a workman had answered. It seemed a bit strange, but then nothing really surprised us any more and I assumed it might be the antique dealer Jeremy had mentioned – a day early.

When we arrived, the first thing I noticed was that the painting of Granny Bamber had gone. On looking in the dining-room, I found that the other painting and the boxes of glass had also gone. I wanted to have a proper look round for the other photographs and things, but something didn't feel quite right. Apart from that, I was still upset that the place had been stripped and cleaned while I was away, so we quickly gathered the twins' belongings and a pile of Bambs's letters and left.

That was the last time I went into her flat for over eighteen months. I had intended to go back and sort out the rest, but circumstances put me off.

On the Monday morning, I was looking forward to seeing Jan at the cemetery when the phone rang. It was David Boutflour, Bambs's cousin. At first he asked me about Norway and whether we'd had a good holiday; he also commented on the twins' funeral, saying how special it had been. At the same time, he seemed to be beating around the bush. Even though I didn't know him very well, I knew him well enough to know it was out of character for him to telephone me at nine o'clock on a Monday morning just to make small talk. Eventually, he said that the main reason he was calling was to prepare me for a bit of a shock. 'I want to warn you that there is going to be a bit of a bombshell in tomorrow morning's newspapers.'

'What do you mean! What sort of a bombshell?'

'I'm afraid I can't tell you at the moment,' he said, but added, 'The only thing I can say is that we all know Sheila couldn't possibly have pulled that trigger, and we have been making statements to the police to that effect.'

I thanked him for telling me and then said, 'But if Sheila didn't do it, who did?' He couldn't tell me that either; the police wouldn't allow him to say any more than he had for the moment. He wished he could.

'Does Jeremy know about all this,' I asked, 'because he didn't say anything the other day when I saw him?'

'Oh yes, Jeremy knows alright,' said David.

I tried to pump him for more information, but couldn't get anything else out of him. He just told me to keep my chin up and said that they were all thinking of me. When he rang off, I put the phone down very slowly and sat there wondering about it. I later found out that David had really intended to call Nevill's other nephew, Anthony

Pargeter, but had dialled my number by accident. Thank God he did! So what the hell was going on? Why couldn't he tell me anything?

I had never had such a disturbing and evasive telephone call in my life and immediately called Witham Police to try and find out. Stan Jones wasn't there, so I was put through to a Detective Inspector Miller, who denied, categorically, that anything unusual was happening – flatly refusing to say any more to me. I received the same brush-off my father had been given weeks before. This was crazy, something had to be going on, so I telephoned Heather and told her what had been said. I was in a terrible state by this time and began to slip back into all my earlier turmoil and confusion. Heather called the police, but didn't get any further than I had. Sergeant Jones, who was there this time, would only say, 'Just be patient.'

Thank heavens Jan was to tell me her extraordinary story later that morning at the cemetery. It was to give me so much of the strength I now needed to carry on. By the time I met her, however, I had already started turning things over in my mind; finally asking myself all the proper questions.

Given the assumption that Bambs couldn't possibly have done it, then who did? And how was her death made to look like suicide when, as a mother, she would have been trying to save the lives of her children? My immediate feeling was that she had either been asleep, and the first to die, or she had been held. And if that was the case, then there must have been two assailants – one person couldn't have done it alone. Also, Bambs couldn't have been drugged, because the police had said they could find no traces of anything unexpected in her blood. So if there had been two assailants, who were they?

Jeremy had told me that he'd had a phone call from his father, who told him that Bambs had gone berserk and had a gun. He had also said that he felt Nevill was already wounded at the time of talking to him. When told the murder weapon was small-bore and that Jeremy had been out shooting rabbits with it that afternoon, I had made the assumption that they were referring to the small-bore shotgun I had seen Jeremy use many years before, on a Boxing Day shoot. What an odd coincidence that two half-torn photographs of that day were the only other pictures Jeremy left amongst the carrier bag of Bambs's letters in her flat. Bambs and I had been the beaters that day.

So, all I had to go on was that if Bambs couldn't have done it, Jeremy's story about a telephone call had to be a lie. I didn't need to know any more, because then I had only one question to answer: why should Jeremy make up a story about a phone call unless he had something to hide? Unless he was involved in some way?

By killing only his parents, Jeremy would still have had to share their estate with his sister. So, as well as having her illness as a smokescreen for his involvement, in killing her he could also get hold of her share. But why kill the twins? Unless, of course, he already knew that some form of clause or change in the wills precluded the rights of their next of kin – that being me – if they didn't reach maturity. What other reason could he have had, and why the apparent urgency to get such large sums of money together? It was at this point I began to realise how much I could also be considered a suspect, and possibly why Stan Jones had pressed me so hard on that first day.

The only other thing which bothered me, now that I allowed myself to think about it, was that Bambs's body had been found next to June, and that if she had really taken her own life, she would never have been found beside her mother, but would have laid down next to her sons.

Even though I am still looking for some of the answers, the first came in the following morning's newspapers. Jeremy had appeared at a special court in Chelmsford accused of stealing £980 from the family's caravan site in Goldhanger on 25 March. It was understood that he was one of two men detained by police, who were also holding a woman. Bail was refused. Apart from that, the papers said little more than we already knew, reporting restrictions had now been imposed.

Back on the phone to Witham Police, Stan Jones said that he still couldn't tell us anything, except that they had arrested Jeremy and his friend Brett at seven o'clock on Sunday morning, at Bambs's flat, but they were not holding Brett. At least we now knew who the 'workman' was that had answered the phone. The press were also back in force outside my front door, so I told Stan I intended to go away again, to Cornwall this time, at the end of the week. If they wanted to ask me any more questions or take another statement, they would have to be quick about it. I now felt I had an awful lot more to say about things.

Two detectives came round the following afternoon, full of questions but still no information. They said they had only just joined the case and didn't know any more than us. This time they wanted me to tell them everything I knew about Jeremy. How long had I known him? Did I know him well? What had we spoken about at my party and when had I previously seen him? Did we speak often? What was his sister's reaction to him? And so on. It was quite an interrogation; certainly as intense as the one about Bambs, if not more so.

After an hour or so of these questions, each punctuated by a long silence as the male officer wrote it all down in my statement – very slowly and precisely – they asked me where exactly I would be staying in Cornwall, who with and what was my vehicle registration number; just in case they had to find me. It would be several more weeks before they turned up again, to fingerprint me.

Within days of Jeremy's arrest, newspapers, my only source of information at that time, were rife with new rumours. On 11 September we read that detectives were investigating the possibility that Bambs was involved in drug-trafficking. They alleged that police were trying to discover if the slaughter had followed an argument over a deal which had gone wrong.

On the 12th, they went further and said: **'Detectives think model Bambi Caffell and her family could have been massacred by a Mafia-style hit-man. Police started probing the possibility amid revelations that the 27-year-old beauty owed drug barons £40,000.'**

Now I *knew* something was wrong! Nobody would ever trust Bambs with that kind of money; she was far too scatterbrained and dizzy! As far as I know, this story was originally uncovered by the *Daily Mirror* and has been a major contributing factor in destroying Bambs's reputation. Even after the trial proved her innocence, the *Mirror* continued to defend this, vehemently, as a fact; still claiming to have proof of it.

On the 13th it was reported that villagers living near the 'death scene' told of sealed envelopes full of cash dropping through their letter-boxes. They were all addressed, it was said, 'To a member of Sheila's family' and contained £100 or more. This was the same day Jeremy was released from police custody. At an appearance in court he was released on bail, despite police objections. Apparently the money had been put up by members of his family – obviously not those who had condemned him – so they weren't all against him.

Everything was going crazy, but I still wasn't completely satisfied that it wasn't just his relations ganging up on him. After all, he was about to inherit substantial control of their biggest money spinner – the caravan site. It was only when I reached Cornwall and spoke with the friend I was staying with, who happened to be an ex-policeman and marksman, that my suspicions were finally confirmed.

He asked me if Bambs was a good shot and when I said no, and that she had never used a gun, he said that she couldn't possibly have done it. He then explained that a .22 calibre rifle, of the type which had been used, is a very accurate weapon which uses very small bullets. To kill someone with such a weapon, the person would have to have been a very good shot and know what they were doing; especially with a moving target. We have since learned that nearly every one of the twenty-five bullets fired found its target. I hadn't, up to this point, considered whether Bambs was a good enough shot because I assumed that, apart from Nevill, they were all asleep and killed at close range with a shotgun.

By Tuesday, 17 September, news of a silencer had been leaked, as had the fact that Bambs had been shot twice. Some reports also said that villagers had told police of torches found mysteriously planted in hedgerows near the farm. The torches, all facing upwards, appeared to form a pattern. The police were probing the possibility that they could have been marking the dropping zone for a light aircraft passing overhead. With all this new information, plus what I already knew, I went for long walks along the cliffs near Land's End. That particular piece of coastline has always been one of those places where I feel completely in touch with the earth and able to think more clearly. Although rapidly becoming convinced of Jeremy's guilt, I still needed to mull the whole thing over and cross-examine my own theories.

The whole issue had been confused with rumours about drug smuggling, hit-men and dropping zones. So who had this debt? Who had the link, if there was one at all, with drug barons? Jeremy had boasted about going on weekend trips to Amsterdam to buy drugs. Perhaps the debt was really his. From the way Jeremy was behaving, it seemed as if he was the one who was in a desperate hurry to raise large sums of money. As for the torches and light aircraft, he was also in the perfect position, as farm manager, to take advantage of the large areas of land at his disposal and collect small packages dropped from light aircraft.

I have since learned that the police were of the opinion that the children were responsible for leaving the torches in the hedge, 'after a game'. I really cannot accept this because in the countryside, especially on farms, torches are used all the time; so the boys would never have been allowed to play with them, let alone not put them back.

With all this in mind, I began to worry about the nude photographs again. If Jeremy was that desperate, I wouldn't put it past him to try and sell them. As everything started to click and fall into place, I put all my fears into a letter, confronting him and once again demanding the slides. I got it off my chest, but I was also too late; within minutes of having posted the letter at St Just Post Office, I wandered into the local sweetshop to buy some chocolate where, to my horror, I saw the front page of the *Sun*:

BAMBI BROTHER IN PHOTO SCANDAL
He tried to peddle sex snaps of model.

When I read the article, I knew it had to be true. The way they described him talking about the pictures was exactly the way he had talked to me about them. In anger, I wrote him another letter, but then started to worry about my own safety – having confronted him with all my suspicions in the first letter, I had told him that I had been spending a lot of time sitting alone on the cliffs at Land's End and, in my confusion and depression, felt like throwing myself off.

In sudden fear for my own life, of an accident made to look like suicide, I decided to leave Cornwall the very next day and went to stay with some other friends in Somerset. That day several papers reported that Nevill had been savagely beaten before he died. Bambs could never have done that. She was so small compared with her father, a very fit farmer of six foot four.

Everything went quiet for over a week, until the evening of Sunday, 29 September, when, just before midnight, Stan Jones phoned to say that he and another officer had arrested Jeremy at Dover – on his way back from a holiday in St Tropez in the South of France. He had been charged with all five murders. Five minutes later, news of his arrest was on a late radio news bulletin. The weeks of speculation and silence had finally ended.

According to newspaper reports, Essex police had been protecting a mystery woman in connection with the case. I was eventually told that this had been Jeremy's girlfriend, Julie Mugford. Unable to contain a terrible secret any longer, she had walked into Witham Police Station the day before Jeremy's first arrest and given evidence against him.

Desperate to find out the truth because, even weeks later, I was still being kept in the dark, I asked Stan Jones to pass on a message of support to her. I also said that I would like to see Julie at some point; I wanted to thank her for having had the courage to come forward. On 17 October, finally satisfied that I was not an accomplice, as I very much felt they had suspected, the police allowed Julie to visit me at my flat. She came with her friend Liz Rimmington and not, as some newspapers suggested, guarded by two armed Cagney and Lacey-style policewomen.

CHAPTER NINE

SHAKING A LITTLE as she talked, Julie explained that she was only allowed to tell me so much and would only be able to answer certain of my questions. As it is, much of what she could tell me is still unpublishable. She looked frightened and worn out as she told me about Jeremy's gruesome plans and how they had developed several months before the shootings. At the time, however, she hadn't taken him seriously, thinking he was just venting his frustrations over what he saw as his parents' unjustified attempts to control his life; even to the extent that his mother, he said, had threatened to cut him out of her will in favour of the twins if he didn't toe the line.

One of the conditions set down by his mother was not having Julie to stay overnight in the cottage his parents had provided for him. As far as his mother was concerned, sex before marriage was 'a sin in the eyes of God' – or certainly in the eyes of the local community. The Bambers had offered to set Julie up with a little flat in Colchester, where their son could visit *her* instead. She actually lived in south London, where she was in teacher training. There was no doubt in Julie's mind that June's ceaseless proselytising was steadily driving Jeremy crazy. What made it worse for him, really fuelling his hatred and almost certainly putting a nail in *their* coffin, was the fact that June idolised the twins; in her eyes, they could do no wrong.

That was all very well, I thought, but why kill them? Did she know that?

At this point Julie's friend Liz joined in. She said that money was very important to Jeremy, but when he was encouraged to resume working on the farm, the shortage of it really began to rankle, especially when, in his opinion, he put in very long hours. She added that he felt very embittered by the feeling that he was not being given the just recognition and reward for his efforts. Jeremy was paid about eighty pounds a week, an average farm manager's wage at that time – which included the cottage and car – but for the kind of lifestyle he wanted to lead, that wasn't enough. He wanted to be out every night, drinking champagne and getting in on the London club scene; to have a flat in London, like his sister; take his friends out for dinner and go abroad, much as his father was free to do.

Jeremy had once said to Liz that it was very important to have money when you were young, but he also resented having to ask his parents whenever he needed it. With this restriction, Jeremy turned his mind to more illegal resources: mail-order marijuana, which he either grew himself or smuggled in from Amsterdam when he went there (hence the envelopes of cash mentioned earlier); cheque-book fraud (in which the girls had been involved, but had since repaid the defrauded amounts in full); and breaking and entering.

When I asked Julie why she hadn't said anything to the police when it first happened, she told me that she hadn't wanted to believe that Jeremy was the killer, because she was still very much in love with him. She also said that she was frightened – not only for her own safety but because, having tried to challenge him about it afterwards, he had told her that knowing so much about everything, his plans and her own involvement in his illegal activities, she was also implicated in the crime.

She said that Jeremy had originally intended to drug everybody and then, once they were asleep, set fire to the house, but he dumped that idea when he later discovered that the contents of the farm, the antiques and paintings, were grossly under-insured. He also teased her about his ability to kill, saying that he killed rats behind the barn with his bare hands.

Remembering the occasions Jeremy flared up at the tiniest provocation, she then spoke about how – although a relentless tease himself – he hated even a taste of his own medicine; to the extent that on the occasion of her twenty-first birthday party, he pushed her birthday cake into the face of the woman who had made it. The friend had simply poked a little fun at him. Julie also spoke of her own desire to kill Jeremy, how she even tried to suffocate him one night with a pillow, as he slept; she had reached the point where she could no longer bear any physical contact with him, or the terrible pressure of carrying his ghastly secret.

Julie had originally met Jeremy when she took a part-time Christmas job, as a waitress, at Sloppy Joe's, an American-style pizza parlour in Colchester, where he had been working as a cocktail barman since his return from New Zealand. Their relationship had been intense, but always difficult for her in that Jeremy maintained more than a passing interest in other women. Things were then made even harder by the arrival, a month or so before the shootings, of Jeremy's friend Brett; a man he had formed a very deep friendship with during his time in Australia and New Zealand. There was an instant change in Jeremy's personality, as Brett seemed to have an extremely powerful hold over him. He also clearly didn't like Julie being around and was openly coming between them.

Jeremy's travels to the Continent and Australasia had been financed by his father in the hope that it might eventually quell his restlessness and wanderlust, but it only seemed to get him into more trouble. Although Nevill had cousins who farmed in New Zealand, Jeremy didn't spend any more time with them than he had to. Rather than help out on yet another farm, he took jobs in restaurants and bars.

For some reason, according to David Boutflour, he also had to leave New Zealand in a tremendous hurry, catching the first plane out and calling his father from somewhere else in the Far East, asking for money. Nevill sent him an airline ticket home. David couldn't remember if he had heard this from *his* father or from Nevill directly, but Jeremy, who never gave the reason for his sudden departure, clearly felt the need to get away fast.

According to Liz, Jeremy never believed murder was a crime and thought that morality and social conscience, like religion, were only for the weak. When she told Jeremy she thought he was a psychopath, he had said to her something like, 'I know, I'm sick, I have such evil thoughts, I can't help it.'

To my horror, Julie then explained how he had justified each of the five murders to himself, and that he believed he was doing it as 'a mercy killing'. He had told her that his father was getting 'old and spent', his mother was mad anyway and 'needed putting out of her misery'; Bambs was also mad and, although he loved her, her illness frightened him. He didn't understand it. As for the twins, he was convinced that they also had to be disturbed and emotionally unbalanced, having been brought up around all that madness. I began to feel sick and didn't take much notice of anything that was said after that. My only thought was that *he* had to be completely mad.

On the following Wednesday, 24 October, newspapers were once again reporting Jeremy's court appearance – but with a difference: Jeremy, who was on legal aid, had now demanded the services of Sir David Napley, Britain's most expensive lawyer. Even though his request was refused by magistrates, on the grounds that it would cost the local authorities too much, Sir David took up the cause and their decision was overturned a week later.

I still didn't know what to believe. I had already begun to realise that so much of the little I was being told, or had heard, was pure speculation or rumour. I was even told at one point, by Mr Ainsley, the Detective Superintendent now in charge of the case, that because of the many leaks to the press, apparently emanating from police sources, he had been putting out red herrings in order to trace the culprits. But that didn't help me or my family and friends much.

CHAPTER TEN

The Sculptor's Armature

The armature stands
before me,
tall,
slim,
defiant.
A dark daunting figure;
like a ghost
from the past.
The ever mysterious
finger of destiny.
She is attractive
and teasing;
What delights
and pain
will she bring me?
What mysteries
do you keep
secret?
You catch my eye;
mesmerise me
command me.
'Command me!'

DURING THE WEEKS following Jeremy's arrest, I made my first pieces of sculpture. They came about, not through any desire to become a sculptor but quite by accident, through a need to express all the painful and unpleasant emotions that were now crashing around inside me; tearing me apart because it seemed there was nothing else I could do about them. I had spent much of my life doing everything I could to avoid pain and darkness and here I was confronted with it, in its totality.

I was full of rage, not only at Jeremy but also at myself for falling for his deception; sick at the implication that my conversation with him at the party gave him the last pieces of information he needed to bring his terrible scheme to reality. Out of a primal need for revenge, I yearned for a crowbar in my hands and five minutes alone in his cell with him – to break every bone in his body. But because I had been brought up to be so nice, a gentle man, I could never tell anybody else that this was how I felt – except once when a likeable old tramp started talking to me at the graveside one afternoon. Up to that point I had been in total denial about my anger. I was so terrified of losing control, but I could no longer maintain what I realise now was a very false sense of composure.

That old man taught me something very important that afternoon, in that he was very open about his feelings. He knew why Bambs and the boys were buried there, and he didn't hide the fact that had he himself still been in prison, and given the chance, he would have killed Jeremy. He didn't know I was the father at first, but his tears and anger gave me permission to have mine. So we both just stood there – two strangers on a cold day – and shed our tears together.

I didn't want to kill Jeremy – death was far too good for him – but I wanted him to suffer, to feel the pain that I was feeling; to endure the life sentence I was now condemned to, but much more so. For that reason alone, I was glad there was no longer a death sentence in Great Britain. The real punishment for Jeremy Bamber would be to grow old watching life and the world outside carrying on without him.

More than anything, though, I was beginning to carry around my own feelings of guilt, shame and remorse; that dreadful feeling inside that I could never put the clock back for any of those much-needed second chances.

After the funerals, I started to have tremendous regrets at not having seen the twins myself; I hadn't even visited the funeral parlour to sit with them in the Chapel of Rest. I began to feel ashamed of myself for being frightened of my own children – wishing I'd had the courage to touch or hold them one last time.

As an artist, my initial reaction was to draw. I felt I had to somehow give shape to this wretchedness in order to recognise and, hopefully, transform it in some way. I couldn't carry on the way I was. The resulting images were not only therapeutic in working out those feelings, they became my way of recreating what I didn't have the courage to actually do; to show them how much I'd really wanted to hold them and say goodbye.

The first drawings portrayed two emotional aspects that I wished to express in a theme of holding the boys in my arms. One was of sadness and tenderness; the children in the limp sleeping position they so often fell into when being carried off to bed at the end of a late evening. I am holding them close, my cheek on one of their chests, crying quietly and listening for an absent heartbeat. I wanted it to appear, on first viewing, as if they were 'just asleep', but to create that nagging doubt that they were in fact dead. The feeling tone is inward and intimate, concentrating on the torsos and faces of the figures..

The other aspect showed a more angry stance, with the full-length figure of a man, holding the children in the same way, but standing with his head thrown back in an anguished cry; that silent scream I had experienced when they first told me. The feeling here was much more intensely expressive, outward and extrovert.

Further drawings came out on the night Jeremy was charged with the murders. Even though his arrest was inevitable, I still went into deeper shock. The musing had finally become reality. After the phone call from Stan Jones, giving us the news, Heather and I opened a bottle of whisky left over from the funeral and got very drunk. I also began to take all my aggression and confusion out on paper, with a series of raw, angry pastel drawings on the same theme as before; this time accentuating my anguish with the added impact of colour. The next day I returned to the quiet reflective pose, once again enhancing the image with that raw use of colour.

The mood that most suited my ideas of reconciliation with the twins and my shame seemed to be the more tender one and far more important, at that time, to develop further. I hadn't intended to make a sculpture at first – I wanted to do a painting – but I had such difficulty in translating my thoughts on to paper in the way I wanted, I decided to make a rough clay model from which I could do further drawings. The clay model, however, took up so much of my attention, it quickly became a finished work. It seemed the most natural thing for me to do in the circumstances, because I realised that our experience of the world is primarily three-dimensional – not two-dimensional and flat as we are predominantly encouraged to represent it from an early age.

On completion, I was not only surprised at the result, but I think I have captured that dual feeling of sleep and death in the children's figures, and the weight carried physically and emotionally by the man. The piece has a certain naïvety, which in a way enhances much of the feeling I am trying to express. Because it was made entirely from my mental picture – without any preparatory life drawings – there are also some inevitable anatomical inaccuracies; hands are different sizes, arms different lengths and backs too long, but the composition seems to work. It feels right and that is all that really matters to me.

Having successfully made that first sculpture, it wasn't long before I began work on another piece – but this time of Bambs as a woman heavy in pregnancy; a theme I was to repeat a number of times in the future. Again, the emergence of the image had a rather accidental nature to it, which soon brought me in touch with even more of those locked-up feelings that were sitting just below that feeling of total numbness.

I had originally planned to make a more complex piece of the two boys dancing around their mother, emphasising that constant physical contact there always was between them. But this was easier said than done – the clay, which had a habit of drying out too much, too quickly, kept cracking off the wire armatures of the smaller child figures.

Not to be beaten, I took those figures away, leaving only the one of the woman, which I began playing around with, not knowing what to do with it – until I came to her stomach. It brought back all the memories of Bambs when she was last pregnant; constantly cradling her ever growing belly in fear of losing her precious babies. With this in mind I started filling her out, adding arms and hands to support the weight of that lovely rounded form.

I tried to recreate that feel, when viewed from behind, of the slim woman she'd remained all through pregnancy. But on turning the figure, you see the huge bulge delicately cupped in her hands; her face tilted towards the physical transformation of her body, in awe, but with an added hint of anxiety in her face, just as she had been.

I have always found the image of a pregnant woman so very attractive, and what I will always remember about Bambs is that she was especially serene and beautiful during that time. It was a joy to look at her, a joy to touch and to hold her, even though I later went on to betray her; first in our marriage, and then when the loss of the twins had been such a shock, all the memories of her anguish and obsession to be a mother went right out of my head. Had they not, I would never have accepted what I was told on *that* day so easily. In the light of events, these thoughts were to come up time and time again, with resounding intensity during my more desolate moments – but it was all too late.

Finding myself lost in the circling thoughts of the 'If only . . .' syndrome, my visits to the cemetery increased. The only thing that made it bearable was the delightful song of the robins, who would always dance around the gravestones and through the branches of the wild rosebush only feet from where I sat.

I suppose what really saved me, initially, was this overwhelming desire to make figurative sculptures, an activity which was almost completely new to me. I had attempted only one other piece in adult life, two years earlier when Jan and I first parted, but that was all. My work in ceramics, until then, had been of an entirely traditional nature, specialising in wheel-thrown pottery. There was also a symbolic side to my making sculpture, which I wasn't aware of at the time, and it was all to do with the fact that, as a sculptor, I would always be able to cast more copies. With Bambs dead, I would never be able to replicate Daniel and Nicholas. Half of the mould had been broken.

*　　*　　*

Within days of completing those first sculptures, late in October, I received a letter from journalist Yvonne Roberts, telling me she wanted to write a book about the case and was seeking my approval and help. She had also been angered by the way in which Bambs was treated by the press. Having seen them at their worst, my initial reactions to another reporter were of suspicion and contempt; even though intentions were honourable, it felt like another invasion. Never having written myself, I once again felt powerless, but I was damned if I was going to allow yet another stranger to pass comment on such an intimate and sensitive story without my control – no matter how sympathetic they were.

Subsequent meetings with Yvonne greatly modified my opinion and I am now very grateful for the help she gave me then. After a great deal of thought and a lot of encouragement from family and friends as well, I decided to try and write my own 'story', and started immediately. I had, in an indirect way, been given my second chance!

Naturally, I spent much of the next week writing up those events most relevant to the investigation (the police had also asked me to keep a notebook), but had terrible difficulty in allowing myself to relive that afternoon of 7 August. It was far too painful a memory to write down. In desperation, I borrowed Herbie's pocket cassette-recorder, to see if I could release it more easily on to tape, but that didn't help much at first either. When I sat down that evening, I found the *new* batteries had gone flat during the day, the machine was completely dead, so I had to do the account straight on to paper after all. Having now psyched myself up for the task, I couldn't wait any longer.

Working in this way, thinking about each word and layer of shock, brought everything back all the more clearly. It seemed that to face again those moments of trauma, yet in my own time, piece by piece, allowed me a much-needed healthy release of emotion.

The following day, I bought some replacement batteries, but before I changed them, for no rational reason, I pushed the start button once more. This time the machine burst into life as it should with fresh batteries. There was no longer anything wrong. Needless to say, I was rather surprised.

Around that time, maybe a few days earlier, I awoke with a start one night having heard – in a dream, I suppose – Bambs's voice speak softly in my ear something about my own death. I cannot remember the words but now realise, in retrospect, that the death to which she had referred must have been a symbolic one, and the book I needed to write was not about her, but an obituary to the person who had lain dead on my living-room floor since the day of the shootings – myself. And while that obituary remained unwritten inside that corpse, my old ways and patterns would hang around my new form like the strong, sticky gossamer threads of a spider's web; tying me to that old body like a putrified umbilical cord that no longer provides nourishment.

Curiously enough, within days of writing this section at the end of 1992, I was faced with a condition I thought was the first stage of a potentially life-threatening illness. Fortunately, this turned out to be something relatively minor, but during the weeks awaiting hospital tests, I experienced, in my imagination, the reality of my own imminent death. I was not overly frightened by the possibility – or the earlier 'dream' experience with Bambs – but on both occasions fired with a sense of urgency to complete what I had begun. In being faced with death, either real or imagined, I am reminded, once again, that the only moment we can really be sure of is the one we are living right now.

On having had that 'dream', I also decided to make my first visit to the farm since the shootings. There was no further trouble with the tape recorder.

Whitehouse Farm, 12 November 1985:

It was on a beautiful, clear, crisp autumn day in November such as this, that I first came to Whitehouse Farm. It was just as cold and bright with the frozen leaves on the ground crunching underfoot. This is the first time I have been down here since those terrible events three months ago. I had to come, just to try and bring back old memories, old thoughts.

I can now just hear the tractor in the field, humming in the background. When I arrived it was silent, the place was deserted.

There was a strange calm when I got here today, a sort of loud silence. It is very much the same when I arrive at the graveside in Highgate.

I haven't come here to look inside the farmhouse, but I can't help looking up at the window of that room in which the twins slept and died. I suppose I came here in the hope that they might make contact with me, being the last place they were alive. I wish, if they were going to talk to me, they would talk to me now. I want so much to hear their voices and listen again to their innocent wisdom.

It's hard to believe that it's over three months since they were all murdered. I suppose if their spirits had been here, they would have gone on by now; it's too far away in time. Why should they stay with this world when there are probably more exciting planes of existence to look forward to. Even so, I wish they'd come and talk to me, let me know they're all right.

I had quite a surprise this morning when I visited Witham Police Station and was speaking to Mr Ainsley, the Detective Superintendent who is now leading the investigations. He said that he had never worked on such a 'bizarre' case in all his career. What did he mean by that? It's not that bizarre! That word has been used too many times in recent weeks. It would almost suggest that what we've been told is only the tip of the iceberg.

Being on murder investigations all the time, Mr Ainsley remarked that he could normally leave his work behind when he closes his office door in the evening. On this case, however, he lies awake at night thinking about it all; the pictures of my children; the photographs of their bodies – stark images in his mind. More than anything, though, the police photographs of Bambs: 'Her face is a picture of pure innocence.' Those were his very words and, I thought, a surprisingly sensitive statement for a hardened police-man with twenty-eight years' service.

The police must have shown considerably less sensitivity getting into the house; there is a different kitchen door. They must have smashed the old one down to get in. I had wondered whether Jeremy had let them in or not. It helps to build up a better picture of that night.

There is such a feeling of calm here now. Peaceful. But on the eve of the murders, while I was at Heather's, I felt the horror. Like a mother, I felt it instinctively; blind panic struck me. I realise now that it must have been happening at that very time. It was followed by a tremendous feeling of calm and peace, almost as if the boys came straight to me for protection. Or maybe they were protecting me. It was as if their spirits stayed inside me from then on, until they were ready to go . . .

Sitting here on the doorstep, looking around at it all – the farmyard, the fields and woods, the farmhouse and garden – I think of Bambs and our insatiable appetite for each other when we were first here together. I remember how we used to sneak off into the woods or the barn at every opportunity. Those were happy days.

Then there are my memories of the times we were all here together. I can almost hear the sounds of their laughter, the jovial evenings of Christmases past; the long walks with Nevill as he showed me new irrigators and the like in the hope that, one day, his son-in-law might show an interest in farming. I can also remember the twins playing in the haystacks more recently, or driving Grandad's lawnmower, but then, these are just echos from the past.

It seems as if someone has been here to keep the garden nice but I won't wait; I think I'll just leave the flowers on the doorstep and go back home. I don't think I am going to get any signs at all, am I?

A few days later I added to this:

It's very strange but as I begin writing, I feel that in trying to remember the way Bambs and I were, the things we had together – our loves and laughs and everything – I almost feel I'm having to fall in love with her all over again. And as I do that, memories come back to me. I start to relive our most intimate times. It is a curious experience – to fall in love with someone who is dead, someone who has gone . . . yet at the same time a person I knew very well. Not like falling for a projected celluloid image, as I had done in my youth for Marilyn Monroe. Strange how, to use the words of the Elton John song, Bambs, too, was 'like a candle in the wind'.

PART THREE
The Journey

CHAPTER ELEVEN

Absence in November

And Autumn now, as everywhere,
Drips down to Winter from the bare
Cold stalactites of hedge and tree,
And makes a stalagmitic me.

Spring, like as not, will come one day
And rivers wash the world away,
Clouds from the hilltops lift the snows
And dwindle to a summer rose.

But I in Time's forgotten woods
Imprisoned under frozen moods
Shall bear no blossom, lift no leaf,
To die, as these have died, of grief.

Stanley Richardson

So I HAD finally reached the bottom of the pit – or was it just another ledge which would suddenly give way beneath me, like the last one? I really didn't know any longer. All I knew was that it was dark and it was lonely, even though there were still many people around me. I could not stay in that desolate place for very long, I had to keep moving. But the terrain was so unfamiliar to me; I had no road-map for my emotions, I had little choice but to follow that tunnel; feeling my way blindly along its sides. I didn't realise it then, but through beginning to write and making those first sculptures, the journey had already begun . . . The choices had been made.

I also soon discovered that, in writing everything down, I no longer needed the sleeping pills my doctor had prescribed. It seemed that the activity of putting my thoughts on paper effectively let them out of my system and allowed me to sleep naturally again; it broke the pattern of destructive thoughts circling around in my head. It was the same when I made the sculptures.

With now considerably more experience, I realise that drawing or writing in this way – tapping our often unexplored creativity – can be of tremendous help to anyone trying to come to terms with some form of loss or trauma. It was far better to get all that turmoil out of my system in some way, rather than push it all back inside where it could fester and eventually cause illness. Because that's how it felt when I kept it in: I began to feel sick. It really doesn't matter if we don't know how to draw or write, the results don't have to be seen by others. It is the activity itself that is most important.

Clay in particular seemed to me to have an incredibly healing effect, because it can take us back to a form of creative expression which predates the stigma many of us acquire around our ability to draw; about being forced, too early in life, to translate our three-dimensional experience of the world into solely two-dimensional images. Sadly, this flat, two-dimensional emphasis on our experience is heavily reinforced by the pre-eminence of television in our culture. Real life, unfortunately, is not a television screen that can be switched on or off when the content becomes too painful, or, conversely, desirable.

I had also begun to notice, during this time, that my greatest periods of inspiration and creative insight seemed to accompany equally intense moments of despair. In the same week I completed the figure of Bambs, I was to learn of the death, some eighteen months earlier, of a very good friend of ours whom I had lost touch with.

After receiving the news, I went to a framed photo-montage I had brought home from Bambs's flat and looked at all the faces. As well as the many pictures of Bambs and the boys, it included those of Nick, the man I had just had news of, and another friend, Ollie, who had taken his own life a few years earlier. I was devastated. I couldn't understand what kind of a world could take away so many of its real characters, so young. All the lively, happy, good people; it just wasn't fair.

I cried for several days after this and, in an odd sort of way, it was really good for me, because that news was the catalyst that finally opened my floodgates in a big way. On every other occasion, someone or something had shut me down; reporters, clergy, the wrong words at the wrong time, all contributed. It had never felt safe before. In my despondency, I found it tragic in that, for the most part, I had to cry on my own.

In an attempt to bring all of them back to life in some way, I threw myself into writing and drawing even more and, as a result, found tremendous salvation; some further sparks of the truth, isolated moments of joy and inspiration I couldn't understand but had to accept. It wasn't long after this that I had one of those magical creative experiences that stayed with me for a long time after.

I was alone one Sunday afternoon and decided that I wanted to do a picture of Bambs and the boys that I could reproduce to give as presents to my family and closest friends. Daniel had always been the hardest to pose, so I set out to draw him first. He had always been really embarrassed by me looking at him so intensely, causing him to fidget and giggle, that all other attempts had failed to capture his innate wide-open look. Nicholas, on the other hand, was much more confident and always sat incredibly still, with little concern for my scrutiny of his face.

Using the school photograph as a model, I quickly achieved the basic layout of Daniel's face, but soon noticed that the drawing looked more like Nicholas – as if he was trying to get in first – and no matter how hard I tried, it continued to look like him. It was only when faced with drawing both of them that I began to realise how similar their features were. The only thing that made them different was their uniquely individual facial expressions, which developed with their very different personalities. The only time they were ever really alike was when they were asleep and relaxed.

I struggled for a couple of hours, tightening up on detail and quality of line, but it was only when, in frustration, I put the photograph away and relied on my feelings and memory that it all fell into place. The portrait suddenly came to life before my eyes. Somehow, the drawing is very different from the photograph I had used, yet more like Daniel than any photograph I have ever seen; it was as if the eyes had taken on that far-away light of his. Several people have said that it's as if he has come to life again in my drawing, as if he was really there: 'He seems to look straight through you.'

The following day I went to the farm again; by then, Jeremy was being held in Norwich Prison awaiting committal for trial. I hadn't planned to go on that particular trip to Essex, but after a very encouraging chat with Auntie Pam on the telephone, I felt I could. After thinking about it, I told myself that my initial reaction not to go was just the same as my not wanting to see the twins after their deaths, and that this was something I had to find the courage to do. Fortunately, the experience of making that drawing had given me all the courage I needed. All the same, I still wanted some moral support and asked Jill, as one of my oldest and closest friends, to come with me.

On reaching Tolleshunt D'Arcy, I began to feel nervous and wanted to turn back, but with Jill there, and Ann Eaton's car in front, leading, I was committed to going. When we arrived, everything was much the same as I remembered. The kitchen was still the same – with shelves filled with jam, sugar and biscuits, correspondence and notes still on the side – except, perhaps, the place was that little bit tidier; unlived in, but with a lived-in look, like a time capsule with everything frozen in place.

I felt rather ridiculous standing there, almost as if waiting for something to happen; as if both Jill and Ann were waiting for *me* to do something. Suddenly it seemed strange to want to see an empty house. Ann led us into the front hallway, where I saw the twins' anoraks hanging on the coat hook, and just for a second I thought, 'Ah, they must be in.' I shuddered and went to get them down, to take home. I looked at Jill, caressed the fabric and decided to leave them there for a little while longer, where they belonged.

In a way, I wish Ann hadn't been with us; I felt somewhat inhibited, as if on a guided tour – and being watched. When we went into the living-room, she pointed out the small posy of flowers I had left on the doorstep some five weeks earlier. They were now on the mantelpiece, still looking as fresh as the day I had left them.

It seemed sad that many of the smaller contents had been removed, but it was unimportant, the rooms still had their memories; the fabric of a building holds those. That old house must hold hundreds of memories both happy and sad, and at least one terrible one which may never be erased; I could feel it. I felt calm and at home, yet uneasy.

'Would you like to go upstairs and look around?' said Ann.

'No, I'd rather not,' I said. I was nervous of going up there, especially into Bambs's old bedroom – the one the boys slept in. I didn't know what to expect. The fear of the unknown, I suppose. I didn't, at that time, know who was found where and in what condition. Perhaps I was frightened of seeing ghosts.

'It's quite all right, there is nothing to be afraid of,' said Ann. 'Would you prefer to go up on your own?'

I thought about it, took a deep breath and said, 'Yes, if you don't mind, I think I would.' She went to put the kettle on. As I walked up the stairs, Jill stood at the bottom, watching me with concern. As soon as Ann had gone, I beckoned her to come with me. I didn't really want to go alone, just in private with someone I cared about, someone close. On that one day, I disliked Ann intensely; it felt like *she* was the intruder. It remains inconceivable to me, given the history of the place, that she and her husband, Peter, now hold the tenancy of Whitehouse Farm and are living there with their two children.

The first thing I noticed, when I reached the landing, was the smell – different to the way the house always used to smell. It was some sort of air freshener used to cover up another smell. The one it was *trying* to cover was one I didn't like at all, one I had never smelt before but I knew instantly and would never forget: the smell of death. Jill was now beside me, I took her hand and led her to the room the boys always slept in; Bambs's old bedroom. The door was closed.

When I opened it, I was relieved to see there was now only one bed in the room; thankfully, not the small ones the twins had slept and died in. It now looked a bit like it had when I first came to Whitehouse, when it had been Bambs's room. We walked in and sat on the bed, where I explained all this to Jill. She said nothing but simply put her arms around me and held me very tight. I wanted to cry but I couldn't, so I put my head on her shoulder and just felt very empty. I stared at faint splash marks on the wall. Were they remnants of bloodstains or spilt drinks? I hoped it was the latter. I was so glad Jill was with me, I knew I couldn't have done it on my own.

All of a sudden, Ann broke into our thoughts and came in. She said they had thought it better to put the room back the way Bambs had had it. Rather than leave it empty, after the twins' beds had been removed, they brought Bambs's old bed back in. 'Have you seen this?' asked Ann, pointing out some words scratched into what looked like new paint on the wardrobe door. 'I HATE THIS PLACE,' it said. I then remembered the police asking me about it, but on seeing those words I felt as if I had seen them before, in the last year or so – probably when I stayed at Christmas, although I couldn't be absolutely sure. I guess Bambs must have written it out of frustration on one of her earlier, more anguished visits. It seemed sad, but now quite unimportant.

That day left me completely wide open. More came back to me and I began to realise that in reassembling much of the truth about Bambs and her family, I was going to hurt some people. I didn't want to, but circumstances had left me very little choice.

Just before Christmas, I threw a fancy-dress party (for grown-ups) in memory of Bambs and the boys – the theme was Fairy Tales and Fantasy. It was a tremendous success and many of the boys' older friends turned out in colourful array. I also went to the cinema with Chantelle – the little girl who had held my hand at the funeral. I was finding this part of my loss the hardest, because with the twins being taken from me, I also lost contact with most of their friends. There were suddenly very few children in my life. Chantelle and another friend of theirs, Chloe, were the only ones whose parents stayed in contact. I would have loved to have seen the others, maybe take them out too, but all contact was lost.

In a way I could understand why. For many people, especially those with their own children, in seeing me they are confronted with their deepest fears; that feeling of 'it could happen to me' is brought right home to them. Understanding, however, did nothing to ease my loneliness; even some of the old friends were beginning to drift away.

Before I flew off to Norway again, on Christmas Eve, Jan and I climbed the wall into the cemetery to light some candles at dawn and decorate a tiny Christmas tree her father had planted on the grave – a tree that is now at least twelve feet tall! It was a magical moment but did nothing to fill the gap. As for Christmas itself, I don't even want to think about it; even eight years on, it hasn't got much better and tends to pass uneventfully.

Then on New Year's Eve, I got hopelessly drunk for the first and only time since Jeremy's arrest. In fact I passed out in the snow just after midnight, watching the fireworks go off. The temperature had fallen to −18° Centigrade, but I was totally oblivious of the fact; I didn't really want to remember the final hours of 1985. I don't think my hosts wanted me to either; by the same token, however, I don't remember the beginning of 1986.

On 6 January, I returned home to an announcement in the press of June's will having been read. Her estate was valued at approximately £230,000. Within the next two weeks, Nevill's was also published. His estate was valued at approximately £380,000. In both cases, Jeremy was now the major beneficiary. It was also announced that a committal hearing had been set for 10 February.

At this point, Jeremy's relatives and I had been informed that Sir David Napley's firm nearly always called for what is known as an old-style committal, where all prosecution witnesses could be interviewed by the defence solicitor – in the presence of the defendant. It would, in effect, be like a dry run of the main trial but in a small courtroom, and was not something I was looking forward to. In fact I felt sick at the thought of sitting in the same room as Jeremy. On the morning of 10 February, it was suddenly reset for 10 March.

I realised there were going to be certain occasions when I would miss the boys more than any other. The obvious ones like Christmas and our birthdays were almost too painful to think about. Fortunately, I had that wonderful family of friends to take the sting out of my grief and loneliness that first Christmas. There were other times, however, when the memories would sneak up and I found myself, unexpectedly, in situations where I couldn't avoid my desolation and missed the boys desperately.

When it snowed that February, I wandered up to Highgate to visit the grave on my own. The snow was that lovely powdery type that sparkles in the sunlight. I needn't have had any fears about not finding the site under all that snow, because as I came to the bottom of the hill, I was greeted by a sight that made me roar with laughter.

Standing in front of the grave was the loveliest snowman I had ever seen. He wasn't tall by snowman standards, about two feet at the most, had a broad cheeky smile on his face and an upside-down flowerpot with a red rose stuck in the hole, on his head. I was once again over-joyed at people's sensitivity to the way the boys would have liked to be remembered; it didn't surprise me later to learn it was Herbie.

On my way home, I passed Hampstead Heath and decided to stop for a walk in the snow. The sun had come out, lighting up the scene with lovely pale colours contrasted by a deep blue sky and dark silhouettes of the trees. The scene was reassuring, like a Christmas card, but my dream was quickly shattered by the squeals of laughter coming from the happy families playing in the snow, throwing snowballs at each other and racing down hills on makeshift toboggans. All of a sudden, vivid memories of Daniel and Nicholas sprang to mind and I desperately wanted to join in the fun and be part of a family again. Knowing I couldn't, I began to wish the snow would go away.

Back home, and terribly distressed, I played a recording Bernie had made of the boys some months before the shootings – which I had only just heard for the first time – listening, over and over again, to one part in particular. It had been by sheer coincidence that while Daniel was talking, a report on the Ethiopian famine was broadcast on the television news. His reaction to what he saw was so innocent and so perfect.

'Why are the children crying?' said Daniel.

'If you went without food for a couple of days *you'd* be crying,' said Bernie; 'they've been a couple of weeks.'

'Oh gosh!' said Daniel. 'But, but how can they die without food?'

Bernie explained. 'Well, if you don't eat food you die. You need food and you need water. There, look, that one's dying!'

'Oh yes,' said Daniel, who paused and then slowly added, 'Poor little mites.' Pleading for a satisfactory answer to the whole world's problems, he finally said, 'Well, I don't know *what's* happened. I don't know *why* they should die like that. Do you?'

Reading the transcript over, I had a strong feeling he was trying to tell me something, but what? Daniel's sensitivity had moved me, almost as much as the images of suffering in Ethiopia and the Sudan have moved us all. His reactions were saying something very special about children, I was almost surprised at his awareness. The fact that both he and Nicholas talked and worried about the problem for some time after gave me an idea to make a major piece of sculpture as a monument to all children. A celebration of their unity and love for each other, a love which can spread right across the planet; and did when children the world over played such an enormous part in raising money for Band Aid.

It doesn't matter what language they speak, children will always manage to communicate with each other. Through using signs and body language, they do, with far greater ease, what we as adults hardly ever can. Daniel and Nicholas showed me that in Norway, when playing with other children whose language they didn't speak. Daniel's words really brought home to me the fact that our children were not growing up in our world, rather, we were growing old in theirs; and, like those very children, that which has been entrusted to our care – the earth itself – is only on loan.

The idea I came up with was of a strong, well-fed Western child making friends with a child of the Third World; thin, emaciated and too weak to stand up. Food is being offered in friendship; an apple seemed the most universally recognisable and symbolic item of food known to Western children that I could think of. But the offer of food becomes of secondary importance as the starving child touches, instead, the back of his companion's hand, in recognition of that friendship – a statement beyond politics and beyond racism or preju- dice of any kind. It was very important that the body language in the piece be open, friendly and giving; it must not appear condescending in any way. Eye contact and expression were also of utmost import- ance between the two figures.

As the idea formulated in my mind, my drawing of Daniel on the wall seemed to be smiling even more than usual.

To help me become more familiar with the images and shapes of malnutrition, I bought a copy of *Imagine*, David Bailey's photo-journal of the famine. I still wasn't fully prepared for the images which met my eyes; they made the writing of my story then seem so futile compared with the mammoth suffering in so many parts of the world. Every time I saw or thought of those pictures, it brought tears to my eyes and made the idea for that sculpture seem far more important than anything I had ever done. It was not that making a sculpture would do anything to feed the starving millions, but it could be a daily reminder if copies of it were erected in public places.

Today, I see that, like the simple offering of an apple, it's not the grandeur of the act but the focused attention of each person's contribution, however small, that changes the world. All I wanted to do at that moment was pack my bags and fly out on the next supply plane, to try and help; maybe make some drawings from life, from my own experiences, to add a sharper edge to the final piece. The temptation was great but I was also determined that, for once in my life, I was going to finish something I had already started – the earlier manuscript – before running off to begin something else.

I realise now that my desire to run away and attend to the needs of others was very strong in me – as part of my own family's pattern of avoidance and denial. A long time later, after finally making that sculpture, it dawned on me, as I sat looking at the finished bronze one afternoon, that both children symbolised aspects of myself: an inner poverty, and a desire to rescue; something that is common to a major part of our Western culture now.

CHAPTER TWELVE

To speak of the dead is to make them live again.
Temple inscription, Phillae, Egypt

MY LIFE, DURING that first six months, had been somewhat like a yo-yo. I didn't know whether I was coming or going half the time and there didn't seem to be much hope of things settling down for many months to come. At the very time I thought I might begin to get over it all, the pain actually got worse as the state of shock began to wear off. This was further exacerbated by the fact that certain well-meaning but insensitive people, who thought there was some kind of time limit on grief, told me that I ought to be getting over it now and that I should pull myself together.

Others asked me how old I was and then suggested that I had plenty of time to have another family – as if my sons were interchangeable, or replaceable like livestock. 'I know how you feel' was another phrase which angered me, but how could anybody know what it's like unless they have lost children themselves, let alone lose them in such horrendous circumstances? This kind of thoughtless goodwill did nothing to alleviate my terrible pain. Friends who were *not* afraid to talk about Bambs and the boys, as many seemed to be, were of much greater help.

By giving me permission to share my grief and my memories – without being made to feel guilty – I could take one more step towards recovery. The brave few even heard some amusing stories in the process.

I also found that in being encouraged to talk out my memories, I was able to recall many forgotten or missing pieces of the jigsaw puzzle – especially those recollections of Bambs's own stories of childhood, family and boarding school – my main key to understanding Jeremy. And when there were gaps in the picture, or questions, or my memory needed jogging, someone or something – often a letter – would turn up out of the blue, usually within hours, and provide the answer. That's when I really became aware of that spiritual backroom with the guardian angels I spoke about earlier. It happened so frequently, it was uncanny.

As the picture formed, I was drawn more and more to Bambs's illness and couldn't quite piece it together without coming back to her childhood. I kept being asked if she and Jeremy were actual brother and sister – even though they were adopted four years apart.

Apart from the fact that they looked incredibly alike, I suppose this confusion was because it appeared as if Jeremy was also mentally unbalanced and people must have wondered what was the connection. Given that many coincidences are meaningful – especially when connected to such a dramatic event – I must admit that questions of this nature had begun to crowd my mind as well. It is very easy to condemn someone out of hand when by their actions you have lost everything you love. But that had never been the case when we thought Bambs had been the murderer. For her I had only ever felt terrible sadness, nothing more.

Having put Bambs's illness down to some unknown – and now unknowable – trauma in childhood, how then could I condemn Jeremy without asking the very same questions about him that I had been asking in connection with his sister? As a product of that same family environment, I had to apply that same maxim to his life. The coincidences were more than I could accept without further question: genetically unrelated, Bambs was diagnosed psychotic and 'mildly' schizophrenic, June was treated for manic depression and Jeremy, by all appearances, seemed to be some kind of schizophrenic psychopath – a sociopath, who would do anything, even kill, to get what he wanted.

So what was the connection? What made Jeremy so hateful of his family that, 'out of greed', he became a mass murderer? What drove him to that point, and why did I still feel that June and Nevill were behind the whole tragedy? In Jeremy I now had someone else to blame, but it didn't seem to make any difference. Irrational or not, I was still feeling incredible anger towards his parents as well.

Out of a need to understand, I had to follow that thread and look at what it was all connected to. I then realised that with Jeremy's arrest nothing had changed – and it was also nothing to do with gut feelings. The only feeling in my gut was a gnawing rage, added to which a lump in my throat ached with holding in a tremendous scream I didn't feel safe enough to let out. There was never anywhere safe enough to let it out.

I also began to feel a certain amount of compassion towards Jeremy; even strangely connected to him in a way I couldn't at that time fathom. As products of the same environment, it might be safe to assume that he and Bambs probably suffered some of the same or similar psychological wounds. But there was something else going on for me – some of which only began to crystallise further as I gathered all this material.

The theme of pregnancy seems to be the key to many of my memories, so it may also be a good place to begin.

I didn't actually hear about Bambs's adoption until she herself was first faced with becoming a mother, during the early days of our relationship. Initially, I didn't believe her and took it all as fantasy, because I knew how disappointed she was with June as a mother; how she couldn't get on with her and never had. These barriers really worried Bambs. She felt very sad that she didn't have the same relationship with June that so many of her friends had with their mothers. There was one in particular who was more like a sister to her friend than a mother. That meant a lot to Bambs.

She also talked about June always being too busy to sit and talk to her or have coffee together when it was only the two of them. She would say, 'Mum never had time to have time with me. Even as an adult, I would just be in the way.' To make it bearable, she imagined that her biological mother, who we now know as Christine, was everything June wasn't: bright and gay with a sparkling personality. She also *had* to be very beautiful, which, as we later discovered, couldn't have been more true; Christine was all of the things Bambs had imagined. With her adoptive mother, June, Bambs had always experienced the opposite; although June was not an unattractive woman, she hid any hint of it behind a cold and formal exterior.

Referring to her schooldays, Bambs often said she was so upset because her mother would nearly always turn up to meet her very formally dressed, in a tweed suit and brogue shoes, when all her friends' mothers arrived looking very trendy, in jeans or lovely colourful skirts. Such practical clothes in the country were not unusual in themselves, but in June's case they exemplified her nature and acted as an effective barrier to any intimacy. In fact, Bambs talked a great deal about the lack of physical affection between herself and her parents; a distance I more recently observed between them and my own children. Much as June would kick up quite a fuss about the boys coming to stay, once there they were often looked after by a girl from the village during the day while Mrs Bamber did other things, usually with the church.

On the other hand, Bambs felt sure that some kind of physical love would have been there with her real mother – both for herself and for the twins. This actually turned out to be the case; I have a lovely picture of them all sprawled on the floor, playing together, when Christine visited.

When I asked Bambs why she had felt like this, she told me that she had only ever been allowed to play with her mother or sit on her father's knee at certain times of the day; at any other time or place it was never allowed. As a result, Bambs felt she could never run up and throw her arms around them when she wanted or needed to. This surprised me because she was always so physical with everybody else, even down to the gentle touch on your arm as she talked to you. She also spoke of vivid memories of being left in her pram in the garden, screaming her head off for attention or affection – sometimes for the best part of an afternoon.

I thought it quite remarkable, even then, that this should be such a significant memory in a child who could not, by any stretch of the imagination, have been any more than eighteen months old. It might be nearer the truth to say that Bambs was often *told* she was 'a difficult child' – because of her insatiable demands on her parents' attention, which are natural to nearly all children.

From the day she was first brought home, Bambs was also adopted by Jasper, the yellow Labrador dog, who made himself her constant guardian and companion. He would sit by her pram, especially when she was left in the garden to sleep. Bambs had, in fact, a wonderful way with animals and made up special pet voices and languages for them, distinctly different for each animal. Her greatest pet love, however, was Sweepy, who looked like a mop but was, I am told, a dog – a Shih Tzu. He was given to Bambs as her tenth birthday present from June and Nevill, only months before she was sent away to boarding school.

Before then, and later during her school holidays, Bambs would spend her summer days walking in the fields with the dogs, or playing hide-and-seek around the farmhouse or garden with her brother.

Jeremy, who was also adopted soon after birth, was born on 13 January 1961 and, unlike his sister (who could and often did have a temper), he appeared to be a much more placid child who rarely misbehaved. Whether it was a vent for pent-up anger and frustration it's difficult to say, but according to Bambs, he did have one particularly destructive habit that always upset her, and that was to break the stems on all the garden flowers before they could open.

This happened regularly, although, with June being the gardener, it is more likely to be a veiled statement of anger towards her – what psychologists would describe as passive/aggressive behaviour. Bambs viewed it as a dislike of anything beautiful or that which gave pleasure to others. Bambs also gave me the impression that she never really liked Jeremy and was often quick to let him know it; at best she tolerated him.

At five years of age, Bambs was sent to the local kindergarten school, Maldon Court, as was Jeremy several years later. She loved that school, but most of all enjoyed coming home on the bus with all her friends in the evening. As a marked contrast, she loathed Moira House, the boarding school in Eastbourne on the south coast, where she was suddenly sent for her secondary education. She spoke of suffering terrible feelings of rejection at this time, not only by her parents but also by most of the other girls at the school.

Perhaps the reason was that it seemed to coincide with the untimely death of Nevill's sister, Diana; Bambs joined midway through the academic year and, although she eventually made a few friends, had to fight very hard to be accepted by the already established cliques. Bambs had never needed to fight for herself before. The only way it seemed she could be accepted was to take rule-breaking and practical-joking to extremes. Although she later defended this era of her life as helping to build a certain strength in her character, to the extent that she wanted to send the twins to boarding school, it also served to fuel her major feelings of inadequacy and very low self-esteem due to the constant rejection.

Jeremy was to have similar feelings when he was later sent away to Gresham's School in Norfolk.

On one of my first visits to the farm, Bambs was showing me some of her paintings and drawings, which her parents had kept from her schooldays, when one caught my eye as particularly striking. It portrayed three girls wearing long dresses standing on a spiral staircase, another girl at the bottom, kneeling on the floor in dark clothes, looking down and away from the others. Its imagery was both powerful and rather disturbing – not unlike Edvard Munch's painting *The Scream*.

When I asked Bambs about it, she told me she had painted it at Moira House when she was eleven years old. The three girls represented the older pupils who were always 'really nasty' to her and always made out that they were 'so superior and glamorous' and that she was always so 'dowdy and pathetic'. I told her I thought the painting very moving and advanced for the age at which she did it, and asked if she would let me have it.

I still have that painting and keep it as a reminder of how honest and informative children's pictures are. If only we'd look at them with more open eyes, they could tell us so much, before it's too late! Having since attended a number of workshops on the interpretation of spontaneous drawings, I recently turned the picture over and looked at the back of it for the first time. There was a sinister black and white face with bright red lips, which had then been crossed out with two broad daubs of red paint. It is often the case that the aborted attempt at a picture can be even more significant than the one which is presented. The whole thing, which in its entirety is even more reminiscent of *The Scream*, now seems horribly symbolic.

It was on that same afternoon that Bambs first showed me her father's photographs of his late sister, Diana. I wonder to what extent

June and Nevill ever talked to the children about Diana's death? Or were they like my own family and made the decision that such a discussion would be far too distressing for Bambs or Jeremy and hoped that, by not saying anything, the subject of a favourite aunt's death would be quietly forgotten?

Such denial of a child's natural feelings of grief is hard enough, as I know, not only from my own experiences of childhood but also more recently, when my nieces were not allowed to come to the twins' funeral. To then send that child away from home to a hostile boarding school can only further add to the pain and confusion and make that child (in this case, Bambs) believe that her father was not only blaming her for his sister's death, but punishing her for it too.

We tend to believe, far too easily at times, that a child is either totally incapable of understanding or, conversely, understands everything regardless of an adequate explanation. But it really comes down to a denial of our own pain and our own unexpressed feelings. Nevill must have been extremely distressed at the time, but how was *he* dealing with it having already lost his other sister? Was he allowing his full range of emotions or was he 'stuffing it' by losing himself in work or other activities, as was his way, or getting unjustifiably irritable with the children?

Was he able to accept support or did he push those around him away? Or was it that, in an attempt to spare Bambs from their grief, which *is* possible, they sent her away from home and left her, unwittingly, feeling abandoned? The real question, though, is: in what way, if at all, had both he and June dealt with their earlier losses – including the fact that they couldn't have children of their own – and were Bambs and Jeremy carrying all the pain and grief for them? Either way, the effects of the combined events on a child who was already feeling isolated could be catastrophic.

I had wondered for a long time how Nevill fitted into the picture; now it all begins to make more sense. If he was like many men of his generation, including my own father, he would have found it impossible to show his feelings, cry or allow himself to be held in any way. To lose control would have been *too* great a risk.

Every time we fail to have our appropriate feelings – to grieve the 'little deaths' and losses – it adds to our pool of 'unfinished business', a pool that eventually spills over as the result of one hurt or loss too many. It might be the death of a pet or it might be something akin to my own experience, but the result is inevitably the same: the unexpressed feelings connected to *all* the previous hurts come rushing forth in a huge wave of despair and agony.

But at least that's preferable to depression or hatred and rage, which is what can occur as a result of keeping it all in; when things are moving, we no longer have a stagnant pool where the bacteria of negativity can multiply, where disease can fester and take hold.

After nearly a year of unhappiness and pleading with her parents to take her away from Eastbourne, Bambs was moved to Old Hall School at Hethersett in Norfolk, where she was much happier. She was not, as some newspapers have said, expelled from Moira House. If she had been, she would certainly not have been ashamed to say so.

Bambs, having come to Hethersett at the beginning of the school year, made loads of new friends and further developed a wicked sense of fun with some of them. The survival grounding she gained at Moira House held her in good stead, greatly improving her talent for mimicking members of staff. She did, however, occasionally get caught out when the unfortunate victim walked into the room behind her as she stood on her desk amusing everyone else. She was certainly very popular with classmates, if not with the teachers. Bambs was, I have been told, very loyal to her friends and would always own up if group pranks were rumbled. She would never allow her friends to take the blame for anything she did. Jeremy, on the other hand, was quite the opposite and never owned up to anything. (I was much the same, until all this happened.)

One of her closest friends, Jane Davis, said in a letter to me: 'There was nothing except kindness and fun in Bambs – she was one of the few people I knew who never showed any signs of malice. We were very much a team at Hethersett and tended to do things as such.' This was to include getting expelled on their last day at school. Due to some St Trinian's-style, end-of-term hell-raising – which also happened to coincide with Bambs's seventeenth birthday – the whole class was expelled. Their only crime was tearing up their old uniforms and generally having a good time as most teenagers do on their last day; and why not?

Meanwhile, Jeremy, from what I gather, was having a miserable time at Gresham's, although he wouldn't show it to anyone at home. He was feeling as cut-off and lonely as Bambs had been, but as a boy was expected to keep his chin up and be strong.

Like many parents wanting the best for their children, the Bambers had sent them both to boarding school determined to give them a good, middle-class education – as Nevill himself had enjoyed – but as far as Jeremy was concerned, his parents had betrayed him. Years later he was to complain bitterly that he couldn't understand why they had adopted him in the first place, knowing how they intended to send him away when he was only nine years old; especially to such a hostile environment.

As Uncle Bobby recently pointed out, there is a strict 'pecking order' at boarding schools, which would have placed Jeremy amongst the lowest of the low. Gresham's is the school to which most of East Anglia's dignitaries and landed gentry send their sons, but as Jeremy was only the son of a farmer, and a tenant farmer at that, it was inevitable that during his first years there he was to be emotionally, physically and, according to Jeremy, sexually abused by older boys; thereby hardening his character and understandable resentment. It also came out that he was adopted and was hence dubbed 'The Bastard'.

Loathing every minute of his time there, Jeremy found his own methods of survival and started taking his frustrations out on other youngsters. As he progressed through the grades, he was branded an arrogant bully and reported more than once for mistreating younger boys. The headmaster described him as a 'prickly boy who displayed a touch of arrogance at an early age . . . a relentless tease'. And to quote his housemaster: 'He was cold and detached . . . a loner.'

He hadn't even been that popular at primary school, where classmates made his life a misery, teasing *him* about his 'posh voice'. One of them was quoted by a newspaper as saying that he was 'a real wimp', who would 'burst into tears instead of fighting back. His sister stuck up for him a lot and he hated that.' Which says a lot for Bambs, knowing how she felt about Jeremy. It also sounds a lot like me and *my* sister – except I didn't mind being rescued.

In my view, for all the rebuke he got from her as a child, Jeremy thought the world of his sister. He spent much of his last term at

Gresham's making us a dining-table for a wedding present. At the very least, Bambs, who had since become a photographic model, was a status symbol for him amongst the other boys. It was said that he would often show off photographs of her.

It is also worth mentioning that Gresham's is famous for its Cadet School and a high standard in shooting skills, especially target shooting with rifles; an activity in which Jeremy was more than passable.

Coming back to the predicament of Bambs's first pregnancy, we discussed all the possibilities and decided that we would most likely keep the child. That was my preference; I wanted to tie down this butterfly and get married. My ego wanted a replica of myself and the girl I loved. As a father, I could have a piece of her for ever, to love and look upon; I was the one obsessed with having children. Bambs, who felt she was far too young to settle down, was a little more hesitant – certainly far more sensible – but didn't feel good about either of the alternatives. With a termination we were both concerned about the moral issues surrounding it; whether the foetus was already a life with a soul or, as an embryo, did it lack a personality since the brain would not yet have developed. This was something we talked over at length, but for Bambs, her main concern was that the operation might damage her insides and affect her chances of having a baby in the future. To give birth to her own children meant more to her than anything. She couldn't bear the thought of having to adopt, as her parents had. Nor could she face subjecting her own child to an existence that risked the same apparent lack of love and understanding she herself had experienced.

Having made our decision, we realised we would now have to tell our parents. Bambs's mother and father greeted the whole thing with surprising calm. But then they were *always* so level-headed and calm! Mine were far more blunt and my mother gave me a repeat of her 'Why do you have to keep all your brains in your underpants?' speech resurrected from my teenage years.

The following day we took the train out to Witham, where Mrs Bamber picked us up in her Mini. Not to our surprise, she talked about the weather, the garden, the church, in fact everything except our little predicament. This made us even more nervous as we sat in the back of the car tightly holding each other's hand.

When we arrived at the farm, Mrs Bamber banged and busied herself around the kitchen while Bambs and I sat together, grinning sheepishly, until her father came in from the fields. Up till then, nothing was said. You could have cut the atmosphere with a knife.

Bambs had assured me that in all her memory she had never known her father to show anger or lose his temper, but on this occasion I thought there might just be a chance. When Nevill came in, however, he greeted me warmly, made himself a coffee and sat down for an informal chat. I think he was surprised at my coming to see them, and all the more so for coming so soon, but because of it I feel he treated me with a certain amount of respect.

I launched into telling them my proposed plans for taking a year off college and how I would like to marry Bambs if she would have me. All the time, Nevill sat there asking all the right questions in all the right places; listening carefully but knowing full well I was a dreamer and being unrealistic. Ever since our first meeting, I have had great admiration for him as a man who was fair and never made up his mind before listening to all the facts. I think he realised how much courage I'd had to summon up to face them, for never once did he talk down to or reproach me and, for that, I will always be grateful.

Instead, he made suggestions of a more practical nature: had I considered his daughter's age, for example, and the fact that we might both change a lot in the next few years; the high cost of living in relation to the fact that I had yet to find a job; and, of course, the importance of me finishing my degree without the added pressures of supporting a family – wouldn't I be able to find a better job once I had that qualification? He was absolutely right, but I felt that, deep down, he could also understand the dreams of young lovers who weren't too worried about slumming it a bit; he knew when not to tread on our toes.

Mrs Bamber, on the other hand, was less than tolerant and quick to jump on the morality bandwagon, openly reproaching us for having sex before marriage. The Church also crept into the conversation when she told us that she had already been to see the vicar to ask his advice. Was nothing of our life sacred? It was almost as if, in the home, she needed to back herself up with the authority of a higher power. It was not in Nevill's nature to wield it.

On the following day, Bambs and her mother left very early to see the family doctor. When they returned, I was sitting in the garden enjoying the warm spring sunshine. Bambs came out looking pensive and sat down on the grass next to me. She told me that the doctor had explained everything to her about the operation and how safe and simple it was.

'He assured me that it wouldn't upset my chances of having babies in the future,' said Bambs, 'and most girls go on to have successful pregnancies later on.' She also went on to say that she had talked a lot more with her mother, who had spoken a great deal of sense. 'I hope you won't be too upset but I have decided to go through with the termination. I do love you,' she said, 'but I think it's all for the best. Don't you?'

I was sad but knew all along it was the right decision. We were relieved but had tears in our eyes as we held each other very tightly, like two lost children.

It was early summer by the time the operation was due, and Bambs's mind seemed full of doubts and worries. So I took her to Cornwall for the weekend, where we stayed with a friend of mine who was a district nurse. It did her the world of good. As well as taking Bambs on some of my favourite walks, along the cliffs at Land's End, conversations with the nurse did a lot to dispel many of her fears.

When I telephoned Bambs the day after the operation, Mrs Bamber answered and greeted me rather formally, then told me that now 'this business' was over, it would be better if Bambs and I were not to see each other any more.

'Why not?' I demanded. 'Just because we made one mistake, it doesn't mean we've stopped loving each other!'

'I don't think you know the meaning of love, Colin,' she said, 'and my husband and I feel it would be better for both of you if you didn't see each other—'

'I think Sheila and I are the best judge of that!' I said, interrupting her. 'Could I speak to her, please.'

'Yes, all right, but I don't think it'll do you any good. I don't think Sheila will want to see you.'

I waited for a minute or two, wondering what was going on, and then Bambs came to the phone. 'Hello,' she said sleepily, 'are you coming down here soon? I really want to see you. I need a cuddle.'

'Yes, I'd love to come but are you all right?'

'Well, yes, a bit delicate but OK.'

'That's good,' I said, and added, 'Your mother just told me she didn't want us to see each other again, and that you didn't want to see me either.'

'What! How dare she? It's none of her business! Can you take tomorrow off college and come down?'

'Yes, if it's OK with your parents.'

'Don't worry,' she said, 'I'll call you back later after I've had a word with them.' Then she whispered, 'I love you,' and rang off.

The following day was one of those really glorious, balmy summer days that people write songs about; the sort of day that makes you want to sit quietly under a tree and just think. Bambs had called me back the night before to say she had cleared things with her parents and put them straight on a matter or two. Eager to see her, I made an early start and arrived at Witham at around eleven o'clock. Bambs and her mother were at the station to meet me, Bambs looking wonderful in a favourite floral cotton skirt. We were so excited to see each other and couldn't wait to be alone again, just so we could talk freely. We tactfully avoided the rather sore subject of the termination in her mother's presence.

After a light lunch, Mrs Bamber suggested we sunbathe in the garden, but Bambs thought otherwise and suggested taking a picnic out to the fields for the afternoon. As we walked along, in search of a nice spot, Bambs said that she had to get away from the house. 'Mum's been acting really funny with me since I've been here. I feel we would have been watched had we stayed in the garden, I wouldn't have been able to relax.' She then went on to tell me about her experiences at the hospital, to which she now had a rather flippant attitude. Although I was a little put out by this, it was soon forgotten when she diverted my attention to the fact that her bra size had somewhat increased in the process.

It was so hot in the shelter of the hedgerow that, having spread our blankets out, we decided to strip off completely and sunbathe naked.

She looked fabulous and was so proud of her new shape that she asked me to take some photographs of her, just as a reminder of how her figure had been. The same photographs Jeremy had found in his mother's bureau and reminded me about when I last saw him at Bambs's flat before his arrest.

'I do hope I've done the right thing,' she said, resuming our earlier conversation, 'because I'm so worried about being damaged inside. Do you think I'll be OK and be able to have more children?' I tried to assure her that the doctors would have done their utmost to be careful and that everything was bound to be all right in the future. 'I hope so,' she said. 'I don't really trust those doctors half the time. It will be all right though, won't it?'

This was the anxious tone of Bambs's conversation that was to dominate much of our relationship in the coming years; her confidence was ebbing rapidly. The only thing I could do then was to keep repeating variations of my own extremely limited answers until I had persuaded her there was nothing to worry about.

We had been talking like this for an hour or so and were deep in conversation when, all of a sudden, Bambs sat bolt upright, staring over my shoulder in horror.

'Oh no!' she said. 'It's Mum!' I turned around to see Mrs Bamber's little blue Mini bumping angrily along the dirt track towards us – an expression of grim determination on her face. We made a somewhat unsuccessful attempt to put on some underwear before she skidded to a halt in a cloud of dust next to us. But it was too hot to rush anything, and too late anyway, so we just sat there with our towels over our laps. Mrs Bamber leapt out of her car and stood over us shaking with rage.

'How dare you behave like this!' she shouted. 'Fornicating on my land! Wait till my husband hears about this!'

In an attempt to calm Mrs Bamber down, I tried to explain how she had misjudged the situation and that we would hardly be making love in Bambs's present condition. We were only sunbathing.

'I don't care what you were doing,' said Mrs Bamber. 'It's disgusting!'

'Mum, we were only sunbathing in the nude,' said Bambs, who then added that if her mother chose to start looking for us, it was her own fault. If anything, Bambs used much harsher words, so her mother demanded we got dressed and for Bambs to come home in the car immediately. We preferred to get dressed after she'd gone, if she didn't mind.

In a final fit of rage, before she stormed off, Mrs Bamber said, 'Well, be back at the house in ten minutes, or I'll be back for you!' And then added, 'I'll *speak to you* when you get home, young lady.'

Bambs and I stared at each other in total disbelief as her mother restarted the car and rattled off back up the dirt track. 'I can't stay here with this atmosphere,' I said as the dust settled again. 'I'm going back to London. Are you coming?'

That afternoon, for Bambs, was to prove emotionally catastrophic.

What effect did similar proselytising have on Jeremy?

When he began to go out with girls – or, more to the point, stay out with girls – his mother would always be there on his return, with Bible in hand, ready to moralise, judge and list his sins.

It was as information and memories like these began to re-emerge and take their place in the picture that I started to realise that had I been stuck in the same environment, in the same childhood, I myself could have easily been drawn, in a fit of temper, to killing Mrs Bamber. She had incredible power to victimise. Apart from the fact that Nevill didn't seem strong enough to intervene on his children's behalf, I still couldn't understand Jeremy's reasons for killing the others, and perhaps I never will. But June was another matter. She touched so much of my own pain and anger, it often made *me* feel murderous.

As Bambs and I walked back to the farmhouse, I asked if she thought her mother had been able to see us. 'Oh no,' she said. 'It was probably because she couldn't that she came looking.'

When we got back, Bambs went straight upstairs to pack her things, followed rapidly by her mother, who soon came down and attempted to lecture me in the kitchen. Nevill was only just coming in from work when we were ready to leave.

Totally unaware of the conflict, he was disappointed that we were leaving so soon. Bambs, determined not to be outdone by her mother, and knowing he would no doubt be told later, told her father how and why they had fallen out again. Nevill didn't seem shocked or surprised at anything he was told and just said that he hoped to see her again soon. He then fixed me with his gaze, shook hands and said, 'Look after her, won't you?' The drive back to the station was without conversation from her mother and it was a relief to be back on the train.

'At least we'll now be able to sleep in the same bed tonight,' said Bambs as she snuggled under my arm. Looking back, we found the whole episode rather amusing, but it was far from so at the time. Nor was I aware of the far-reaching effect that confrontation had had on Bambs.

Some years later I was to learn that, in private, Mrs Bamber had branded her 'the Devil's child'; a condemnation which, according to her psychiatrist's testimony at Jeremy's trial, struck very deeply and had a profound and devastating effect at the time Bambs was most emotionally vulnerable and in need of reassurance. From then on she never stopped worrying about her ability to have children: her obsession with being a natural, rather than adoptive mother had taken root.

CHAPTER THIRTEEN

Looking back, Bambs never really stood a chance ... Like the beautiful princess in the myth of Amor and Psyche, her only sins were blind innocence and her God-given beauty. But through other people's projections, being the fairy-tale princess, she was also destroyed. Everything in her strove to be accepted and loved by those she cared for, but more often than not she was left abandoned – or isolated in some way – by those very same people, myself included. Then like Psyche, with deliverance in sight, she fell into a death-like sleep from which only Love – with whom she had fallen in love – could reawaken her. And that's where I failed: Bambs's pain was more than I was then equipped to deal with ...

Another accidental pregnancy, after I had graduated from art school, soon brought all her fears welling to the surface again, but this time we decided to get married. When she miscarried at five and a half months – only weeks after our wedding – it was a bitter blow to both of us. But for Bambs it was also taken as a form of punishment or divine retribution that she continually beat herself up over; proof that she had been wrong to have the earlier termination.

The hardest part was the fact that, being so far gone, she had to go through labour and give birth to a tiny child that she was convinced was still moving, still alive, before they whisked it from her sight. I don't know how true that was, because I had already been asked to leave the room.

Shortly after this she was offered two months' contract work in Tokyo – her first major modelling assignment. We thought it a good idea at first – to get her back into a routine and take her mind off things – but as it turned out, the tough world of modelling was the last place she needed to be. She was thrown in at the deep end at a time she was most in need of support. Even my own reasons for encouraging the trip were selfish: I thought I might join her at some point and use the opportunity to visit the studios of some of the great Japanese potters.

But I was not then aware of the Japanese attitude to life and people, which to most Western sensibilities would be considered heartless bordering on cruel. In business, especially if you are hired by them, they will extract their pound of flesh without feeling. In the modelling world, especially, you become meat, a commodity to be exploited to the full; for Bambs, it was a disaster from start to finish.

She was expected to work two or three assignments a day, starting most days at 5 or 6 a.m. when a car collected her, not getting back to her apartment until very late in the evening (if she was lucky). Often, she was taken straight out to a nightclub, when all she wanted to do was go home and sleep. There were even occasions when her employers tried to get her to sleep with clients that they wished to impress. To these people, models were little more than prostitutes and were treated as such.

What most upset Bambs, however – what really unhinged her – was the fact that if she ever tried to complain about their treatment, or asked for some much-needed time off (at one point she worked seventeen days without a break), those who normally spoke English well, her interpreters, suddenly couldn't manage a single word of it.

Whether this was from shock – that a woman was speaking up in public – or simply the fact that it was not in the Japanese vocabulary or way of thinking to either complain or call in sick, it left Bambs frighteningly isolated. In one of her letters to me, she wrote:

> I'm finding it very difficult to be myself here because in Japan there are only a few English or European models and it's very competitive and everyone looks at you all the time, which makes me nervous because I feel that I'm being compared by people for looks with the other girls, therefore I'm behaving rather nervously. The other girl, who I share the room with, is very beautiful and chic and sophisticated, unlike me.

In another letter a couple of weeks later, with the strain of constant invasion beginning to show, she added:

> I look very tired and they have straightened my hair but today I am going back to the hairdresser's to have it recurled. Don't get worried when I say this but I really think I should go to a psychiatrist when I get back, so could you please arrange an appointment for me as soon as possible and I will be very grateful. I've never felt so confused and unable to control my brain before and I'd like to get myself sorted out as soon as possible.
>
> It's my self-confidence. Some days at jobs I'm happy and self-confident and other days I'm not and you can see the change in people when I'm not. They don't really like me on my bad days, it's almost as if I'm schizophrenic or something. [When she got home she qualified this by telling me that during these down periods her mood seemed to affect everyone around her – almost to the point where she felt she exuded an 'evil aura' which frightened people away.]
>
> I feel so sick of people and stale. It's terrible, I don't know what's happening to me at all. Can't wait to get back and be with you, you're the only person who really cares and understands.

During this time I had moved into the flat her parents had bought us. But her homecoming, although a tremendous relief, was not a pleasant experience. The woman I carried across the threshold was a frail shadow of the one I had married a few months earlier; she was weak and thin and broken. All the bubbles that had made up the person I first knew had gone. In this sensitive mortal, Aphrodite had begun to extract her revenge. There was nothing left of Bambs but a shell.

During the coming weeks, as she regained all her physical strength, anxieties about motherhood resumed and tensions between us grew. Within months she became pregnant again and this time a stitch was put in to support her weak cervix. Then something else went wrong: the foetus became infected through a careless internal examination and the pregnancy once again had to be terminated. With tension and anxiety increasing, we were both in desperate need of a break, but Bambs wouldn't let go and soon became pregnant for the fourth time – this time with the twins.

Needless to say, the physical and emotional pressure not to lose them was a nightmare – as was the pregnancy itself. She spent over four months of her term in hospital having total bed rest. Distressed and jarred by the whole 'journey', she was once again subjected to the intense lack of privacy and constant violation of physical boundaries that make up any hospital stay.

By this time, having endured so many fights between us – not only because of the tensions created by her gynaecological problems, but also by the fact that I could no longer tolerate the almost constant attentions of other men, which she rarely discouraged – I was also just about 'broken' and eventually found myself in the arms of another woman.

That in itself may not have mattered, but I also made the mistake of falling in love. The woman, as I have already said, was Jan. She was everything Bambs had been before the miscarriages, yet at the same time so calm and peaceful – everything I ached for and hadn't had for so long. Out of a desperate need for love and support I may have made a terrible mistake, and one that is hard to defend, but also one that I have more than paid for over the years.

For Bambs, in the wake of her greatest triumph – the birth of her children – it was also one of the greatest betrayals; especially when I decided to leave her five months later. I had been the only person to ever love her in the way she really wanted.

But even that event was almost shadowed by the effect of her mother's response to the births. I will never forget it. The day after the boys were born, both June and my mother came to the hospital to see them. Mum arrived about the same time, but in the middle of all the hugs and smiles that were being exchanged, all the relief and elation, June stood there with her arms hanging by her sides. Then, still making no attempt to touch or hold her daughter, she just smiled and said: 'Who's a clever girl, then.' Nothing more.

Bambs just stared at her, half smiled back and then turned away, looking lost and deflated. I think she had hoped for so much more from her mother, after such a long and painful struggle, some kind of recognition, but that never happened. Regardless of all Bambs's delight at having given birth to two beautiful sons, the knife went in again, and it went in deep; as if she had achieved nothing.

I have this image of Bambs at a doorway or threshold in a barren landscape. The door is high up on a precipice and can only be reached along a knife edge. On one side of the door, within the safety of the cliff face, are all her hopes and dreams: her two sons; the parents whose love and approval she needed so much; the love and support of her husband – all of her emotional security. And on the other side, there *she* is: standing on the knife's edge; naked, powerless and bleeding from her feet; fighting, for all her life, to keep the door open against the effortless tide of disapproval and false judgement; desperate to reclaim not only an untainted sexuality and womanhood, but her very identity as well.

Looking back, there was something wonderfully vital and primitive about Bambs – a beautiful and delicate simplicity that those close to her never really understood, but also yearned for. And, one by one, we each took a piece of it from her; Jeremy's actions the final and ultimate betrayal.

As I said before, she was just like 'a candle in the wind' and never really stood a chance . . .

CHAPTER FOURTEEN

A diary note, 6 December 1992:

The journey is as much now as it was then. I must never forget that.

THERE ARE ANY number of events and incidents, similar to those I have described, that might serve to illustrate the relationships within the Bamber household. But to catalogue all of them does little to further the purpose of this book, the purpose being to understand rather than blame or denigrate. We all have our weaknesses and short-comings – it is part of human nature – and June, Nevill, Bambs and Jeremy all had their fair share, regardless of how they presented themselves to the world. That also applies to me and my own family. None of us in our society are completely without fault, without aspects of ourselves that cause other people pain. What is most important right now is to establish the emotional climate in which a domestic mass murder took place.

I still have the strong feeling, though, that out of loyalty to Bambs I need to present more of her story. It is important that the public, who have read and generally believed the media images of her, finally see Bambs for the beautiful and compassionate person she was; a woman who was horribly violated in her lifetime, in the most sinister of ways, through tyranny, deep shaming and the threat of 'hell-fire and damnation'.

Bambs is no longer on trial. I cannot emphasise that too much.

When I first approached writing this story back in 1985, my feelings were raw and came from a place of incredible pain and naïvety. I had a lot of anger which I didn't understand then, but I knew where most of it belonged – with the Bamber family. The rest belonged with me and my own family, and I was later to do a lot of work on that. But right now, on having reread my original biographical section in full, I am once again enraged at the injustices and level of abuse that Bambs suffered. This time, however, my intense fury comes not from ignorance but from conscious, full awareness.

Eventually, I was to train with Dr Elisabeth Kübler-Ross as a facilitator in her 'Life, Death and Transition' workshops. This training also led me to staffing a number of women's abuse workshops, in which I also had the unenviable but enlightening experience of working with a disturbing number of adult survivors of cult and ritual abuse in childhood.

What happened to Bambs at the hands of her mother – who also endeavoured to subjugate the twins in the same way, with her excessive prayer sessions – was nothing less than ritualised abuse; by the very nature of its enforced repetition, a form of brainwashing. I am referring to the fact that June would define everything Bambs ever did wrong – which in her eyes was nearly everything she ever did – as the work of the Devil, as if Bambs herself was wrong; bludgeoning her with it at every opportunity.

I mentioned earlier that Bambs had rather a fiery temper; a temper that we both shared and which erupted with increasing frequency as her anxieties became greater. But there were also references in the press to these tempers being violent; references for which I am mainly responsible. If anything, I was the violent one, not her. I realise now that my accounts of certain events were greatly coloured by my initial acceptance of the murder and suicide theory and did in fact give an unrealistic impression. Any display of physical violence I ever witnessed was directed, without exception, towards inanimate objects or, on one extreme occasion, to herself. Desperate to gain my attention, after some particularly callous behaviour on my part during her twenty-first birthday party, she put her hand through our bedroom windowpane.

Her quite justifiable reason, in my eyes, was down to the fact that I had left the party, earlier in the evening, with a young woman from my office – with obvious carnal intent – and did not return for a couple of hours. Later, in an endeavour to pretend nothing had happened during that time, I ignored all her questions and was trying to sleep it all off.

After such cruel behaviour on my part, she would have been quite justified in hitting me with something very hard in order to gain my attention – as I am sure many women have in response to such infuriating treatment from a man – but Bambs didn't. Nor does her action make her either a murderer or suicidal. Just as in her child-hood, Bambs needed to be heard and would do anything to gain a response. I don't think I'll ever forget that sickening crash of her fist smashing through glass, or the blood and those permanent scars on the back of her hand; scars she would often thrust under my nose whenever she wanted to make me feel bad.

I feel very strongly that this is an important episode to mention, not only because it was later brought up during the trial, but because it clearly illustrates that, even when she was provoked or in terrible emotional pain, she would not and could not cause physical harm to another. The only form of retribution she knew or would use was always on an emotional level, based on the model of her own child-hood experience.

On the physical side it was always restricted to damaging those things of most value to others. Apart from hurting herself on this occasion – which is why I had initially been able to accept the suicide theory – she had never harmed another living creature. In yet another coincidence, Jeremy, who was staying overnight, was the only other person present – and *he* took her to the hospital. I was too drunk to respond.

At the point where I began to think more clearly, memories like this helped to convince me that Bambs couldn't possibly have turned a gun on her own children or, for that matter, her parents either. I can only see this episode as another of her desperate cries for help, a plea to be noticed and listened to. Even when we first lived together, it was not uncommon for Bambs to provoke an argument by either digging around for a weak spot, then picking at it mercilessly until I reacted or, if that failed, she would destroy items from my collection of studio pottery, much of which was irreplaceable. These were not, as one might expect, thrown at me in anger, but defiantly dropped from shoulder height in order to cause a reaction. On one occasion that reaction from me resulted in a black eye for Bambs.

It seemed to me that Bambs's constant goading was simply to find out if I was as unshakeable as her parents. In fact, she often told me that she wished I was more like her father, who could never be roused to a temper. It felt to me like I was being constantly tested to see if I'd lose mine. Something I did with increasing frequency as our life together continued and her insecurities became greater; insecurities that were to increase the more I pulled back to a safe distance. For me to lose control in that way – to become violent – was a side of myself that I could not accept, much less knew how to deal with. These confrontations brought my own childhood anger and fear to the surface so quickly and with such force, it really frightened me.

At that time, I didn't have the emotional strength Bambs expected of me. I also began to realise that when I did lose my temper it seemed to be almost a comfort to her, because it showed I cared and was getting upset by what was happening. Where I would be left shattered and shaken, remorseful of my loss of control, Bambs would appear almost invigorated, as if nourished by it. She would say things like, 'I needed that. I needed to know you cared. I had to get you to react because you're so easygoing and docile. I needed to fight for you.'

This was something I was never fully able to understand or come to terms with, but it became part of our way of life. It was as if Bambs was craving a physical reaction as a way of gaining some form of emotional security. She craved physical affection so much that any physical attention meant something to her; whether it be a gentle touch of the hand in conversation, making love or a physical fight.

When the tide had turned from these emotional outbursts, we would sit in our room for hours, just talking. More often than not, Bambs would begin to speak about her feelings towards her mother and father. She spoke a great deal about Nevill's very lively social character and how, as a couple, her parents attended fewer and fewer social events as June became increasingly introverted and religious. Bambs had become aware of what a totally different man her father was when he was out without June. She talked about going to golf club functions with him herself and feeling very warm and special, as any daughter would on the arm of her father.

These occasions, however, were rare and, more often than not, the barriers would be up again in the presence of her mother. I clearly remember Bambs's growing resentment for June because she, June, seemed to be causing not only a rift in her own marriage but one between Bambs and her father as well. As far as Bambs was concerned, he was desperately unhappy and she used to cry out, 'Why the hell does he stay with her!'

I often spent hours reassuring Bambs that if she felt that way, she herself could make the effort to close the gap with him. I said, 'Look, you can't relate to your mother, but your dad obviously thinks the world of you. He loves and needs you as much as you need him. So maybe you can do things to bring him out and make him feel better. Put your arm round him or give him a hug occasionally. Don't wait for him to make the first move.' I told her it sounded as though he almost needed the physical reassurance that he was loved as much as she did. 'You love him, for God's sake, so let him know you love him; you're his daughter and that's all that really matters.'

As someone pointed out to me more recently, Nevill always looks so happy in photographs of him with the twins snuggling up on either side. He really seemed to appreciate their physical closeness, so why was there this barrier with his children, and could it have been the result of some form of jealousy on June's part? Jealousy because of Nevill's ease and general sociability? He was a naturally more likeable person, more easygoing and at times even improper or *risqué*.

June on the other hand was intense, shy and always extremely proper. Her rare attempts at spontaneity usually came over as somewhat contrived. She may also have been very jealous of the relationship between Nevill and their daughter who, as a woman, was not only incredibly pretty but also carried much of her father's gregariousness and popularity.

It is sad really, because I find it extremely hard to write anything nice about June – even now. The face she presented in public, which was always very pleasant and caring, was not the one I knew in private; not the person that, having fucked up her own children's minds, attempted to do the same to mine.

It doesn't matter which one of them was infertile, or whatever their problem was; June was still left without children of her own and that must create a certain amount of anguish and resentment in anyone who wants a family. Although my portrayal of June Bamber might appear harsh at times, I also see her as being just as much a victim in her life as everybody else concerned; there are no real monsters in this story, only victims of circumstance.

Somehow I don't think June and Nevill really knew how to show their children the love they needed, which is why, certainly in Bambs's case, she was constantly testing them to get a reaction, as she did with me. I feel her only problem, when charged with being a difficult child, was that she had a bright and lively personality which her parents didn't know how to handle. She craved some form of attention and feeling, responses which she very rarely got from them.

For my part, the fear of anger was connected to shame in that, as a child, whenever I expressed anger, I was quickly informed, either verbally or non-verbally, that I was drawing unfavourable attention to whichever parent I was with; I was making them look foolish in public; *I* was shaming *them*, which is the last thing I wanted to do. I adored my parents − as most children do − so, instead of shaming them, I took the shame into myself. This can be done so easily, even without words, by simply walking away from the distraught child, adding further feelings of threatened abandonment to the shame. It didn't take long before a simple 'nil response' had the very same effect. In one fell swoop we learn how to shame and be shamed.

My own spontaneous but unnatural response to Bambs's anger was the same: either silence or abandonment − both of which led her into further reaction. How many of us know that pattern? One of the great human tragedies is our natural tendency to seek out and be with those people who have learned to speak the same language − by which I mean the emotional languages of love and abuse; to be with those people who have received the same or similar messages in childhood, thereby perpetuating the patterns throughout countless generations.

At least Bambs was able to release some of her anger and frustration − *that* was never a problem to her. Jeremy, on the other hand, like me, seemed to bottle it up and often walked out on any disagreement that didn't go his way, seething with inner rage. I remember once, on a visit to Carbonells, Pam and Bobby's farm, Jeremy had deliberately upset his sister by picking at one of her sensitive spots and, as a result, got a justifiable ticking off from Auntie Pam. He had said to Bambs, as they were being shown around their cousin David Boutflour's impressive new house, that she would never have anything like that while she was with me.

Jeremy didn't stick around to listen to his aunt's reprimand but, very red-faced, stormed out of the house and off the farm. When Pam told Nevill what had happened, he just brushed it aside telling her not to worry; Jeremy would probably walk it off, walking back home the twenty miles, as he often did when things didn't go his way.

That seems to be it: Nevill always seemed to let things go rather than use the authority he appeared to have. Again, like my own father, who as a young man built up lots of muscle in the hope that nobody would ever pick on him, I wonder to what extent Nevill cultivated an appearance of authority so that nobody would ever question him?

To a growing child, discipline (especially firm *consistent* discipline) provides as much security as being cuddled and, from what I have heard, I don't think Bambs or Jeremy got enough of either from where it was needed – until it was too late. Children cannot feel secure without clear boundaries. They have to know the fences are there and, as thinking human beings, they also have to know why they are there. To attempt to survive in a vacuum (which is what it must feel like without them) one can only suffocate or go mad. The ideal is to expand the boundaries as children are ready to accept greater limits and need more space; to give more room as they grow.

If the boundaries are too close – which was the case in my own childhood, in that I was *over*-protected – the child will again feel suffocated, as in the vacuum. And if they are too loose or non-existent, the child has nothing to push against and has to resort to screaming in the hope of a response – any response, even an echo. Contrary to the view of many Freudians, I don't feel children are naturally naughty or bad – wicked – these words are bred into or projected on to them, like movies on a screen, by parents who were given similar messages in their own childhoods. Children are simply inquisitive and keen to identify a sense of their separateness from their mother; trying to establish just what their boundaries are as they explore what to them is a new and wonderful world.

I suspect that when June and Nevill adopted, they were not sufficiently prepared for Bambs and Jeremy being much more than living dolls. They didn't take into account the possibility of them having their own strong personalities, wanting to scream and shout, demand things and ask all sorts of trying questions. When they did exercise their personality muscles – their natural exuberance – it was suppressed with negativity and alienation. In fact, Auntie Pam summed it up perfectly one afternoon, as my mother and I were leaving Vaulty, Granny Speakman's house, after a family gathering some time after Jeremy's conviction.

'I really can't understand why it all happened,' said Pam. 'Junie and Nevill provided such a nice home for them – good food, nice clothes, a fine education – what more could they want?' Apart from noticing the explicit plurality of Pam's accusation, I felt like saying, 'And what about love?' But Mum saw my anger rising and nodded for me to get in the car. There was really no point in saying anything right then – the family had just buried June and Nevill's ashes.

It certainly backs up what Bambs often told me about always having felt like an outsider. She had always felt that she *had* to be grateful – as if any complaint would be met, by all those around her, with incredulity and defence of her parents. It must have been the same for Jeremy.

As adoptees, Bambs and Jeremy almost needed more physical love than children with their natural parents; having already been rejected once, they now needed extra reassurance. The trouble was, June and Nevill didn't seem to have that natural connection with parenthood essential to a healthy upbringing. There certainly didn't seem to be any of that true parental bonding which even the Bible talks about in the 'Judgement of Solomon'.

I might also add that Bambs' childhood tantrums never went unchecked with either Granny Speakman or Auntie Pam, both of whom she felt much closer to than her mother. Bambs got many of the responses she needed, and often deserved, from them.

Leading psychologist Alice Miller speaks about the need for all children to have an adult witness to the hurts or injustices of their lives. Without this support, the unbearable loneliness compels us to put a lid on our feelings, repress all memory of the trauma and idealise those who inflicted the abuse; like all children, we need to look up to and have the respect of those who care for us. Thus dissociated from the original cause, feelings of anger, helplessness and despair eventually find expression in destructive acts against others (Dr Miller cites criminal behaviour, mass murder and rape as typical), or against themselves (alcoholism, drug addiction, prostitution, psychic disorders and suicide).

She then goes on to say that if mistreated children are not to become like this, it is essential that at least once in their life they come in contact with someone who knows, beyond a shadow of a doubt, that the environment – not the helpless child – is at fault. 'In this regard,' she said, 'knowledge or ignorance on the part of society can be instrumental in either saving or destroying a life.'

I am pleased to say that Daniel and Nicholas were blessed in the number of adults around them (especially with the Flowers family) who, for the most part, listened to and respected their feelings when they felt they had suffered an injustice. To have even one adult believe a child who feels hurt really can make a difference. It certainly gave the twins a sense of inner authority when they felt persecuted. They were never mollycoddled, but instead allowed to have their anger or tears without anybody saying they were wrong to feel that way; that maybe they were right to be upset. Just because a grown-up says something, doesn't mean to say that person is right.

In Bambs and Jeremy's case, they were surrounded by people who would only expound their parents' virtues and never saw why *they* were hurting. There was nobody in their environment who supported their distress and said, 'Maybe you're right to feel angry.' They never had, it would seem, the intervention of an adult witness.

Even before Bambs's first breakdown, the twins, especially Daniel, had been bothered by June's religiousness. They would return from the farm complaining that she was always making them say prayers. At this time, even with reassurances that Granny didn't really mean any harm, it was not unusual for Daniel to stab a finger at the sky and say things like, 'Well, I think Granny is too much in love with him up there,' which Nicholas found really hilarious.

After their mother's second breakdown, however, it became apparent that June's religious fervour was having a greater effect on them than I originally thought. Comments like the one above became far less amusing. Seeing their mother's depression manifesting in much the same religious way as June's, but making proclamations far stronger than those of their granny – 'hearing voices from God', etc. – Church became an institution which had sinister overtones and began to frighten them.

To illustrate this more clearly, there was one particular occasion when Jan and the twins had an unfortunate encounter with June and Nevill, which led to them expressing their quite justifiable disgust at what had happened. It certainly became a turning-point in my own determination to face up to June's apparently malevolent manipulation.

While Bambs was still in hospital, after her second breakdown, June telephoned one Thursday morning to say that she and Nevill would be visiting Bambs's flat that day and would like to take the boys to the farm for the weekend. Regardless of the fact that they would have to miss a day at school, at a time they most needed a sound routine to keep them grounded, I had also already arranged for the boys to have tea and an overnight stay with Ann Flowers. Added to which it would be impossible to contact Jan before she picked them up at the school gate.

Unfortunately, I was still easily intimidated by June and eventually gave in to her persistence, mucking up all prior arrangements. Much as June seemed hell-bent on causing disruption, the tea party at Ann's could not be changed. For myself, rather than preparing for an important meeting that evening, I spent the whole afternoon running all over the place, trying to reorganise everything. I had not, however, allowed for Nicholas and Daniel's reactions.

'There has been a slight change of plan,' I told them when we met outside the school. Jan had also arrived by this time. 'Granny is at Mummy's house and wants to take you to the farm for the weekend.'

'No!' they screamed in unison, bursting into tears. 'We're going to Ann's house for tea!'

'That hasn't changed,' I said, 'you'll still have tea at Ann's, but afterwards Jan will take you to meet Granny.'

'But we don't want to go to Granny's,' they cried. 'She shouts at us!'

'Yes, she's always shouting at us when we don't eat our meat,' sobbed Daniel, 'and she never stops making us say our prayers. Please don't make us go!' Then, in a woeful voice, Nicholas added, 'She even makes us say prayers while we are trying to clean our teeth!'

'You mean bedtime prayers?'

'No!' replied Nicholas angrily. 'As well as bedtime!'

Jan and I were quite taken aback. Normally, we would stand our ground and talk them round, but because of current circumstances I was not going to ignore their pleas or turn my back on them. I decided then to stick to my original plan.

When I told June, she was furious and said they were 'only children and had to do what they were told'. I made it clear to her that under normal circumstances I might agree, but they were obviously nervous because they had not seen their mother for several weeks and didn't fully understand why.

'I know you're their grandmother,' I said, 'and I understand how disappointed you are, but they obviously need to remain here at the moment. So please respect their wishes!' Even after I had said this, she still insisted on seeing them before she went back. Eventually, I agreed but insisted that she didn't put any pressure on them. They had made a decision and had made it quite clear how they felt. If she couldn't respect their wishes, then they wouldn't be brought to see her at all. June reluctantly gave me her word, but when I spoke to Jan later, I wished I had cancelled my plans and taken them myself.

Apparently, June totally ignored her the whole time they were there.

On arrival they were taken to the living-room, where Nevill was waiting and where Jan was immediately interrogated about what was happening and *who* exactly was looking after the boys for the weekend; almost implying that they felt whoever it was, wasn't good enough.

Jan, now beginning to get annoyed, pointed out that she was under the impression that I had arranged everything with them earlier, and had only brought Daniel and Nicholas on that understanding. To the best of her knowledge, the boys were spending the weekend with me, because they didn't want to be away from home. At this point, June backed down and Nevill left the room. With Nevill out of the way, and now ignoring Jan, June then began to put pressure on the twins to change their minds.

'Wouldn't you like to come to the farm with us, rather than stay here?' she said, looking at Jan. The boys became very self-conscious and looked to Jan for reassurance. When Nevill came back in, looking rather embarrassed, June said to the boys, 'Come with me a minute, I want to do something with you,' and took them into their bedroom. They were in there for about five minutes and when they came out, June said, 'Now don't forget what I told you.' Jan was really fed up by this time, having done this as a favour, but did point out that although June had refused to acknowledge her, Nevill had been very polite and pleasant from start to finish.

When Jan finally got outside with the boys, she asked them what they had been doing in their room and they said that Granny had made them kneel down to say their prayers again.

'Why does she always make us say prayers?' said Daniel. 'I don't like it very much. Why does Granny always go on about God?'

Jan was furious at how rudely she had been treated and said that Daniel and Nicholas were very distressed by the time she got them away. They were still very angry and upset when I saw them the next day. In some ways, this doesn't seem very much until one becomes aware that these pleas and complaints began to come with alarming regularity, and increased in frequency whenever a meeting with Granny was imminent. They loved her dearly, but also felt threatened by her behaviour.

By way of contrast, they felt absolute trust and safety with my own mother. So much so, that on their last visit to her house – only weeks before their deaths and with the visit to Whitehouse Farm imminent – Daniel made a series of very disturbing drawings which he urged my mother to take into her safe-keeping. There were eight altogether. They also had a specific sequence – which my mother kept them in – and a story which, unfortunately, she had forgotten most of by the time she showed them to me six months after their deaths.

When he gave them to her, Daniel was also extremely emphatic about what she had to do with them: 'You will make them into a book for me, won't you, Grandma. It's very important. You must promise!'

The drawings included images of 'Whitehouse Farm turned dark' (No. 5) or with the sun crying over it (No. 3). Sometimes the sun was being sick (No. 4) or had red pouring from its mouth (No. 1). In fact, every portrayal of the sun – which in spontaneous drawings usually represents the father, God or a higher spiritual power – is afflicted in some way. It is also interesting to note that the farmhouse motif is repeated in every other drawing of the sequence (Nos. 1, 3, 5 and 7) – emphasising, through sequential repetition, his anxiety around the house itself – with the final representation (No. 7) showing Granny, having taken on that form, with teeth bared and red gushing from her head in several places.

The final picture in the sequence (No. 8) gives an extremely disturbing and graphic image of 'naked Granny (June)' which, once again, Nicholas found hilarious as Daniel described it to my mother. Daniel, however, was not laughing. What I find most disturbing is the fact that in both images of 'Granny' – the last two of the sequence – she appears to have a mask covering part of her face. Why is that? I find it very sinister.

I am also curious about the fact that 'Granny' in the last picture – who is naked apart from a pair of red shoes – is holding four unspecified creatures on leashes. Two of these are very much smaller than the others, like insects that could well be crushed by those shoes immediately above them, red shoes like those worn by the 'Wicked Witch of the East' before *she* was crushed by the falling house in *The Wizard of Oz* – a film the boys often watched on video at Herbie's.

As I said before, children's drawings – using non-verbal symbolic language – do not lie. Daniel was desperate to get a message over in a way that his childhood vocabulary could not adequately express. The feeling tone of the entire set is full of fear and anxiety, with many more images I haven't even mentioned; so many that a whole chapter could be written just about this set of drawings.

When I later showed these and other pictures by both Bambs and the twins to Gregg Furth, a leading drawing analyst from New York, he came to the conclusion – after asking numerous questions about all our relationships, as well as about what had happened – that it was unlikely Bambs was schizophrenic and suggested instead that she was carrying her mother's illness for the entire family. The psychosis being her only means of escape from an extremely painful reality. With reference to her letter from Japan in which she described herself as possibly being 'schizophrenic', schizophrenia tends *not* to be a condition that elicits insight into itself, but is more typically recognised by the tendency of sufferers to see all their problems as external to themselves – they are not notably 'self-referring'.

With the term falling into general misusage, it is more likely that, in the same way Bambs was *told* she was a 'difficult child', she may also have been *told* she was 'schizophrenic' by someone who found her moods 'difficult'. She was very good at taking on board other people's beliefs about her.

In their book *The Family Crucible*, family therapists Augustus Napier and Carl Whitaker talk about the family as a 'system' in which all members actively participate – albeit unconsciously – as in a biological organism. For example, if one part is 'sick', then all the parts are sick, and the person referred to as the 'presenting problem' is often not really sick, but a manifestation of the entire family dynamic – like the fruiting body of a fungus being only the outer representation of something that inhabits and eats away the fabric of an entire tree. It can also emerge on any part of the tree, or family.

This all begins to back up my own suspicion that the sickness in the Bamber family had little if anything to do with Bambs's and Jeremy's families of origin but was connected, instead, to their environment – the home they grew up in. In that respect, it was obviously *not* congenital.

The unfortunate knock-on effect – I see this now but could not have known then – is that by keeping Bambs away from June as much as possible, giving her both space and time to heal, the disturbance was likely to break out in the next weakest link of the family structure, that being Jeremy. It was unlikely to re-emerge in June, because her condition had been effectively contained through medical treatment rather than worked out through a process of psychotherapy; the underlying emotional causes having still not been dealt with.

A suitable metaphor for this might be that of badly hung wallpaper, whereby any attempt to just flatten an air bubble will only result in it popping up somewhere else. To hang wallpaper well, the bubbles have to be worked out carefully or vented in some way that doesn't damage the paper. It would be the same with the wounds that are carried in families.

When Dr Ferguson explained about the medication he had been giving Bambs (during her first hospitalisation), he told me that although she would show some improvement, there would be relapses which would become more frequent and more intense as time went on. I was shocked and horrified at this news; it was the last thing I wanted for my children's mother and I felt sure there must be some alternative.

Privately, I thought he was just wallpapering over the cracks. I realise now that the pharmacologically based psychiatric approach has its limitations in that, by its very nature, it will lead the patient along the downward path to drug dependency. It is, however, both cost-effective and quick, in the short term. Psychotherapy, on the other hand, being more like an archaeological dig – carefully uncovering and healing underlying unconscious material – can be extremely slow and, therefore, comparatively expensive.

Part of the problem for patients and their families, I feel, is that, on the whole, we are not made aware of some of the basic facts: all psychiatrists are medical doctors who are trained to treat psychological difficulties – what *they* define as 'mental illness' – as physical ailments; added to which, the general belief of the majority is that *all* psychiatric disorders are biological or genetic in origin. Sadly, the two fields of psychiatry and psychotherapy are generally lumped together in the public mind, making the idea of consultation, of any sort, a taboo subject; something to be fearful of.

In the case of psychiatry, the fear is quite justifiable. What Bambs's psychiatrist, Dr Ferguson, did not explain to me at either of our meetings were the usual side-effects of these major tranquillisers, also known as neuroleptics, and a neuroleptic-induced brain disease called Tardive Dyskinesia (T.D.), which would develop as a result of prolonged use of them; something that, along with Daniel's 'book', I was not to hear about until many months after the shootings, when I watched a British television documentary entitled *The Price of Tranquillity*.

The basic symptoms of T.D. are loss of muscle control causing involuntary movement such as shakes, tongue-rolling and difficulty of speech amongst other things. It can afflict any of the voluntary muscles, from the eyelids to the neck, arms, legs and torso. To make things worse, the drugs which are then prescribed to counteract such disorders have equally horrendous side-effects of their own. While some symptoms can improve or even disappear after removal from the 'offending medication' – as Dr Peter Breggin described it in his book *Toxic Psychiatry* – most cases are permanent. There is no known treatment for this disease, yet doctors still continue to prescribe these drugs in such a way – high doses or combinations of them known as 'cocktails' – that research has proved increases the risk of T.D.

Bambs had been on various combinations, in often high doses, for the best part of two years.

During that documentary, an eminent Harley Street psychiatrist said something to the effect of, 'It takes only ten seconds to write out a prescription, but it takes a great deal longer trying to work out a programme of psychotherapy.' I couldn't believe what I was hearing. It seemed that even with all our modern understanding, a large number of people with mental illnesses are still put on the scrapheap. The only difference now is that instead of containing sufferers in asylums, as we used to before the 1950s when these 'miracle drugs' first became available, doctors are now imprisoning patients within their own bodies, which cease to function as required because of them.

In very simple terms, according to Dr Breggin, so-called schizophrenia, along with other mental disorders, is what he calls a *psychospiritual* crisis generated by past social and spiritual defeats which, when we are in the middle of it, can seem like a terrible affliction in which the whole body can be affected. The ancients called this madness 'the dark night of the soul'; something we are all faced with, to some degree, at some stage in our lives. The use of chemically lobotomising drugs and ECT (electroconvulsive therapy) not only takes away a person's ability to face challenges, by destroying much of their capacity for love, empathy, self-insight, determination, autonomy, rationality, abstract reasoning, will-power and, most frightening for me, creativity, but also spares the patient's family any need to look at or even acknowledge their own role in the disturbance.

Maybe that is the problem: in our endeavour to become a pain-free society, we would still rather bury pain than deal with it. Hence all the thousands of subterranean volcanoes which erupt daily as murder, suicide, incest, wife beatings, racial and sexual harassment and so on. Or we suppress the pain with every sort of addiction one can imagine. Unfortunately, the more I became aware of this, as the blinkers of my own childhood perceptions, which were still very much in place, fell away, the greater became my depression and sense of grief.

CHAPTER FIFTEEN

IT WOULD BE easy to imagine, after some of the earlier chapters, that my two sons, Daniel and Nicholas, had a pretty screwed-up life. The press apparently thought so; it served their purposes to create an image of two children abused by a schizophrenic 'drug-crazed' mother and abandoned by both parents. As it was, they couldn't be further from the truth. I have never known two individuals to pack so much *living* into six years of life. There didn't seem to be a moment that wasn't an adventure – or at least full in some way.

We owe much of this to the Flowers family, especially to Herbie, who is a big kid himself. It was as if he had been waiting for them to come along. Jan and I were worried about telling him about them at first. We thought he might react badly to the fact his eighteen-year-old daughter had fallen in love and was now living with a man newly estranged from his wife and two babies.

When we finally did tell him, he was over the moon and couldn't wait to meet them. The man who wrote the song 'Grandad' suddenly started behaving like one and looked for every opportunity to take 'The Boys', as he called them, out on his own. In many ways, Herbie became their third grandfather, giving endless hours of pleasure, larking about and getting into all sorts of trouble with them.

It was Herbie who also set me up with my first pottery studio: Sky had just had a number one hit record in the album charts, so, to share his success, he gave me the use of the garage at his home in Uxbridge and the money to buy all the equipment I needed. This was a break I will always be grateful for.

The two little babies had, by that time, grown into very energetic toddlers who never stopped laughing and talking. They were a joy to have around. They were inquisitive, everything fascinated them, and their manners and speech, thanks to Bambs, were always impeccable. The more they grew, the more they became attached to the Flowers family, who gave them an abundance of love, laughter and music. But without a doubt, Jan was really the most special. She gave herself to them in such a way that she was like a mother, but at the same time young enough in spirit to be their best friend, superseding both Bambs and myself in their affections.

There was a wholeness in her relationship with us that I had never experienced before, uninhibited. Naturally, this caused some resentment in Bambs – being excluded from this part of the boys' lives – but in children, as I saw it then, there are no real divisions; it's not in their nature. The boys rarely saw me without Jan, so they always associated her equally with me.

For Bambs's sake, I didn't encourage these displays of affection, but I wasn't going to discourage them either. The depth of love in Daniel and Nicholas was so natural and in such abundance, it was something for everyone and I wasn't going to be the one to spoil it – or let anyone else for that matter. They had a way of making everyone feel like the most special person in the world, as I have often been reminded.

After their funeral, one friend wrote:

Nicholas and Daniel were such vibrant, vital and engaging boys and we have such sweet memories of the few times we enjoyed their company. If our boys enjoy life half as much as they did, they will be two very happy, beautiful children.

For the first couple of years they were much like any other children, making everybody laugh with their funny learning experiences. The more they made people laugh, the more they learned the art of it, especially Nicholas. For some crazy reason, just because he was a few minutes younger and slightly smaller, he was always referred to as the little brother, which instantly put pressure and responsibility on Daniel to be the big brother which, in turn, let Nicholas off the hook completely. In this role, he could happily develop other talents safe in the knowledge that he was being looked after by Daniel. Nicholas even nurtured a babyish voice on the strength of it. On the other hand, he also felt the need to distinguish his identity, as Nicholas, which never seemed to bother Daniel. *He* didn't mind if people got them muddled up.

I sometimes wonder if this was part of the reason their personalities began to show quite marked differences as they grew up. They were both very creative and outgoing, sensitive but in different ways. Nicholas, like me, was enchanted with nature. Flowers, birds and butterflies fascinated him; little girls were even more interesting. His expression of love was for the world outside of himself, in things he could see as well as imagine. He loved to play with my collection of crystals, getting lost in their myriad facets. His paintings were always bright and colourful, full of smiles and rainbows and fairies.

Daniel, on the other hand, was a little more serious but just as loving. His sensitivity was much deeper and inward – more towards people and their feelings. From an early age, he was aware of other people's suffering, and even before I was given his 'book' of drawings, I was very much aware that he suffered a little himself. Like Nicholas, Daniel also liked to play with the girls, but at the same time desperately wanted to be accepted by the other boys, which never worried Nicholas.

Daniel played football and talked about the cartoon character He-Man, but away from all but his closest friends, preferred to be playing with much less macho dolls. He had his own special doll which he called his 'baby' and took almost everywhere he went. If there was ever a real baby around, one could guarantee that Daniel would soon be found sitting on the sofa holding it. His greatest ambition when he grew up, he said, was to be 'a mummy'. He understood that this wasn't possible, but he wanted to all the same. His paintings were usually about homes and houses, family and friends, but this didn't mean they were any less imaginative than his brother's or that Nicholas liked people any less than Daniel. They were just different; like two sides of the same coin.

Shortly before our divorce, when Bambs sold and moved out of our marital home, Jan and I also moved from our studio apartment in Hampstead village to a larger mews flat in West Hampstead. This came about because Herbie wished to invest in some property, so he bought this place with the idea that Jan and I live in the flat and that

I set up my pottery studio in the garage below. Having moved in, we realised the garage was far too big for my needs, so Herbie decided to build himself a small recording studio at the back.

From then on, life was always busy with all sorts of people coming and going all the time. The only downside of this windfall was an increasing lack of privacy and the realisation that I was once again in the pocket of my partner's father and so I experienced yet another loss of my own self-esteem. In those days, however, I was too unconscious to recognise it as such and simply obliterated any doubts that might have emerged by having a good time.

The boys, delighting in this new environment, loved to meet new people and were never shy of saying hello or asking someone's name. They also enjoyed going on visits or staying with one of their many grown-up friends. Wherever they went, they were always welcomed. Nobody was ever trying to pass them on, but wanted instead to see them. Like their mother, however, the only stipulation Daniel and Nicholas ever made was that they had to know, well in advance, when, where and who they would be seeing, and also that any such arrangement must never be changed. Woe betide anybody who did.

This was probably part of an inbuilt protective mechanism, where, as they changed from my world to their mother's, and vice versa, they would shut off the one they were leaving till next time. For example, when they were with Jan and me, they rarely talked about Mummy, and when they were with Bambs, they rarely talked about me or Jan. If I ever stopped for a coffee and a chat with Bambs when dropping them off, they could get extremely uncomfortable and fidgety, even bad-tempered to the point where they would hurry me out of the door if I stayed too long. Five minutes was fine, any longer, unthinkable. As far as they were concerned, I didn't belong in that world, so they didn't want me there. Even so, they were always pleased to see me if I ever dropped by on the off-chance. On those occasions, however, Bambs wasn't; she hated me just turning up.

Food was another thing which always featured high on their list of priorities and, wherever they went, the first place they would check out was the fridge; they had to know what was on offer. But then they had good reason to. Bambs and Jan often prepared wonderful puddings and surprises for them. Whenever Jan was cooking

– especially cakes and biscuits – the boys would always be in the kitchen 'helping' her. It was not uncommon to hear hysterical giggling coming from that direction and find, on investigation, Daniel and Nicholas sitting on the work surface and all three of them covered with flour!

For me, though, one of the most memorable moments has to be the first time Jan and I took the twins to a live concert; it was both an amusing and moving experience for us all. They must have been only three years old, but even then they were familiar with the music of Sky. We had told them that Herbie was going to play on stage in front of thousands of people, but as small children they had no real idea of what to expect.

We arrived at the Royal Albert Hall about half an hour before the doors were opened to the public. Nicholas and Daniel had been frantically talking about it all day and were bubbling with excitement as we went in. On entering the building we could hear the band doing a sound check. New questions began flying ten-to-the-dozen and their excitement was reaching fever pitch as we entered the auditorium. Then, silence.

Their mouths dropped open in complete and utter amazement. Wide-eyed, they looked up, they looked around, they looked at Jan, they looked at me and then they looked up and around again. It was such a magical moment as they took in the red plush of the upholstery, the 'flying saucers' in the ceiling and the sheer immensity of the place. They had never seen such a huge room before. The Royal Albert Hall always makes *me* shrink in awe but they must have felt like Alice in Wonderland did, shrinking in the long corridor. I think they were also a little frightened at first, because they had been so busy talking as they went in, they hadn't noticed how big the building was from the outside.

'Hello, boys!' shouted Herbie from the stage. They looked round quickly, then saw him in the distance.

'Herbie!' they squealed in unison, running up to him and hurling hundreds of questions all at once.

'Are you going to play your bass guitar here tonight?' said Nicholas.

'I certainly am.'

'And your tuba?'

'Yep.'

'With these people?' added Daniel, pointing at the rest of the band.

'That's right.'

'Where are all the rest of the people? How many people are coming? Why is this place so big? What are those flying saucer things? Why are they there? What's *he* doing? How do we get up on the stage?'

'Come on, I'll help you,' said Herbie, lifting them up one by one, 'then I'll take you downstairs for some lemonade and Smarties.'

'Oooh goody, Smarties!' they yelled, as all three trotted off backstage.

While we were all in the dressing-rooms, the hall had been filling up. That buzz of expectation before a concert was building, but not as much as it was in two small newcomers. Five minutes before the start, we took them to the auditorium to find our seats.

'When did all these people come?' shouted Nicholas.

'While you were stuffing yourself with cakes,' I said.

'Gosh! What a lot of people!' said Daniel. 'Have they all come to see Herbie?'

'Yes,' said Jan, 'and the rest of the band as well.'

'Cor!' they whispered. 'When are they going to start?'

'Right now,' I said as the lights went down and the band came on to the stage.

'Oh my!' they yelped, panicking. 'What's that noise? Why is everybody clapping their hands?'

'It's OK,' said Jan. 'That's how the audience welcome the musicians and show they are pleased.'

'What's an audience?' asked Nicholas.

'You're part of it,' I said quietly. 'Now be quiet and listen.'

'OK,' whispered Daniel. 'That clapping was too noisy anyway.'

Somebody behind us was still talking as John Williams quietly played the introduction to 'Sister Rose'.

'Ssshhh!' hissed Nicholas, glaring over his shoulder.

We could hardly contain our laughter; in less than five minutes, he was already behaving like a true concert veteran. The boys sat quietly through each and every number, adding appreciative comments as they applauded gleefully with the rest of the audience. By the second half, when Herbie played 'Tuba Smarties', the tune they had been waiting for, they were really getting into it, even though Nicholas repeatedly felt the need to turn round and tell the woman behind us to 'Shut up!'

From this early age they became aware of the real excitement generated by live music and this grew more and more as the studio downstairs became increasingly productive. They would often go down in their pyjamas just to listen on the headphones or watch somebody play. With their bedroom immediately above the studio, it was hard to keep them in bed if there was something really good happening. That's how they met Patrick Rös, the man who conducted their funeral for me.

Another reason they spent so much time in the studio was because Herbie always had a constant supply of biscuits and cakes down there. Unfortunately, Jan was getting really fed up with him always ruining their appetites before supper. In the end, she gave strict instructions to both Herbie and her brother, Nick, not to do this, or else. But then, with those two, her breath was wasted. Ten minutes after such a warning, as Jan had just finished cooking supper, Nicholas and Daniel wandered upstairs each finishing off a Bakewell tart. Jan was furious!

'Where did you get those?' she demanded.

'Herbie gave them to us,' they said, swallowing the last bits quickly. Jan stormed downstairs to give her dad another, even stronger telling off, to which he first took offence and then, as a joke, took the last Bakewell tart from its packet and nailed it to the cork wall – right through the cherry!

As a permanent reminder never to do it again, the note to which it was nailed said, 'I promise never to feed Daniel and Nicholas before supper,' signed 'Herbie'.

The point was finally taken and the tart remained for another six months.

CHAPTER SIXTEEN

WITH SO MANY wonderful memories, and so much pain in the remembering, I began to wonder how and if I would ever get over it. It didn't seem possible, even with the healing I seemed to be getting from writing, but at the same time I felt strangely comforted by something I couldn't explain.

So much of what had been happening around me, in the form of what I would now describe as 'synchronistic information gathering', or was being presented to me in the form of the children's drawings, began to make me wonder how much of this was not just wishful thinking and really was predestined or spiritually guided in some way. The most terrible pain was that I was being torn between what I had always accepted as reality and what I was beginning to experience as such. Even though I desperately wanted to find 'something', I was also very suspicious of my experience.

The more I looked, however, to prove myself deluded, the more I found, especially in the twins' more recent drawings, that there was more to all this than I could logically explain; even to the extent – as I was to learn much later when I met drawing analyst Gregg Furth – that, on some level, they knew they were going to die.

I was to read many books during this time, but the first to really grab my attention was Michael Bentine's autobiography *The Door Marked Summer*. As one of the original Goons, and a well-known comedy scriptwriter, I was surprised to find him writing with such authority about his little-known research into the paranormal. But what most affected me was his account of how his own son, Gus (who was killed in a light aeroplane crash), had appeared to him in the family garden some hours after his son must have died, but *before he knew of the death*.

This began to confirm my own feelings that Daniel and Nicholas had come to me after their deaths. It also made me want to find out more. For the first time in my life, I began to ask questions and search for those deeper answers about our existence – rather than just accepting everything as I always had done. I also began to think back to when Bambs and I first lived together – and to Maggie, our curious clairvoyant landlady . . .

At the beginning of my last year at art school, I decided to leave my father's flat and move into digs nearer college in south London. There were a couple of other students on my course who were in the same boat, so we decided to look for a place together. The college social worker gave us the address of a Mrs H. near Peckham Rye, who was keen to let part of her house to students for twenty-five pounds a week.

There was no way one could be prepared for the sight that welcomed us when Mrs H. opened her front door. She had jet-black hair, heavily made-up dark eyes, very colourful clothes and was slightly drunk. She had obviously once been quite stunning but now, in her late forties, she came over as a trifle eccentric. Her mannerisms reminded me somewhat of Bette Davis in the film *What Ever Happened to Baby Jane?* when she opened her door to the songwriter.

'Well, that's what I call service,' she said in a very deep husky voice. 'I only telephoned this morning and they've already sent me three lovely young men!' I think I can safely vouch for the other two that we all wanted to turn and run at this point, but she smiled and invited us in. 'Please excuse this mess,' she said as she stepped over an enormous pile of old clothes that spilled into the hallway from the front room. 'I bought up the end of a jumble sale last weekend and the bastards delivered it all this afternoon! By the way, call me Maggie.'

She led us straight upstairs to the rooms she was letting, but we couldn't help noticing that all the rooms downstairs were in much the same state as the hallway except, perhaps, the first one, which was also very dark and mysterious. When we reached the top landing, the sight that greeted us was much the same as below, but mixed with a general selection of books as well.

'I write Gothic horror stories for a living,' she said as she fished a paperback from the pile on the floor (our hearts made another bolt for the door!) and added, 'As you can see, I've recently decorated and put some posters up, to make it nice.'

The rooms actually weren't quite so bad and showed great potential so, having tactfully gained her permission to make alterations, we looked at each other, winced slightly at the thought of living with her and said, 'OK, when can we move in?'

Later that same evening, I telephoned Bambs with the good news. Then, in preparation, I told her about Maggie, saying, 'The landlady's a bit strange, though.' But Bambs didn't seem too concerned. She was really excited and couldn't wait to see the place. Even with my warning she wasn't quite prepared for what she found the next day, but once she had got over the shock, we spent the next couple of evenings cleaning up and painting. We were all quite ruthless, throwing everything we didn't want downstairs to Maggie.

Over the months, however, during her blacker moments, Maggie sometimes found occasion to hurl some of it back up at us. So we each quietly decided to put bolts on our doors. Within a few more weeks, Bambs had moved most of her things in and we were, inevitably, living together. We hadn't planned to, but that's how it turned out.

Life at Maggie's was, to say the least, interesting, often unpredictable. We soon settled into the life of students in digs – sharing cheap meals of spaghetti bolognese, discussing life, art, sex and generally enjoying ourselves.

As we got to know our somewhat eccentric landlady, we discovered all sorts of weird and wonderful things about her. Over the years she had been responsible for drawing a famous strip cartoon in a national newspaper, as well as writing several successful novels under a pseudonym. Most fascinating of all, though, were her talents as a clairvoyant – which she was always eager to talk about.

This side of her didn't surprise any of us in the least, as her environment was a reflection of all our wildest images of such a person. Apart from the jumble-sale remnants one had to wade through to enter her rooms, her walls and cupboards were adorned with many strange artefacts. There were unusual candelabra and a large crystal ball on the sideboard; a musky smell hung in the air. Pinned to the wall amongst broken mirror tiles were faded newspaper cuttings of the days of her success. And, finally, in an armchair in the corner of her living-room sat Alphonse, a very lifelike, life-sized dummy with a beard.

Maggie's only other companions were Nancy, the cat, and a black and tan mongrel puppy called Bootle. He was named, so we were told, after one of the rougher districts of Liverpool and whenever Maggie called his name, it sounded more like a swear word than an object of her affection. She had great hopes of him growing into a large dog, but somehow this never happened. She did have a family, of whom she often talked affectionately, but they never seemed to give her much of their time.

With all her talk about her life and achievements, Maggie came across as a very disappointed and lonely woman. When talking about her clairvoyant abilities, she would often tell us how she had helped so many people over the years. They wrote to her from all over the world; well-known actors, writers, even politicians, but she had never been able to help herself. That ability, unfortunately, didn't come with the gift.

Over the months, we all got to know Maggie much better, but Bambs and I, especially, became much closer to her; it seemed she almost took us under her wing. When Maggie talked about palmistry and the tarot, we were all fascinated and very keen to have our hands read but personally, I was very reticent about the tarot cards; they frightened the shit out of me. In fact, ever since I could remember, I had steered well clear of anything relating to what I thought of as the occult, black magic or death. To my mind, the tarot fitted into the heavier side of the occult and, as such, commanded a lot of respect.

I didn't realise then that the term 'occult' meant virtually anything esoteric that was not connected to the Christian dogma – including Gnosticism, which was one of the earliest forms of Christianity. The tarot, for example, has its origins in the cabbala, which is an esoteric philosophy within Judaism. And astrology is an ancient science of energies as obscure to the layman as modern quantum physics. Much of the fear, I realise now, is connected to medieval superstition and basic ignorance of the facts.

The real question, in my opinion, is down to the motives behind the use of these tools: whether the practitioner is using them to *empower*, in that they are helping an individual to access unique information about themselves (like a modern computer database), which might enable that person to prepare for oncoming challenges – information they have every right to. Or whether those practices are being used to *have power over* another person or group.

Without a doubt, it is the latter that causes me concern – even more so now. The same goes for ritual. There are both positive and negative rituals, which either serve to celebrate a higher purpose or to have power over others. My fear of black magic was a healthy fear and remains so. By the same token, I am equally fearful of extremism within any established religion. There is not a lot of difference.

With Maggie, I felt no such threat. She revelled in our attention and would often keep us sitting up half the night with the promise of a reading. When we finally did strike lucky, at about six o'clock one morning, Maggie read my hands first and then Bambs's; the other two had given up and gone to bed. For some reason she seemed totally uninterested in doing theirs, yet very keen to do ours.

I had tremendous feelings of apprehension as we sat in Maggie's semi-darkened living-room and she reached across the dark velvet-covered table for my hands. One thing I always loved about Maggie was her wonderful sense of the theatrical, but I also noticed that her personality changed quite dramatically when she was working. She lost her normal disorganised and affected nature and took on a persona which was both serious and quite formidable. She had already explained that anybody could learn to read hands or the tarot, but that she used them only as a focus to tune in, clairvoyantly, to her subject.

'The reading I'll be giving you consists of three parts,' she said. 'The first will relate to the past, the second to the present and the third to the future.' She then told us that in order to gauge the distance in time any one reading goes into the future, it is necessary to measure how far back into the past the first part goes. This can only be done by relating recognisable incidents to the sitter. The time span between the past and the present will always be the same as the present in relation to the future. It was all to do with Time being like a continuous spiral across the loops of which she could pick up echoes. She later explained that with most people the time span in a reading was only a year or so at the most, but with Bambs and me it seemed to go much further back.

As Maggie looked at my hands, she would occasionally stop talking, close her eyes and start rocking gently from side to side for short periods; sometimes she rocked backwards and forwards. Every time she opened her eyes and came out of these little trances she would make some quite astounding revelations about my past, things she couldn't possibly have known about. The one that finally convinced me was to do with the circumstances surrounding an incident in my early teens when I broke a finger. I should first explain, however, that the little finger on my right hand is crooked and looks as if it has been broken at some point, but is not actually the one that was broken.

As she held my hands, she told me that I had once broken the bone in my little finger and I thought, 'Aha, I've caught you!'

'The one on the left hand,' she said, 'and you broke it during a game of football which you didn't want to be part of; in fact you were bullied into the game.' I sat there speechless as she rocked a little more and then said, 'You weren't in goal, were you? That's what I'm getting.' Then she added, 'To look at you, I would have put you as a centre forward.'

She had just described exactly an event going back to when I was about eleven or twelve years old. I had in fact been bullied into a game of football by one of the worst local thugs, who told me to stand in goal. On my first attempt to stop a ball, it hit my left hand against the fence behind me and broke the little finger; an insignificant fracture but a significant revelation, after which Bambs and I sat and listened intently to everything else she had to say.

Maggie then told me that I would be successful but not in the field I was then studying; she was getting images of what looked to her like a sculptor's armature and that this related, very strongly, to an unexpected achievement of mine during my early teens. I had, apparently, done or made something in such a way that my family were surprised I even had the knowledge, at that age, to do it. Of the many things she told me, most of which I can't remember, this stuck in my mind as a bit of a mystery and – apart from the fact that I had made a figure of a semi-naked Native American girl kneeling on the ground about then – in many ways it still does.

Maggie then went on to say that I would have two children, both boys, although one of them might be a girl or certainly very feminine. She also said that I would live into my mid-eighties. At this point, Bambs asked her if she could see how a person was going to die, or whether she would actually tell anyone the circumstances of their death.

'I can see an awful lot of things,' said Maggie, 'but I will only tell a person what they mainly need to know. There is no constructive purpose in knowing how one is going to die, it would be too distressing and could even prevent someone from getting on with their life properly. In the circumstances of an early or traumatic death, I would probably tell a lie if I had to or not mention it at all.'

Before she finished she said, 'I really think you should let me do your tarot. There is nothing to be afraid of, it's just another way of focusing for me.' She added, 'I feel that one day you will benefit from the advice that comes from it. I also get that you have latent psychic ability yourself.'

When it came to Bambs's turn, she preferred to have hers done in private, so I went upstairs to bed. When she came up, half an hour later, she told me quite a lot of what had been revealed and was excited to tell me that it looked likely that we would have children together. She had been told that she too would have two boys and, like me, there was confusion about one of them being a girl. 'And I'm going to live into my nineties,' she said proudly. 'Maggie said I would live almost as long as my grandmother is going to, Granny Speakman that is.' Such well-chosen words in the circumstances, considering I wasn't to realise the significance of them until *after I had written down this part of the story*: Bambs died six months before Gran – so she really did live 'almost as long'!

The deluge of information for both of us that morning, and in subsequent tarot readings, was quite staggering but also hard to remember. Maggie assured us, however, that as each thing came to pass, even though some of it may sound like riddles now, we would recognise it. Looking back, it hadn't really sunk in just how far into the future those predictions would go, if at all. Many years were to pass before it all began to fall into place and when it did, I started to wish it hadn't.

Maggie was a strange yet comforting interlude in our lives and I've often thought of her over the years. Sadly she died a few years later when the house in which we all lived burnt down, with her in it. Somehow, in the light of that, I will never forget the haunting echo of her despairing words: 'The one person's future I can't see is my own.'

CHAPTER SEVENTEEN

Except the Heaven had come so near –
So seemed to choose My Door –
The Distance would not haunt me so –
I had not hoped – before –

But just to hear the Grace depart –
I never thought to see –
Afflicts me with a Double loss –
'Tis lost – And lost to me –

Emily Dickinson

WITHIN DAYS OF Maggie coming back into my thoughts, I ran into Caroline Salmon, an old college friend who used to spend a lot of time, when visiting Bambs and me, downstairs chatting to Maggie. On a subsequent dinner date with Caroline, I was talking about my desire to seek the help of a medium when I mentioned Maggie, wishing that she was still alive so that I could go and see her. So much of what she had said all those years before finally seemed to be falling into place and was coming back to me. Even then I could only remember with any clarity a quarter of what she had told me – I had always relied on Bambs to remind me of the rest.

'God, I haven't thought about her in a long time!' said Caroline. 'It's amazing how so many of her predictions came true – especially the way in which she had predicted Bambs's death.'

'What! How do you mean?' I said. 'I didn't know about any of this. What did Maggie say?'

Caroline then told me about the time she came home with me from college and got into conversation with her, while I went upstairs to see Bambs and drop off my things. Maggie, looking very worried, told Caroline that she had just foreseen Bambs having a very violent death and didn't know what to do about it. Maggie had been very fond of Bambs and was obviously very distressed, not being able to tell her what she had seen.

All of a sudden, I remembered Maggie's urgency to do my tarot that afternoon. Bambs had just had hers done, so I agreed to have mine. Caroline then reminded me of several other predictions, including the one about a sculptor's armature, after which a lot more came back to me.

For all it was worth, it didn't make me feel any better.

On 16 February, June's mother, Granny Speakman, passed away peacefully, at the age of ninety-five. I was especially sad because, since the shootings, Pam had not allowed me to visit her in case I caused a traumatic reminder of her family. That weekend I also went for tea at the Pargeters', where I met several of Bambs's cousins and learned a little more about what had been going on – not a lot, but a few things finally began falling into place.

They were all as anxious as I was to see the legal proceedings commence, but none were looking forward to the committal with any relish. There was, however, one thing they said that afternoon which really bothered me; something they had also thought very strange but hadn't yet made a connection. They told me how Jeremy had given instructions that his parents and Bambs should all be cremated with their rings on, and that once he was satisfied that this had happened, he had been laughing and rubbing his hands with glee. The undertaker had, apparently, been really upset at having to do this, because it was not a normal procedure with cremations.

'But they weren't destroyed in the cremation!' I said, and then explained that Nevill's executor, Mr Cock, had told me he had them all in his safe. Not knowing of Jeremy's earlier instructions, I had already asked Mr Cock for Bambs's wedding ring. He must have gone behind Jeremy's back and overruled that decision.

My thoughts immediately went back to what Maggie had told me about psychometry, which is an ability some mediums have to view a whole scenario just by holding an item of jewellery or clothing. It is well known that the police occasionally use clairvoyants to help them in their investigations. Maybe this was what Jeremy was afraid of.

It had troubled me for some time that Jeremy had possibly made what Michael Bentine had described as a 'Faustian pact' with the darker side of his own mind. His description of such a person sent a shudder of recognition through me when I read it – especially when I thought back to the party. Was it also possible that Jeremy had been getting involved in some form of occult practice or ritual magic? In the light of what I had just heard, it was not beyond the bounds of reality.

I was also told, that day, that Jeremy had displayed overt transvestite tendencies, sometimes appearing around the village dressed as a woman. On one occasion, in the supermarket at the family's caravan site, his disguise was so good the woman behind the cash register didn't even recognise him – until he spoke. Could this be another clue? Having seen the copy of an extremely angry letter June had written to the Archbishop of Canterbury, complaining of the Church's decision to allow homosexual vicars, I could only wonder if this was another possible reason June and Nevill might have threatened to cut Jeremy out of their wills. The other possibility which occurs to me is that, as a disguise, this could be how Jeremy moved between the two houses on the night of the shooting, without being recognised.

I learned another surprising story that afternoon. Apparently, only weeks after the shootings, while the family were all at Whitehouse trying to decide which window Jeremy had used to get out, a robin flew in through the back door and landed on the kitchen windowsill. When Anthony tried to capture it and put it outside, the robin flew past the open door and landed by the scullery window – the other one they had been debating over. On each attempt to catch it the robin flew past the open door and back to the other windowsill. This kept happening until someone voiced the opinion that it might be trying to help them come to a decision. At this point, the robin 'left its signature' on the kitchen windowsill and finally allowed Anthony to pick it up and put it outside.

'The really strange thing was,' said Anthony, 'that after all that chasing, it didn't struggle in my hands.' Julie Mugford later confirmed that Jeremy had told her the kitchen window was the one he had actually used to get out.

Within less than a week, the very same thing happened to other members of the family when robins flew into all their kitchens. Finally, when the undertaker came to collect Gran's body that week, a robin flew in through the open front door at Vaulty and stood on the chest, singing its heart out in the sunlit hallway. Ann and her father watched it for some time before it was disturbed and flew away.

I then told them my own robin story: how during a guided tour of Highgate's older Western Cemetery, the guide had led our group to the family grave of the famous Pre-Raphaelite painter and poet, Dante Gabriel Rossetti, where we were told the tragic story of his beautiful wife and model, Elizabeth Siddal. She had been most admired for her profusion of luscious red hair and featured in many well-known Pre-Raphaelite paintings, the most notable being *Ophelia* by John Everett Millais. Sadly, she died very soon after their wedding and, broken-hearted, Rossetti buried with her a manuscript of poems that she had inspired him to write.

As the guide tried to tell us the story, and of how later, during hard times, Rossetti had the poems retrieved for publication, a robin landed on her gravestone in the middle of our group and joined in the lecture. It literally shouted its song at us, causing the guide to pause and start again. She didn't know why, but this seemed to be a regular occurrence at this grave, it not being the first time it had happened to her. For some inexplicable reason, I was not in the least surprised and pointed out that the painting she had just mentioned, as far as I could remember, also featured a robin.

On hearing this, the others were as excited as I had been and it became another of those episodes that helped lift me, briefly, from my depression awaiting the dreaded committal. It seemed the question of our little red-breasted friends had gone far beyond coincidence. The last occasion I heard one outside my own window – for the first time in a long while – was recently, on the morning of a very close friend's funeral. I haven't heard one since.

The new date set for Jeremy's committal proceedings to begin, 10th March, passed uneventfully. There was no mention of it in the press until the following day, when it was announced that they were now expected to start in May! The ongoing tension of it all was more than I could stand. I was desperate to get that part over. I had just about reached the point of giving up, added to which nothing made sense to me any more. I couldn't understand why I was being given so much, in a kind of spiritual sense, yet had to lose so much in order to gain it. What sort of a god, if there really was such a thing, could play such cruel games – because that's how it seemed.

I don't think I was really suicidal then, as some of my words might suggest, but the depression was awful. I'd had enough. The following extract from my diary, dated 15th March, seems so strange to me, reading it now, in that I have moved on so far:

There are many periods when I feel desperately lonely and sad at the loss of Bambs and the boys. The harsh realities of what really happened to them come flooding in. My beautiful, loving family; MURDERED; shot with bullets – in cold blood; executed in their sleep. They never did any harm to anyone, they were just innocent obstacles to someone's monstrous greed. They never asked to be part of that family, in fact the boys weren't even aware of being heirs to a fortune. Life is so empty now without them and seems to lack any purpose. The boys were everything I lived for.

The only thing that really keeps me going is writing this book and working on my ideas for the sculptures; they are the only things that still have any meaning for me. Hopefully, work on them will last till well after the trial and I will be over the worst of my grief by then. If I didn't have these tasks and challenges I don't know what I would do.

I often think about the bottle of pills in the cupboard and think how easy it would be to just take them all but then again I have never felt that suicide resolves anything. There are times, however, when the depths of despair blind me to this. I can't deny that the thought hasn't crossed my mind many times in recent months. I want to be back with my family again, even if it is just our bodies rotting in the ground together. I often wish I had also been there that night, then at least we would still be together or maybe I could have helped prevent it happening or saved them. Somehow I think I would have been a victim too, had Bambs and I still been married.

So many people have said to me, 'It's unbelievable that you are so calm, you have been so strong since it all happened.' All I can say is that whatever it was that gave me strength in the beginning, seems to have deserted me now. I continue to show this optimistic side in public, and when I'm with my friends, I am, in fact, genuinely happy. Once alone, however, I can't cope; I get listless, morose and just want to fall apart. This is a side I don't wish my friends to see, they have done enough for me already and it only serves to bring back their own pain.

Through my loneliness I am desperately searching for something new in my life, people who will lift me from this darkness. Life, however, is cruel because when I try too hard to fulfil those dreams the attempts always seem fruitless. On the other hand, if the answer is staring me in the face, it is either invisible or untouchable. I often think how nice it would be to meet people who don't connect me with the shootings, just so that I can be relaxed and normal; to keep it a secret for a while at least and get to know them without that tragedy hanging over my head; to bring my conversation out of the frame of its recent existence and make me become aware of other things. In a way, I have come to rely on it to hold me up, socially. I feel almost vulnerable without it. What an awful thing to have as a social crutch. I can hide behind it all too easily.

We as people all too readily prefer to identify with our woundedness, rather than our strengths. We see it everywhere we look. I saw it then in myself and made the decision to try and break free of it; I didn't like what I saw. I also felt that I could not go on with all the doubts and pain much longer, I had to find a medium to help put my mind at rest.

In desperation, I wrote to Michael Bentine, who I thought might be able to help me. In his book, he had spoken about all the work his family had done over the years, testing hundreds of psychics – more often than not, finding them to be self-deluded or charlatans. Every now and then, however, they found someone truly remarkable and gifted, and I now needed to see such a person. I'd had enough clues of my own to know it was worth a try, but I could not afford to be ripped off, either emotionally or financially, I needed absolute proof.

Having taken that action, things immediately began to look better. Springtime and the Easter weekend, during which I dug up some bulbs from Granny Speakman's garden for the grave at Highgate, brought a breath of fresh air into my life. Bambs and the boys had always loved that garden so much; especially the wonderful spring display of daffodils. I was helped by Ann and Peter's little girl, Janie, and, to our delight, two robins played around us in the flowerbeds as we dug.

I had also begun to realise that my musical tastes had changed dramatically since the shootings. I was no longer listening to the bright, happy tunes I had always shared with the twins. As the months had gone by, and my mood and morale declined awaiting the committal, I had started to indulge my melancholy with music that affected as well as reflected my dark moods; 'Siegfried's Funeral Music' by Wagner had become a real favourite.

I only became aware of this shortly before Easter, when I spent a weekend touring with Herbie's new band. It was then that I realised how much I'd lost touch with that lively kind of music and remembered a tape I had compiled for Nicholas and Daniel of all their favourite tunes. The simply named 'Twins Tape' was found and slotted into the cassette-player, with the immediate effect of lifting me from those doldrums which had clouded my spirits for so long. The music I had so affectionately associated with the twins earlier was to re-emerge as my saving grace.

Towards the end of April, I received another of my regular visits from Stan Jones, but this time with another Detective Sergeant, Winston Bernard. They had come mainly to reassure me about the committal but I also felt they were still fishing for answers to unanswered questions. Winston seemed very suspicious of the fact that I seemed to be handling the whole tragedy so well: why was I so calm? I wished I knew myself, he should have seen me back in March. Looking back, I realise that I wasn't really that calm – I was just very good at putting on a face that didn't cause other people any discomfort; good at hiding my real feelings.

Two weeks later, and quite out of the blue, all the panic about the committal was over; Jeremy was sent for trial after a 'full paper committal' and not, as we'd been led to expect, an 'old-style' one. The hearing was over in eight minutes. A date for the trial was later set for 2 October. We now had a long summer's wait in which to think about it all and keep our memories intact. Mr Ainsley and Stan

Jones called by the next day to tell me about it and put my mind at rest about the trial. Their job now – for the next five months – was to keep all the witnesses at ease.

That same week, I received a very helpful and sympathetic telephone call from Michael Bentine, who even apologised for not calling me sooner; he would have done had he known of my letter before but had just come back from Peru that day. We talked for about half an hour – mainly about the demise of *It's a Square World*, one of his television shows from my childhood – but at the same time he asked me not to tell him too much about myself. The less he knew about me, the more confidence I would ultimately have in the authenticity of information given by the medium. He then gave me the names and phone numbers of two ladies in whom he had absolute confidence but urged me not to build up my hopes too much because there was no guarantee that I would get what I was looking for; he could only offer those he felt were the best. The next question was, which one should I call?

Whether it was her name or what, I don't know, but I was instinctively drawn to Betty Shine and, as it turned out, I couldn't have made a better choice.

CHAPTER EIGHTEEN

The clock of life is wound but once.
No man on earth hath the power
To tell when the hands will stop.
At a sooner or later hour.

NOW is the only time you own,
Live, love, toil with a will.
Place no faith in tomorrow,
For the hands may then be still.

(Written by Nevill on
the back of a wedding
service sheet, April 1979)

WHEN I EVENTUALLY spoke to Betty Shine on the telephone at the end of May, I had made up my mind that if I was going to be at all convinced by anything she told me, I would have to treat the whole thing with more than a degree of scepticism. As a basic precaution, I didn't give any clues to my identity or history, I just said that I had been referred by Michael Bentine and needed her help to answer certain questions that had been on my mind. It is almost impossible to quote the exact words of this conversation, because I was so surprised by what came out that it was some time before I wrote it all down. When she asked my full name, I told her I would prefer to stick with only my first name, for the time being, which didn't seem to bother her at all.

'I quite understand,' said Betty. 'In fact, I really prefer to work with only first names anyway.' Then, before I could say anything else, she added, 'What I'm getting very strongly as I listen to you is that your nervous system is in tatters, it's shot to pieces. Did you come close to some kind of a nervous breakdown about two or three months ago? You know, because I feel you need a lot of healing as well.'

I was quite stunned at her saying that, because I thought I had sounded very calm as we spoke. Anyway she was absolutely right and went on. 'You have a good friend who is with you,' she said, 'and he is with you the whole time and is sort of looking after you.'

'That's right,' I said, thinking she was referring to Chris Precious, who had been an almost constant companion since the shootings.

'Now, he died in a car accident about two years ago.'

'What!'

'And he seems to have been with you for about the last eight months. Does that ring any bells?'

I immediately thought of Nick Rogers, the friend whose death I had learned of a few months after the shootings. He *had* died two years earlier but on a motorcycle, so I questioned Betty further as to his identity. Nick had been one of my favourite, lovable rogues; a man whose intense love of cricket and good-looking women made him a cross between Errol Flynn and Ian Botham.

'Well, the impression I am getting is that he is quite tall, fairly dark, a very good-looking, debonair sort of character. He was someone you had a certain rapport with.' The description fitted. She continued, 'He is telling me that whatever it is that you are doing at the moment, the project you are working on, is very important and you will probably have to go out on a limb over it. Even if it means living in a hovel, in poverty, to achieve the finished article; you must stick with it. He is saying that the time for playing is over and you have got to "get up off your butt".' Sounding slightly surprised, she added, 'Now that is not an expression I would ever use!'

Now the description definitely fitted! Curiously enough, I had been attempting to survive on social security, and the flat I had moved into, since speaking with Michael Bentine, was riddled with damp and seemed like a hovel. Betty continued, 'He is also saying that he is guiding you and has been for some time, and that he will stay with you until you are back on your feet and heading in the right direction. Does that make any sense?'

'All too much sense,' I told her. It linked very closely with every-thing I had suspected about receiving some kind of spirit help. In a way, I was glad if it was Nick, because he had also been one of the nicer men Bambs had spent time with after we split up.

Before we finally rang off and had made the arrangements for our meeting, Betty floored me, one last time, when she mentioned a ring that had been weighing heavily on my mind for some time.

'Perhaps we could come back to that when I see you,' said Betty, who had picked up on my thoughts about Bambs's wedding ring which, even now, has not been returned to me.

When I went to see Betty, about four months before the trial, I still held this image of all mediums being rather eccentric and theatrical, with homes to match, like Maggie or Madame Arcati in George Bernard Shaw's *Blithe Spirit*. But this was not to be the case with Betty. She was a fair-haired, motherly woman in her mid-fifties, whose most outstanding feature was her wonderful laugh. The room she led me to was equally unpretentious, simple – much like a doctor's surgery, with a desk and a treatment table. Most surprising, though, was the fact that there was no hint of her going into a trance or anything like that – she didn't even close her eyes. She said she didn't need to.

The session was taped:

'With you, as I'm talking to you . . . I'm getting a terrible tragedy – a really terrible tragedy! Does this involve two children? And your ex-wife? [I had already mentioned to her, on the telephone – almost to throw her off the scent – that I had lost my ex-wife. I gave no other clues.] But there were two or three other people involved . . . older people . . . two men and a woman, but the young man . . . a young one . . . he's still alive. Is he in a mental home?'

Somewhat surprised, I responded immediately. 'No, he's in Norwich Prison.'

'He's where?'

'Norwich Prison – if it's the man I'm thinking of.'

'Oh, well, he's mad. I mean . . . I get that he should be in a mental home.'

I nodded.

Betty then went on to describe the two children, one of whom sounded much younger than the other. Also that she was not sure if one of them was a little girl, just as Maggie had also described them – it was not uncommon for either Daniel or Nicholas to run around with a dress on.

'I'm getting a child's voice shouting at me,' said Betty, 'saying, "Come on, Dad, cheer up, we're all right!" And although he was only small, I think he'd been here . . . back here so many times, he's an old soul and I think that he is around you all the time. Was there a girl involved, a little girl? Did you have a daughter or was it another son? Two boys.'

'Twin boys.'

'Twin boys! Well, one of them was more feminine than the other.'

'Yes.'

'Yes, because that one is shyer and he's hiding behind the other one that's a bit forceful and so I get the feeling that it's either a girl or he was shyer, more feminine, than the other one. Very artistic he would have been, you know? But these children are around you the whole time, they are, er . . . it may be funny to say so, but they are laughing here.'

'I feel they are.'

'This kiddy really shouted to me, "Come on, Dad, come on, Dad! Come on, Dad, we're all right!"'

'He always put on a baby voice, the other one was wiser.'

'Yes, but all I can say is although it's tragic, they're very happy. It's almost as though they made the transition so quickly that they didn't have time to think about anything. It wasn't tragic, because I think they didn't know. Do you know anything about that? It's almost as though they could have been asleep and so they made the transition while they were asleep. That's what I get – so that nothing was known about it.'

Betty then went on to talk about Bambs, when she suddenly stopped and said, 'Who's Nicholas? Someone's just called out, "You'll know that I'm Nicholas!" So I wondered who Nicholas was.'

'Well, there's quite a few Nicholases I know.'

'No, no, this is the child's voice and I didn't know if it's another child involved or anything like that.'

In that moment I knew, without a doubt, it was the boys. Daniel had never felt a need to make the distinction. Betty continued, 'Um . . . but your own life . . . Your ex-wife . . . you will not get into communication with her for a long, long time and someone is saying to me, "Please tell him not to try!"'

'I don't want to really try . . .'

'No?'

'I just wanted to know . . . I was wondering about what you were saying, that the twins made the transition very easily. Did she?' I was desperate to find out if Bambs had known anything about it or whether, as I now suspected, she had also been asleep.

'Um . . . I feel that she still doesn't know what's happening to her. I just feel that she wouldn't be suffering, because I feel the mind is energy and it's the mind and what we achieve that goes with us. With her, her mind was already disturbed and so therefore the shock of leaving her physical body . . . It's another shock on top of her already disturbed mind, so, therefore, she would be in a state of peace for quite a long time. I feel that she is being looked after and she needs a long period of rest and I believe that is what she's having. The information I'm getting through is that she is at peace and when she does eventually come out of this peaceful rest, everything will be so beautiful that she will automatically accept it, that this has happened.

'There is another man coming through, a rather forceful man, um . . . and he, I am afraid, is still angry but that is something he will have to deal with. He's talking about his son who, um . . . [long pause]. He's saying to me about you as well, that . . . "We were mistaken about you. We see things in a different light and we were wrong." Now I don't know what that means. It's about your relation- ship with your wife and he's just saying to you, he's a very positive man and there is no way he would say he was wrong if he hadn't found out he was wrong, through all sorts of ways, and he's just saying to you, "We were wrong." Who's David? "David," he's saying, "David knows all the answers." Now I don't know who David is.'

'That would be his nephew. David is the one person I haven't really talked to and I feel that he has an awful lot to say, but he's got to keep it to himself.'

'Well, what he is saying to you is, David knows all the answers and at some time or another David is going to have to tell you.'

'Yes.'

'For his own progression, he has held back.'

By this time both Betty and I were holding back the tears, but she had also finally said enough to convince me that what she was telling me was authentic; the part about David having swung it conclusively. At this point in time, I had been told that Bambs's cousin, David Boutflour, was going to be one of the most important witnesses at the trial, but that was all I knew. None of his evidence, including the fact that *he* had found the bloodstained silencer at the back of Nevill's gun cupboard, was public knowledge. I certainly didn't know it.

The message from the man I took to be Nevill also meant an awful lot to me – as an acknowledgement that what I had been trying to do for Bambs was on the right track. It is also interesting to note that June herself did not come through to me, but was referred to as part of the 'we' – as was their way in life. The only thing I couldn't understand was Betty's opening reference to Nevill's anger, that it was something *he* would have to deal with. Why did Betty make that distinction?

The answer to that question was to elude me for another year and came not from the family but from Nevill's secretary, who I had never formally met. The answer was worth waiting for, and worth telling here, if only to assure me that the whole session with Betty had been more than just telepathy.

Barbara had worked for Nevill for many years and, as his secretary, knew more about the troubles within the family than anyone. She described their relationship as being more like a father and daughter than a formal working one. She was one of the few people Nevill shared *all* his problems with. Fearful of Jeremy's release, and because of police instructions, Barbara had kept her entire story to herself before the trial – and even then, much of it was too prejudicial to be heard. It was only after June and Nevill's ashes had been buried, some months later, that she finally gave her full story to the family. Like me, she had nothing to gain from her testimony but to see justice done.

When I saw Barbara, rather than asking direct questions, I told her all about my session with Betty. But when I came to the part about

Nevill's anger, she immediately said, 'That's because he knew he was going to die!' She then told me how Nevill had suspected for some months that Jeremy was planning to kill him – but thought he would be the only victim. He was convinced his death would come as the result of a shooting accident during the hunting season and never envisaged the entire family being at risk. For this reason he thought he had plenty of time and was in the process of tidying up all the loose ends regarding the farm and his financial affairs, just in case.

He was also, apparently, preparing some sort of dossier on Jeremy and had told Barbara that he would soon have to do something very unpleasant that he wasn't looking forward to. He had been referring to handing over the dossier to the authorities. Nevill was angry with himself, because his thoroughness and reluctance to turn in his son had led to the deaths of his entire family.

What amazes me is that even when Nevill learned of Jeremy's attempts to buy a five-shot automatic shotgun, which Barbara told me about, he had said nothing more than, 'If he gets one of those we'll all have to look out.' On another occasion, he had been heard to say, 'I must never turn my back on that young man.'

In another conversation, with Uncle Bobby, I got a similar reaction to the piece about Nevill's anger. He told me that three weeks before the shootings, following a caravan-site director's meeting, he and Nevill were together at Whitehouse Farm discussing their retirement. During their conversation, Bobby had asked Nevill to show him his newly built office, and on their way through what now remained of the scullery, Nevill spotted *the* automatic rifle and its ammunition lying on the settee there. On picking it up, to put it away in the gun cupboard, Nevill had said, 'We mustn't make it too easy for the next generation to step into my shoes!' To which Bobby exclaimed, 'You can't be serious!' Turning towards him, with a knowing nod of the head, Nevill said quietly, 'You never know, you never know!'

'I was alarmed,' said Bobby, 'but knowing that Jeremy, the next generation to which he had referred, was no match for a man like Nevill, I didn't pursue the discussion further.'

Bobby also told me that very shortly after a stormy christening party for David's son Simon, June had asked him, 'What would you think if you saw Jeremy trying to get Sheila to load bullets into that thing that goes on the rifle?' (June had been referring to the magazine.)

'I would think he was trying to get Sheila's fingerprints all over the cartridges,' said Bobby, to me, but to June he said, 'Did she do it?' When June said no and that Bambs had told Jeremy not to be so silly, Bobby again thought no more about it until much later.

Could this be the reason why both Bambs and her mother had been so jumpy around that time? I was to hear a whole string of stories like this.

Coming back to Betty, she was far from finished. Following her first revelations, I told her the full story, confirming all the points I have mentioned so far. Then she said, 'Do you know someone called Peggy?'

Confused silence . . .

'There's a lady called Peggy who used to know you as a child. You will have to possibly ask your mother about this. I feel she . . .'

'The name's familiar.'

'I feel that she was either a next-door neighbour or she was a friend of your mother's – she's dead – and she's just come through and said to mention Peggy to you because, what she's come here to say is that (the twins were with her and that) she's part of a group which helps children and because of her connection with you when you were a child, there is a connection all round.'

When I asked my mother who Peggy was, she had to think for a while and then remembered a woman whose son I had played with regularly as a child. She then told me that Peggy was a sad story, because she had a nervous breakdown *after losing twins at birth*. I then remembered who Mum was talking about and told her what Betty had said.

I have, on a number of occasions, been given predictions about my future, of which some of the most unlikely have come true. For example, Betty later told me that, in the future, my success would come through helping people – through writing and lecturing. The first part of this I found questionable, the second, laughable. My fear of making a fool of myself inhibited even a drunken speech in front of friends, let alone what she suggested. She also told me that I would find myself mixing with people with whom I would never have dreamed of coming in contact before.

It is now not uncommon for me to give informal lectures on 'drawing interpretation' or 'natural and distorted emotions' in front of ninety or more people in a workshop. I have also been working with murderers — and finding many of them likeable ·people. But most recently, at a conference on 'Relationships in Prison', I found myself on first-name terms with a bishop, senior judges and prison governors, *and* telling my story to an audience of two hundred.

Many more pieces of survival evidence came through during that two-hour session, as did the inevitable abundance of inspiring predictions — most of which I have chosen to leave out. There were some, however, with reference to what Maggie had spoken of all those years before, that are well worth including.

Betty said, 'I don't know what all this is about, but you are going to be asked to do sculpture. Do you do sculpture?' Once again I was flabbergasted, but she didn't stop there and went on to talk about an idea that I hadn't even mentioned to anyone at that time. I am referring here to two individual sculptures of the boys, which I still haven't made for reasons that will soon become apparent.

She went on: 'It's almost as though the living minds of these children are going to enter these pieces.' She could see them finished. 'They are going to be beautiful pieces and the minds and spirits of the children will be in them, and then that will be the finish of that part of your life. You will have paid a debt, as it were — not that you owe them anything, but it's your debt to yourself.'

I felt tremendously comforted by this, but five minutes later she pulled the rug from under my feet when she added that, once I had completed them, the sculpting would stop; there would be no more. 'You are being given the gift of sculpturing for that purpose and that purpose alone.' She then explained that I was being guided by someone who was good at it; for their, as much as my own, progression. 'The whole force of these things is being given to you through somebody else's gift, if that makes sense.' Several months later, Betty gave me the name.

Funnily enough, the idea had crossed my mind that someone was helping me, because nobody was more surprised at the results of my efforts than I myself have been. This sculptor's identity was then confirmed over a year later when I consulted an American medium on his visit to this country. Before that I had taken Betty's suggestion with a large pinch of salt. Once again, the medium was given no idea of my connection with sculpture, but in the middle of my session the 'entity' (or spirit) who spoke through him said:

'There is a master with you, who served in the creative arts [the same sculptor's name was given]. His vibrations are with you and if you call upon them actively with your mind, who knows, perhaps you shall become aware of thoughts and impressions and words. Who knows? For most assuredly all who are in the creative arts have been guided to some measure – I believe you call it inspiration, which is a synonym for spiritual master.'

All I can say is the 'master' must have been having a very perplexing time with his pupil, because it was many months before I had the time to do any more sculptural work. When I did start, however, I was staggered at not only the results, but the experience too. In starting work on the 'Monument to Children', mentioned at the end of Chapter Eleven, I once again experienced the phenomenon of my earlier psychic drawing, but this time in three dimensions.

From the moment I bent the first wire armature into shape, it had presence – almost as if a small boy had taken up residence in the form. All I had to do then, it seemed, was hold that image in my mind's eye and fill it up with clay. Within just five days, the boy holding out an apple was complete in every detail; life-sized and remarkably lifelike. His companion, complicated in his emaciated form, took a lot longer. This was only my third piece of sculpture.

Finally, Betty began to answer that one big, unspoken question: why did it all happen, and why to me?

Had I not already made a major shift in my own level of consciousness – through my own spiritual experiences – I would have found some of it extremely hard to swallow. She said, 'You were brought into this world, not to do what you wanted to do, but what you elected to do before you were born. You have been thrown into the cauldron because you were living your life for yourself, and somebody had to throw you in and say, "You didn't come here for this, you came here for something totally different and that is what you are going to do." And it is being forced on you, to find the path of knowledge.'

The one thing I hadn't been able to understand was that, for most of my life, everything I needed had always landed in my lap, so to speak. The loss of the twins had been the only really bad thing to happen to me and, since then, things have continued to fall into my lap. Now I am emotionally stronger, however, things have not been quite so easy. Betty continued:

'I feel it is very easy for someone else to talk, and it's a terrible thing that you went through, you never psychically get over it, the scars remain – but you have got to make them pay for themselves as it were; you've got to make it mean something to you, and to mean something to mankind. As I talk to you, what I get very much is that (the twins) were martyrs to your progression, in as far as they came into and went out of this world for a purpose, because they had served their purpose.

'With you being a younger soul than they are, you've got more to learn. It's almost as though they threw you into the cauldron and said, "Now get on with it because we know it already." For some people who don't understand, this kind of thing might seem terribly cruel, but with progression of the mind you can only – when you've reached your purpose – show somebody else the path; then you have done your job.'

At first, I found this all very difficult to assimilate, even hard to accept, but at least I could understand it far more than anything else I had ever been taught. Much of what had happened to me could be described as religious experience, but it was more Gnostic in form; I was developing my own direct relationship with the divine – something the Church would not have us do, at all costs! And quite understandably so. There are many dangers and one can get burnt out.

It is also dangerous to over-identify with the experience and begin to believe that we alone can save the world; a trap other visitors to Betty have fallen into. I call this a 'Messiah Complex'. A lot of spiritual teachers have it, and that can be their downfall. I fell into that trap for a while myself, but my anger towards June, another deluded Messiah or martyr, helped me to identify and deal with it. In that sense, she was a wonderful teacher, a gift – her 'holier than thou' stuff rubbed up against my own. It just took me a long time to admit or even realise it.

Some weeks after seeing Betty, as if to screw the lid down on any doubts I might have had, Herbie asked me for her telephone number and arranged to make a visit himself. Like me, he was completely 'blown away' by the information she gave him during their telephone conversation, and his visit well and truly dispelled any doubts either of us still had. I know for a fact that I didn't prime Betty about him and, as a result, she has proved herself, in my eyes, a truly remarkable lady.

Like me, Herbie was very sceptical at first, probably more so. For this reason he hadn't given Betty any clues as to his identity or connection with me; he even gave his real, rather than stage name. When Nicky and I met him after, in a nearby tea room, he was full of so many things to tell us.

'She came out with so many amazing things,' said Herbie, 'things she couldn't possibly have known about!' He then told us about some very moving and personal reunions with significant people, including the twins. Betty had told him that there was a little boy called Daniel who was talking about something he only ever did with Herbie, which was sitting on his shoulders. He had spoken about a time he had sat on Herbie's shoulders so he could reach a 'big silver balloon up in the air'.

'Then,' said Herbie, 'she said it seemed to be in a huge place with lots of flashing lights, like in the film *Close Encounters*, and another little boy was squealing and laughing hysterically, because the balloon kept moving out of reach whenever Daniel tried to touch it. "These two little boys," she said, "are they anything to do with Colin? I can see a connection now. The other one, on the ground, is also showing me a small pendant or something, which he is swinging to and fro in front of his face. He says it's something you, or someone close to you, gave him and he says to tell you, it's his one special treasure."'

Nick and I had sat there listening in silence, but almost simultaneously, I said, 'The mirror ball for the "Bathroom Song"!' and Nicky said, 'The little elf pendant I gave Colin to have placed in their coffin for me!'

'Cor blimey, is that right, Nick!' said Herbie, who added, 'You're right about the silver balloon bit as well.' He then explained that Big Bob, one of Sky's road crew, had once had a great big mirror ball hanging from the ceiling of the Royal Albert Hall, on about thirty yards of chain, and had lowered it to just above their heads, to amuse the kids.

'Well, every time Daniel, who was on my shoulders, tried to touch it,' said Herbie, 'or look at his reflections in it, Bob would pull the chain so it moved out of reach. The boys loved it. It's funny how Nicholas would never allow me to put him on my shoulders. There was also another message for you, Colin,' said Herbie. 'They said to tell you again that they are very happy where they are and not to worry, in fact they're the happiest they have ever been. They also said to tell you they can't wait to see the book finished and read all their funny stories!'

CHAPTER NINETEEN

OVER THE MONTHS, there had been a number of occasions when I seriously considered shelving the whole book idea; it was proving far too painful at times. But after the somewhat unusual encouragement that concluded the last chapter, I no longer had any real choice. I had to continue. It had also occurred to me that either Betty or Herbie could be the real source of such a message, but it didn't really matter: living or dead, I was being given genuine encouragement by people who cared.

Well, the book, like many aspects of this strange journey, took a long time to find its present form and the light of day. I now stand as a very different person to the one who walked out of Betty's house towards a murder trial. And like the book, which has existed in numerous forms, I have gone through many transitions since then. I had also reached a point in the journey where I was to discover there were many different tunnels to explore, all of them in my own psyche; tunnels that interlinked in strange and diverse ways.

But like Theseus with Ariadne's 'magical thread', there was still only one route to follow: the one which led to the centre of the Labyrinth, to the monster that lurked therein; to my own Shadow, as Carl Jung described it. I didn't know, then, where I was heading, but *something* in me knew that if I didn't go in to meet that unknown creature, '*It*' would eventually come out to find me.

This was brought to the fore, I realise now, by my impending confrontation with Jeremy at his trial – not that I was required to speak to him, but I still had no wish to see him. I was afraid of the feelings it might bring up in me. I was still very much in denial on very many levels: denial about the deaths and the brutal reality of them, but also of my own murderous feelings, especially towards

Jeremy. As 'a nice guy' this did not sit too well with my own self-image: he, Jeremy, did things like that, not me!

In Chetwynd's *Dictionary of Symbols*, the Shadow, which is the opposite *unconscious* counterpart of the Ego (what I have described as 'my own self-image'), is defined as the 'modern psychological name for an ancient symbolic figure, the embodiment and epitome of all that is most vicious, brutal and vile in the human character'. It is also made up of all those parts of ourselves that we would much rather not know about, or indeed want others to see; all those parts that cause us to feel embarrassed, uncomfortable or ashamed. In that sense the Shadow is not necessarily bad. It only gets in the way if it is ignored.

For example, the very serious person, who has never been allowed to have fun or be reckless, may have a very joyful Shadow; one which, if ignored, might come out as the Trickster (another Shadow character) and tip that person into situations where they suffer an attack of uncontrollable giggles when absolute seriousness is required. That is the Shadow at work. Another symbolic example might be the fairy-tale queen who is no longer considered the most beautiful and becomes, instead, the witch. *Snow White* comes to mind as a perfect metaphor for the drama between Bambs and her adoptive mother. They seemed to be a direct manifestation of each other's Shadow.

In its more dangerous aspect, the Shadow might become manifest in the gentle person who has never been allowed to show their anger, has been shamed by any display of it; the person who, pushed or prodded once too often, loses control and explodes with terrible consequences. Prisons, I have since discovered, are full of them. That was the danger with me.

In Jeremy's case, there was something else in action, something slightly different, connected to morality – or rather, to its negative counterpart – as well as anger. His justifiable hatred of moralistic chastisement, amongst other things, had gone so deep it would seem to have invoked the very embodiment of Darkness itself. From his perspective, the family would represent to him everything alien to his survival; his own Shadow.

CHAPTER TWENTY

O N THE MORNING of the first day of the trial, a robin flew into the house of Karen and David Boutflour. They found it in their living-room, singing on top of a glass display cabinet which contained a porcelain robin given to them by Ina and Anthony Pargeter – in memory of their shared earlier experiences.

There were no windows open in that room, which meant, to gain access, the robin must have flown the entire length of the house from the open front door.

The trial was something I had absolutely no desire to attend or, in fact, read about. Unfortunately, at some point I had to give evidence, so it couldn't be totally avoided. Even before it began on 2 October 1986, I had gone into semi-hiding, staying at Jill's flat. My friends, family and the police would know where I was, the press wouldn't. Even though I had moved home by this time, my new address was too near my old place to take chances; I might have been spotted and followed by reporters, who were now hanging around there again. I later heard that my old neighbours were typically helpful and even treated one reporter to the customary bucket of water.

At the same time, I was also being searched out by members of the defence counsel's office, wishing to ask me questions; something I thought to be completely unethical. When I called the police for advice, they told me that I didn't have to speak to these people if I didn't want to. But if I did, I could request the presence of a police officer to make sure that no unfair questions were asked. As it was, I really had no intention of speaking to them, or anybody else for that matter, so I telephoned their office and reminded them that they had all they needed to know in my statements.

During the early days of the trial, the police received a severe public dressing down by the judge, with regards to the slackness of their original investigations. As it was, the officer who originally led them had suffered a fatal accident shortly after he was suspended from the case.

Under cross-examination by the defence counsel, Detective Inspector Ronald Cook, a fingerprints expert, acknowledged a number of errors made during those first few days. As scene-of-crime officer at the farm, he admitted that he had allowed the family's dog (affectionately known as the Pest), found cowering under a bed, to run around the house, disrupting evidence for two hours before they thought to remove it; that officers had failed to wear gloves when handling the rifle and cartridges, even though rubber gloves were available; and that it was seven weeks before the rifle and cartridges were fingerprinted and a further four weeks before the fingerprints were compared with Jeremy's.

He also told the court that the Bible found at Bambs's side was also not fingerprinted until 24 October. Added to this, he told how he had not checked on possible exits to the farmhouse, which they discovered had apparently been locked from the inside, and that he had failed to notice newly made scratches on paintwork on the kitchen mantelpiece.

The main criticism, however, came after Inspector Cook admitted failing to search the gun cupboard where the bloodstained silencer, a vital clue, was discovered three days later by David Boutflour; and that they then lost a grey hair which had been attached to it while taking the silencer to the forensic laboratory. He had also then failed to warn the laboratory about the contents of what he was sending them.

Despite this seeming catalogue of errors, however, the examination of the evidence had been thorough and was later presented in detail. The mechanism of the rifle found on Bambs's body was found to be stiff and the gentleman testing it had broken a fingernail while trying to reload it, yet it would have been necessary for Sheila to reload twice. It was also pointed out that her fingernails had appeared freshly manicured as well as her hands and feet being clean; there were no traces of lead or gun oil on her nightdress. These facts are inconsistent with somebody running barefoot round a house shooting people.

Experiments were conducted using women of the same height and build, to see if it would have been possible for her to have shot herself using the rifle with the silencer fitted. They had found it difficult to get the rifle into a position whereby the wounds Bambs had received could be duplicated. When they did manage to do so, they found they could not reach the trigger or, when they could, they could not apply sufficient pressure to discharge the rifle.

One of the women who had carried out these experiments appeared as a witness at the trial and, at the request of the defence, lay on the floor of the court to demonstrate the various positions they had worked out. For the defence's benefit, the demonstration was done without the silencer to show that without it the rifle could be fired.

It was established that the silencer *was* attached to the rifle during the fierce fight in the kitchen, when Nevill was killed, and that blood found on the inside of the silencer matched Bambs's blood group, indicating that it had been fitted to the rifle when she was shot. It had got there by a process known as 'back-spattering' – a phenomenon which occurs when a firearm is discharged against flesh beneath which blood is flowing. There was no blood found in the muzzle of the barrel of the rifle, only in the silencer. Of all the twenty-five wounds, the only one that could produce such a large quantity of 'back-spatter' was the final, fatal wound to the soft tissue below Bambs's chin, an area that had been saturated with blood from an earlier shot that had lacerated the jugular vein in her neck. This was the only certain contact wound with an available supply of blood.

It was also pointed out to me later, by David Boutflour, that a small textured, washer-like attachment, normally fitted to the end of the gun barrel to protect the screw thread when the silencer is not attached, was found by police officers on their second inspection of the gun cupboard in the box which had contained the silencer. Without either that or the silencer attached, the thread on the end of the barrel would have been marked or damaged in much the same way that the end of the silencer was; however, it was clean and undamaged, further indicating that the silencer was attached throughout the five killings.

To answer a point raised by the defence, it was pointed out that there was a remote possibility of the blood being a mixture of June and Nevill's, although the absence of an enzyme found in June's blood, in the blood in the silencer, made it most unlikely.

My own appearance in court, even though it carried over two days, was quite short. This was simply because I was the last witness to be called on that day.

While members of the family were giving evidence, I was sitting in the waiting-room, awaiting my turn. None of us were allowed to talk to each other: Stan Jones and the Clerk of the Court made sure of that – so the atmosphere was very charged. We were reduced to small talk when there were so many vital questions to ask of each other. And I knew less than the rest of them! In an effort to keep myself calm, I tried to read a copy of *Jonathan Livingston Seagull*, which somebody had lent me. Others who had already given evidence were whispering to each other at the other end of the room about what they had been asked.

The only high point of the wait came when Uncle Bobby was hustled, red-faced, out of the courtroom by the clerk over a point of law. 'What's going on?' said Bobby. 'What did I say wrong?' Ann thought her father had had a heart attack. I had the strong impression that the family were trying almost too hard to tell everything, even if they weren't asked; I would even say, almost to the point where they risked turning the jury against them, such was their hatred of Jeremy.

Finally, late in the afternoon, the last family witness came out and they all left together. Before I knew it, I was completely on my own. They just left me there with the whole waiting-room to myself. This non-verbal statement said everything: I was *not* one of them.

A uniformed police officer, who had also been waiting, was now giving evidence. Knowing I was to be the next witness to be called, I was petrified – just sitting there, waiting. In a final effort to calm myself, I thought about Nicholas and Daniel and tried to get a sense of them being there with me, so that when my name was called, I imagined them holding my hands as I walked into the courtroom.

It's a strange feeling to be standing in a witness box for the very first time. I felt vulnerable and awkward, naked. Which, I suppose, is the way one is meant to feel. To be the only person speaking in that room – such a large room full of complete strangers, knowing they were all listening to me – was quite horrifying. My voice suddenly seemed very loud in my ears and I began to feel very small – like a little boy made to stand up in front of the whole school. My legs would not stop shaking. In fact, just like the teachers at school, I was reminded a number of times by the judge to speak up and to address my answers to the jury not the prosecution.

To be confronted face to face, across that same room, with the man accused of murdering my family was even stranger. I cannot even think of words to describe it; not all the feelings I was having made sense to me in the circumstances.

From where I was standing, Jeremy was seated a long way back, behind but almost directly in line with Mr Arlidge, the prosecuting barrister – so it was very difficult not to look him straight in the face when answering questions from the prosecution bench. His penetrating gaze was unflinching. The only thought which kept going through my head – and also kept me going as I listened to and answered each question – was 'That's right, Jeremy, look at me. I am so fucking honest it makes you sick!' In fact, I was often so preoccupied with that thought, I didn't hear the questions at all and had to have them repeated.

Having said that, I also found it really hard to look at him directly, which is where the confusion came in. Something inside of me, in my body responses, made me break eye contact and drop my head, almost as if in shame.

In looking into Jeremy's eyes, I realise now, I saw something of myself and my own fears. I also saw the betrayer in me, in that I had once promised (albeit in ignorance of the truth) to stand by him, as a brother. Regardless of what had happened, of what he did to my children and their mother, my deeply inbred sense of honour – of never betraying a promise – was being betrayed. It is a paradox, but something in me still felt some shame in that.

In that paradox, however – which I am only now able to see sufficiently enough to verbalise – I also gained those clues to where my journey would next take me.

So what else did I see of myself as I looked into those eyes – into the eyes of a cold-blooded murderer? Part of the key has to be in the fact that there had been many occasions I had also wished his sister dead – as I did on the night of the killings – and times I had felt murderous towards his mother, for the way in which she violated everybody, especially her daughter. Had June still been alive and continued the abuses to my children that I am now more aware of, I myself might have been tempted to kill her.

In that respect, Jeremy had saved me the trouble and was standing trial for something I had also wished for. How then could I stand as an accuser? In fact, that is another probable reason why my testimony had to be so clear and lacking in malice. Although I didn't understand why at the time, I could not point my finger at another human being, when those same destructive urges were stirring in me.

In the witness box I was asked to describe how I had been told of the shootings and then the sequence of events which followed. In doing so, I confirmed that Jeremy was the first to tell me about the telephone call and that he had told me his father had said, 'Sheila has gone berserk and she's got a gun.' I also confirmed that within minutes of arrival at his home, Jeremy had told me about the family row and that his parents wished to have the children fostered. And that within a few days of this, Jeremy had asked me whether I knew if Bambs had made a will.

Another point I made, when questioned, was that although Bambs had what I had described as a Latin temper, she would always direct any violent actions towards inanimate objects, or herself, rather than other people. The example of her putting her hand through a window was brought up.

In cross-examination by Mr Rivlin, the defence barrister, I was asked whether Bambs had ever hit me or the children, which I denied in the case of the children. I demonstrated that in the few times she had hit me, it had been a slap round the face with the flat of her hand and not, as I felt they were hoping I would say, with her fist. Although he was careful to deny casting aspersions on Bambs, I felt that the defence was weighting all his questions in such a way as to make it look as if Bambs, and not Jeremy, was on trial.

In many ways I was glad his cross-examination of my evidence was held over till the following morning, because I was less nervous than before; I felt less intimidated and didn't feel like I was walking into the unknown. With Julie Mugford being the next to be called, we passed each other at the door as I left the courtroom. I hadn't seen her for nearly a year, so I wished her luck as she went in. It was also the last time I ever saw her.

As Jeremy's ex-girlfriend, Julie Mugford was a key witness for the prosecution case. About a month after the shootings, she had walked into a police station and informed them that Jeremy had planned the whole thing. In court she related the full story. Jeremy had first thought of burning down the house with his family inside and making it look as if his father had fallen asleep with a lighted cigarette. He had abandoned that plan when he had realised that the house and its contents were under-insured.

When Julie confronted him, shortly after the shootings, with the question of whether or not he had done it, Jeremy claimed he had hired a mercenary, to whom he had agreed to pay the sum of £2,000. The 'mercenary' was later called as a witness and turned out to be a plumber who, as it proved, on that night was being unfaithful to his wife with two other women, albeit separately.

Jeremy had gone on to give Julie details of how everybody had been found in the house, details which the defence attempted to show she had got from the newspapers. When Mr Rivlin accused her of trying to make her evidence sound as black as possible, Julie, who broke down repeatedly during cross-examination, said, 'No! I am telling you only what he has told me. The evidence is black. I don't mean to do anything, I have no intention of doing anything, I don't like saying anything at all.'

Julie admitted to helping Jeremy break into the office of the family's caravan site from which he stole £980 while she kept watch. She also admitted to a cheque fraud of her own, to which she had later confessed and repaid to the bank involved, of her own volition.

She had gone to the police, she said, because she had been unable to live with Jeremy's guilt and wanted him to realise what he had done. The fact that Jeremy had been very much involved with the shootings was confirmed to Julie by Jeremy himself, when he called her half an hour before he called the police and said to her, 'Everything is going well, something is wrong at the farm.' He called her again later that morning, after the police had discovered the bodies. Both calls were confirmed by the other girls living in the house Julie stayed at. Several other people, including Julie's mother, were called to support various parts of her story, and to provide further memories of their own about Jeremy's conversations.

The inevitable question that Mr Rivlin put to Julie was why had she lived with the knowledge that her boyfriend was a murderer for a month before going to the police? Her reply was simple and to the point, 'I was scared.'

Jeremy's statement following his arrest was read out in court by Detective Constable Michael Clark, who had also interviewed him on the morning of the shootings. In it Jeremy claimed that Julie had gone to the police because he had jilted her; he also said that she was capable of lying. Detective Constable Clark said that Jeremy had been surprisingly calm after he was told, and described how Jeremy had refused to allow June's sister, Pamela, to remove some sentimental pieces of jewellery from the farm into safe-keeping. Jeremy had told her that the jewellery was now his responsibility.

When the defence counsel called Jeremy to the stand, he marched across the courtroom from the dock to the witness box, where he stood straight but with his head tilted to one side. After denying all the charges brought against him, Jeremy accused both Robert Boutflour and Julie Mugford of lying, and said that the rest of the witnesses had been exaggerating for the benefit of the media. Robert Boutflour, in his testimony, had spoken about conversations he'd had with Jeremy in which Jeremy had said, amongst other things, that he could 'easily kill his parents'.

When counsel asked Jeremy about his relationship with his family, he described the one with his father as 'very loving', and with his mother as good, although not always easy to cope with because of her religious views. Jeremy also described his relationship with Bambs as 'very good' but added, 'I found it difficult to understand her mental illness. She used to come out with some bizarre things.' He then recalled an occasion where he claims to have seen Bambs punch one of the boys. He said, 'We were travelling to see some friends when one of the twins interrupted Dad, and Sheila turned round and punched him full in the face.'

Jeremy is the only person still alive to have witnessed the alleged attack. In the unlikely event of it being true, I would certainly have known about it; I saw the twins far too often and they would never both manage to keep something like that to themselves.

In another statement, which was read out in the witness's absence, Bambs's Iranian boyfriend, Freddie, spoke about an occasion when he had left my mother with Bambs while he went out to collect her prescription. He said that when he returned, my mother said she was leaving because she had been 'beaten up'.

Needless to say, my mother was absolutely flabbergasted when she read this in the newspapers. In all the time they had known each other, Bambs never once laid a finger on her. Unfortunately, as court procedure would have it, there was nothing my mother could do about it. What on earth could Freddie hope to gain from such an outlandish claim about somebody he supposedly loved, especially when there was another person alive to refute it?

To clarify this point, it is worth looking at my mother's own, illuminating version of the events to which he referred. It was 3 March 1985, the day of Bambs's second nervous breakdown.

At about two o'clock that afternoon, my mother answered her telephone and recognised Bambs's voice, but Bambs said to her, 'Hello, can I speak to Dr Ferguson, please.'

'Hello, Bambs,' said my mother, 'it's Doris here. Are you all right?' With a torrent of words, Bambs started saying how she was hearing voices from God and all sorts of things to that effect. When Mum asked her if she was alone, Bambs said Freddie was with her, so Mum asked to speak to him. Freddie said they were trying to get hold of Dr Ferguson because Bambs was ill again. He said she had been screaming at him all night, hearing all these different voices, saying that he was evil and things like that. Mum could hear the children's voices laughing and giggling in the background, so she told him she would come over straight away.

When she arrived, Bambs kept on saying she was hearing voices from God. She was being told the world was all wrong; she had to put it right. Sometimes she said the voices were from the Devil. She told my mother that as she watched the television, the woman talking would come out of the screen into her. Then she asked Mum if that happened to her. When my mother said 'No', she didn't say any more about the voices until the doctor came. Their attempts to contact either Dr Ferguson or her GP had been unsuccessful, so an emergency doctor was sent for.

While they waited, Bambs just sat very quietly and, as my mother said later, 'Looking very serene and beautiful, but very sad and forlorn at the same time. If you caught her eye, she would give a very quick, bright smile, but it would go immediately and she would be sad again.'

Freddie did most of the talking and when Mum asked if he had phoned her parents, he said, 'No,' and insisted that they were not brought into this at all. After this, whenever my mother tried to pick up the telephone, to make a call out, he prevented her doing so by putting his hand over the receiver and saying very firmly, 'I'd rather you didn't.' He seemed determined to stay in control, but Mum's main concern was for the boys so, at the first opportunity, when Freddie went to let the doctor in, she grabbed the telephone and called my father. She told Freddie, 'It's out of your hands now, I've just sent for Colin.'

When the emergency doctor came in, Bambs started talking about the voices again. Mum went out of the room and left the doctor with her. In the meantime, Daniel and Nicholas were in their bedroom playing with their friend, Chloe. There was hysterical laughter coming from inside and when Mum stuck her head round the door, she found Daniel trying on all Chloe's clothes. Not only that, he'd cut his fringe with a pair of scissors, something they all found hilarious.

Back in the living-room, the doctor wanted to give Bambs an injection to calm her down, but she wouldn't have it, so instead he prescribed pills. Mum explained to him about the clinic Bambs went to before and that her parents would most likely arrange for treatment there again. The doctor agreed that Bambs needed treatment and added that, in his opinion, she was not only a danger to herself, but possibly to others too. (This, I have since discovered, is a standard phrase to describe people in Bambs's condition – especially when the doctor, in this case not a psychiatrist, is unsure.)

After the doctor had left, Freddie said to Bambs, 'Look, Bambi, Doris is your friend. Talk to her, go into her arms and tell her everything. Cry.'

My mother held her, but there was nothing. 'She was like an empty shell.' So while they sat on the sofa together, Freddie went for the prescription. While he was gone, Bambs said she would like my mother to go, she wanted to be on her own and was very polite but firm about it. So Mum did what she asked, but waited outside with the door ajar until Freddie returned.

After seventeen days in court and various other witnesses, the jury was sent out to reach a verdict. At around the same time, during an interview with a radio reporter, I was asked about accusations made during the trial that Bambs was into the occult. This related to Freddie saying that during her illness she thought she was a white witch. All I can say to this is that, to my knowledge, she never dabbled in anything of that nature and, like myself, regarded it with considerable trepidation. The nearest she came to the occult, apart from meeting Maggie, was to open her women's magazine or the newspaper to read her horoscope.

There was also a great deal said about Bambs's attitude to, and relationship with, the twins; especially during her breakdowns. The defence counsel said during his introduction that she had 'suffered loss of contact with reality and also had delusions that the twins were trying to seduce her'. As I pointed out much earlier, this would be a typical Freudian psychiatric response to a majority of patients in treatment. He went on to say that, in particular, Bambs saw Nicholas as becoming a 'woman-hater and murderer'. Her psychiatrist, Dr Ferguson, was called to substantiate all this and said, 'She believed [the twins] had a malign adult intelligence and felt at risk by having to have sex with them, or joining them in some violence.'

As I said before, Bambs is no longer on trial and I can only begin to wonder how much psychiatrists might sometimes overreact to what, in many ways, are completely innocuous situations and stories. Bambs was fully aware of, and talked quite often about, how gentle Daniel and Nicholas were. If anything she wanted them to be tougher.

To everybody who knew them, they had a way about them which was mature, but without loss of their childish innocence; they were almost like men in little boys' bodies, yet still little boys; Bambs affectionately used to call them her 'two little men'.

I would go a stage further and say that Daniel and Nicholas really were remarkable when it came to masculine charm and good manners. Whenever there was a 'nice lady' present – it didn't have to be a young attractive girl – they would always show me up by saying absolutely the right thing at the right time: 'Oh, Grandma, what a lovely dress you're wearing today. You've had your hair done, it does look nice.' Or 'What a lovely scarf you are wearing, Mummy, it goes so nicely with your eyes.' It was both remarkable and perplexing, they were so observant and always said what a woman most wanted to hear. Apart from that, they would come out with these compliments so quickly, it always left me wishing I had thought of them myself. The way they used to ooze charm was almost enough to make even James Bond wilt.

Coming back to Bambs, who, if nothing else, looked for her children to parent *her*, as many of us do, I can only let her speak in her own defence and quote, as final testimony, part of a letter she sent me after her first breakdown:

I'm so worried that [the twins] will, or have, lost their self-confidence; I really do hate myself. I'm probably worse than anyone, I so wanted to carry on as I was before with the boys. I know that I have felt very vulnerable for the last two years and changing flat was not an easy thing. I had a little help but it was me who made the decisions. At the time I enjoyed it but afterwards when I settled down into the flat I began to be depressed and the relationship with Freddie was not all it could be. I should have been stronger and not let him enter my life again after we split up. Now I look back, I was fond of him but never in love. I'm a little angry with him because he told me how to do everything like I'm incapable, now it's got to me and I have completely lost my nerve, even with one person.

When you feel bad you think the opposite way than you should and I've been worried that the boys will have problems in their future life with girlfriends etc. I look so horrible sometimes that they must think I don't want them to have a good time, which is just what I do want them to do.

Please, truthfully, tell me if they do seem OK or have they lost their inno-
cence? It seems that way when they are with me. It's been a nightmare, I
wish I wasn't insecure like I am. I never would have thought I could
become so insular a person, I love the boys as much as I ever did but some-
thing is stopping me from feeling free to be myself.

The doctor is seeing me tomorrow and I'm resting in bed. I even find it
hard to relate to one single person . . . I'm so sorry that this has happened.

Love Bambs X

Unable to reach a decision on the afternoon of the 27th, the jury
spent the night in a nearby hotel; on the following morning, another
case was started in court. At 10.40 a.m. the jury returned at their own
request; they needed clarification on the possibility of the blood in
the silencer being a mixture of June and Nevill's. Mr Justice Drake
went through the evidence from his own notes relating to the discovery of the blood and its analysis. Seemingly satisfied, the jury went
out to continue their deliberations.

At 1.50 p.m., the judge recalled the jury and instructed them that
he was prepared to accept a majority verdict of ten to two. Exactly
one hour later they returned to court with a majority decision; the
verdict was Guilty.

In passing sentence on Jeremy, the judge said, 'I have to consider
when I think it likely it would be safe for you to be released from
prison to live in the community and I find it difficult to foresee
whether it will ever be safe to release into the community someone
who could plan and kill five members of their family and shoot two
little boys aged six while they lay asleep in their beds.'

He sentenced Jeremy to life imprisonment five times over and
recommended that he serve a minimum of twenty-five years, and
stressed that he meant a minimum of twenty-five years. He then said
to Jeremy, 'You used the mental illness of your sister and planned the
murders so that she became the prime suspect and if, as happened
later, you also became a suspect, I don't doubt you thought your
sister's illness was such that it would be difficult for people to become
sure of your guilt.

'It is clear from what we have heard that Sheila was the prime
suspect. Your ideas and plans came near to success.

'It shows that you, young man that you are, have a warped and callous mind concealed behind an outwardly presentable and civilised appearance and manner.'

The judge told him that he had performed the murders out of greed and went on to say, 'But I take the view that you also killed out of an arrogance in your character which made you resent any form of parental restriction or criticism of your behaviour.

'Your conduct in planning and carrying out the killing of five members of your family was evil almost beyond belief.'

Outside the courtroom, a barrage of cameras, microphones and a loud confusion of questions awaited Jeremy's departing family. Seizing their opportunity, the press surrounded David Boutflour, firing questions at him as he kept walking. What he said to them was heartfelt and unrehearsed.

'Nobody wins. Everyone loses. You can't bring them back.'

Within a few words, David had managed to sum up how most of us were feeling; but we were all given a very unpleasant, yet valuable opportunity to learn by this experience. What we each choose to do with it decides on whether or not we lose. Speaking for myself, I still had an awful lot of fighting to do before I finally emerged from the darkness and pain of such a terrible experience. This was not the end of the story by a long way. If anything, it was just the beginning.

CHAPTER TWENTY-ONE

FOR MOST FAMILIES of murder victims, it is after the trial is over that the real pain and struggle begins. We were lucky in a way, because we not only had a conviction but a sentence that was in keeping with the scale of the crime. For many, a charge of murder is transmuted to manslaughter and a perfunctory prison sentence bordering on laughable is given. And for others, the murderer is never caught or the body never found, leaving a pain and sense of futility that is unimaginable.

How we can deal with that – or rather, how I approached that challenge myself – makes up most of the rest of the book. But first I want to tie up the loose ends of the investigation. It was only after the trial was over that I was finally given the full story of the family's fight to keep the case open; Robert Boutflour had kept a detailed file of every event that came to his attention since the day of the shootings.

Almost as soon as the shootings had happened, Uncle Bobby and some of Jeremy's cousins were all having their individual doubts about the conclusions the police had come to. Being much more familiar with the Bambers at home than myself, they weren't to be taken in quite so easily. They were each aware of different things Jeremy had said or done which contradicted the images he was presenting to the police.

On the first day, Bobby, David and Ann all overheard parts of the statement he was giving to the police and recognised it as 'a tissue of lies'. Then on the following day, during conversations between David, Ann, her husband Peter, who is a licensed gun dealer, and Nevill's other nephew, Anthony Pargeter, their doubts turned to conviction as they compared notes. At this point, they decided to approach the police with their suspicions. In the meantime, Uncle

Bobby was quietly working things out on his own, and coming to similar conclusions.

They all knew Bambs couldn't shoot and didn't know one end of a gun from the other, so to speak, but when they were told, by the police, that a rifle and not a shotgun was used, they knew beyond a shadow of a doubt it wasn't her. Anthony, who, as a competition marksman, was much more familiar with that type of gun than the others, and in particular the murder weapon itself, presented them with much the same hypothesis I had been given in Cornwall. He had also, only recently, had an informal shooting competition with Jeremy using the same gun. Jeremy proved himself a more than capable marksman. This was considered strange in one who, even though he went hunting, had always expressed his hatred for guns and shooting.

On Friday, 9 August, two days after the shootings, Ann, David and Anthony requested an interview at Witham Police Station with the detectives in charge. They were surprised when they didn't get a very favourable response and thought, at one point, that the senior officer, Chief Inspector Edwin Jones, was going to storm out on them.

They had explained why they thought Bambs couldn't have done it and presented various questions to which they wanted answers. Up to this point, the cousins had, for some reason, been given the impression that only five shots had been fired. When they were told that there had actually been twenty-five, and that they had nearly all found their target, they said that it was all too efficient for Bambs; she would have had to load the gun three times when she didn't know how to, even once. So they asked further questions. Had Bambs's nails been broken or damaged? Was there lead and gun oil on her nightdress and hands? Had they fingerprinted the cartridge cases?

All the time they were asking questions, Ann was writing down the answers on a piece of paper. The senior detective, now going red in the face, stood up and shouted something like 'I don't have to sit here and listen to rubbish like this! I am a very busy man, you'll have to go.' Luckily, Anthony managed to pacify him, but as he sat down again, he shouted at Ann, 'And stop writing!' He had made up his mind that it was four murders and a suicide and nothing was going to change it. As far as he was concerned, the case was virtually closed and everything else was a formality. He certainly didn't like civilians telling him how to do his job.

The other two detectives remained fairly quiet, except for when Detective Sergeant Stan Jones said to them, 'You might be so wrong.' He was to repeat this many times over the coming weeks. They left, frustrated and intimidated, but determined not to give in.

The next day, Saturday, 10 August, Ann, David and Bobby were allowed access to Whitehouse Farm in the presence of Mr Cock, Nevill's accountant and executor. They were there, ostensibly, to collect up valuables and documents for safe-keeping, but they also had other ideas: they were looking for clues.

Ann had been there earlier in the day to help clean up after the police had handed over the keys. All the bloodstained bedding and carpets from upstairs had already been taken out and burnt, at Jeremy's request, by the police, but the kitchen floor, for example, still needed cleaning.

One of the first things Ann noticed then was that sugar had been upset all over the place and she wondered if Bambs's feet had been clean when they found her: did she have blood and sugar on the soles? Ann had also been puzzled by two other things: she found a Tampax dispenser and a toy pistol together in the lounge. Also a twelve-bore shotgun, in the broken position, leaning up against the wall in Nevill's new downstairs office. Knowing that Nevill was never so slovenly with his guns, she expressed her surprise as she put it away in the presence of the police who were with her at the time. She was later demonstrating this to her father, her brother and Mr Cock, in the office, when they decided to inspect the gun cupboard themselves.

Bobby had been told that Jeremy had said that he had taken the silencer and sights off the rifle because it wouldn't fit in the cupboard with them on.

While Bobby was assessing the size of the inside of the cupboard, David started rummaging around the floor at the back of it and came out with a box containing the silencer. Their immediate reaction was that the police had not been looking. Bobby asked Ann where the rifle was. When she told her father that the police already had it, he said something like, 'Then they had better have this too. Put it in the bag of ammo [which had been on top of the box when it was found] and let them have the lot!' David also found the telescopic sights, so that was also put with the silencer and later taken to Ann and Peter's house for safe-keeping; the police could collect it from there. They also checked the windows and found quite a few which could be easily locked shut from the outside.

Later that evening, at Ann and Peter's house, David was examining the silencer when he noticed a drop of what looked like blood near the exit hole. He also noticed that the silencer had been damaged and spotted the presence of some red paint engrained in the textured end piece. They decided to inform Witham Police of what they had found, immediately.

Having spent several sleepless nights, constantly turning it all over in his mind (things he had seen and heard, conversations he had had), Bobby worked it all out and decided that the police must be asked to treat Jeremy as a suspect. Unbeknown to his children, he went to Witham Police on Monday, with his theories, but didn't get any further than the others had. Detective Inspector Miller told him that they could not accept it as possible and that they had completed all the tests but one. So far all tests pointed towards Bambs being the killer. Miller also said that they were sure that nobody had entered or left the house that night; 'We did some very sophisticated tests.'

Before Bobby left, he told them that they would never be able to convince him that Bambs had done it and asked that they look more closely. He asked how it could have been done without the silencer on the gun, to which the officers showed surprise. They had not been told of a silencer, so Bobby then told them where they could pick it up. Apparently, in a further state of shock from finding the silencer, and seeing the blood on it, none of the cousins had actually telephoned the police; they each thought one of the others had made the call.

As far as Bobby was concerned, the adults, being the biggest threat to the assailant, had to be the first victims; the sound of an unsilenced gun would have woken the children and they appeared to have died in their sleep.

Later that evening, as Peter Eaton was showing Stan Jones the silencer, they both noticed a grey hair stuck to it. The whole lot was then carefully packaged up in a cardboard tube, for safe transit, and Stan took it away in his car. By the time the silencer was delivered to the forensic laboratory, by another officer, the grey hair had gone missing and the small 'blob' had been smudged.

Also on the Monday, Jeremy made his first visit to the farmhouse since the shootings. He didn't want to go at first, but Ann convinced him that there was nothing to be afraid of; the whole family had been in for coffee at some time over the weekend. When he and Julie arrived, he sat on Nevill's chair in the kitchen and put his feet up on the table; his manner was very arrogant, but when Ann suggested that he have a look round the house, his mood changed; Julie started crying.

When they got upstairs, he had seemed frightened of going into June and Nevill's bedroom, but when it came to going into Bambs's, he was petrified. 'His eyes almost came out on stalks,' said Ann, who further described them as going almost black because the pupils were so wide open. She assured him that nothing had happened in that room and then took him to the twins' room, where he almost crawled along the floor to their door, crouching in fear. Once Jeremy saw that their room had been changed round, he was quite normal. He and Julie sat in there for a while, then afterwards went back downstairs, where Jeremy asked where Nevill's wallet was; he wanted the credit cards.

Two things occurred to me when I was told of Jeremy's unusual behaviour upstairs: he was either seeing, or believed he was seeing, ghosts, or putting on an act to scare Julie, who he knew believed in them. On the following day, Julie, who went with Ann to order the flowers, spent much more time and care over selecting those for Bambs's coffin than she did for the others. What did she know then?

During the next few days, several things happened. On Wednesday, 14 August, Jeremy's friend Brett Collins arrived at the farm driving Nevill's blue Citroën. He supervised the stocktake of the farmhouse contents and displayed a remarkable knowledge of antiques and their value. The inquest was held at Braintree Coroner's Court and postponed for two months pending the results of further tests. Also the bodies were released to the undertakers.

Later that same evening, Stan Jones called at Whitehouse Farm with some other officers and did another extensive inspection of the house; they found the scratchmarks on the red-painted mantelpiece in the kitchen. Ann Eaton, who was there to let them in, used the opportunity to do a bit more snooping herself. She thought they were doing rather a lot considering the case was apparently closed. Before he left, Stan – who was later to dub her Miss Marple – said to Ann something like, 'You've not seen any of this, but if anybody asks, we were just doing a bit of measuring up.' Ann did as instructed and told nobody except her immediate family.

Another police officer who seemed to be sympathetic to the family's pleas was a Detective Constable Barlow who, with Detective Inspector Miller, came to the D'Arcy funeral and mixed with mourners at Jeremy's house. Stan Jones had gone on leave by this time. As far as most people were concerned, including myself, the policemen were there just in case of trouble with the press. As far as the Boutflours were concerned, they were there to watch Jeremy and his friends.

In fact, everybody was watching Jeremy except me and my family. Remarks made during the proceedings by the two officers convinced Bobby that Jeremy was now under suspicion. They had both wandered up to him at some point and quietly said, 'He's putting on a good performance, isn't he?' Or words to that effect.

Looking back at this period, in the light of what I have since learned, I can see that once the family had sown the seeds of doubt in the minds of the police, they had also unwittingly put themselves up as suspects, because they too stood to gain by the murders – especially if Jeremy was convicted. They also had good reason and opportunity to plant evidence against Jeremy, if they chose to. When I made this suggestion, informally, to the Eatons, they were horrified at even the thought of it. But when I suggested it to Bobby, he could see the possibility; it is easy to see the delicate situation the police were in.

They were being presented with evidence by people of whom any number were possible suspects, including myself. Although the local police knew them through dealings with the campsite as respectable people, it didn't necessarily prevent them being suspects – some of the most respectable families in history have far darker secrets tucked away in their closets; so the police had to go through the procedure of finding further evidence without raising too much suspicion.

Having already allowed some of the evidence to be destroyed, they almost had to allow the killer enough rope to hang himself. By claiming to have received the telephone call from Nevill, Jeremy gave the rest of us the best alibi in the world: his undeniable guilt.

During the weeks following the funerals, while Heather and I were in Norway, the family took every opportunity to pester the police. On the day after the twins' funeral, they were told that the drug squad was making its own independent investigations on Jeremy's house, as a source of drugs. The family were also persistently asking questions, for example: did the police have the results of the blood tests on the silencer yet, and was it human blood or not?

They were told that tests would take about three weeks, but also felt like they were constantly being fobbed off with excuses. While they waited for answers, they kept themselves busy. Ann worked out which window had been used to get out and demonstrated how to close it from the outside. This was later confirmed when Julie gave her statement, as Jeremy had boasted to her about how easily he could get in and out of the house undetected, and told her how he did it.

Bobby suggested the use of June's bicycle, which had been found outside Jeremy's house after the shootings. He also suggested possible routes between Jeremy's house and the farm which he could follow undetected. He came up with a theory about the empty Tampax dispenser, suggesting that the tampon had been used to clean the silencer then flushed down the loo. He asked if there were traces of tampon fibre on the silencer and could they be made to match?

The police must have taken notice because, as Ann remembered it, they had all the manhole covers up on the following day. And so it went on, but the family were still not convinced the police were investigating Jeremy seriously until 30 August, twenty-four days after the shootings. On a visit to Witham Police Station, Bobby learned that officers could not make any sense of the telephone times.

On 4 September, nearly four weeks after they found the silencer, Ann and Bobby once again visited Witham Police Station, to find out if the results were through. Stan Jones informed them that there was no information on the blood tests available to the family and, quite bluntly, asked them to explain what business it was of theirs anyway. He told them that they could give their opinions at the time of the coroner's inquest – the enquiry would not be complete until the coroner was satisfied as to the cause of death.

Finally, like a man who was tied up in red tape, he told them to remember that he was only a small cog in a very large machine, and that one day he would hope to be able to tell them the whole story. He explained that blood is tricky stuff to analyse, and that after a certain amount of time it is of little value. Forensic could be holding back on the silencer because the case was still classified as a suicide rather than a murder case.

Apparently, forensic testing of suicide cases will nearly always be superseded by cases of a more criminal nature and could therefore take months, if ever, to reach the top of the pile. It seems that the officer who finally delivered the silencer to the laboratory had failed to explain the contents of the package to them, or the importance of it as evidence, so it joined the rest of the Whitehouse Farm samples at the bottom of the pile.

This situation would probably have continued had Bobby, seeing justice slipping away, not gone over the heads of those at Witham and written to the Chief Constable of Essex Police. Later that same evening, he telephoned Stan Jones to tell him that Jeremy had been seen unloading furniture into an antique shop near Bambs's flat – he had been ferrying stuff out of the farm for weeks. Bobby also told Stan of his letter to the Chief Constable. Stan didn't try to discourage him. In fact, he thanked Bobby and said that it might help to finally get things moving.

On the following day, 5 September, Bobby handed in the letter at police headquarters. In it he pointed out that it was now four weeks since the murders and explained about the silencer. He also pointed out what his family had been through in order to have the case reopened. He said that he had been given to understand that forensic evidence attached to a suicide case is given low priority. He also pointed out that because of this the prime suspect was still unchallenged and the trail was going cold. Bobby urged that if nothing was done about it, he was prepared to go to the Commissioner of New Scotland Yard. He was granted an interview that afternoon with Peter Simpson, the Assistant Chief Constable.

Mr Simpson was very sympathetic as he listened to the full story, and told Bobby that they would start again from square one with a new team. Later that day, a Detective Superintendent Kinneally rang to say he was in charge of the case. Stan Jones, having stuck his neck out earlier, was given the opportunity to lead the investigations. To give him credit, Stan, more than any other of the many detectives involved, was to live and breathe this case for the next twelve months.

On 8 September, Detective Superintendent Ainsley, fresh from his holidays, took over from Mr Kinneally. He later telephoned the Boutflours, to introduce himself, and told them he would be sending two of his best men to take their statements in detail; the two detectives were with the family for the next ten days. Jeremy was picked up and charged with the burglary at the caravan site, that same day, and held for further questioning. His girlfriend, Julie, had walked into the police station with her own confession the day before.

Stan later told me that he wished Julie had waited just a couple more days, because they were about to bring her in for questioning anyway. It would have looked better for the police, publicly, if they had extracted the truth from her under interrogation. Instead, they were given the truth and had to decide whether or not she was lying. Looking back, I really wish somebody had been telling me the truth. It would have saved my family and myself a lot of heartache and pain of speculation – all we had to go on were spurious newspaper stories and rumours.

CHAPTER TWENTY-TWO

ASSAULT, ENTERING, TRESPASS and deceit are not words one would normally like to associate with members of the press as guardians of a nation's right to free speech; but this, sadly, was the face they presented. With the echoed, hollow excuse of 'the public's right to know', these words can barely begin to describe the abominable behaviour of reporters as they laid siege to many of our homes, during our time of greatest distress.

Callously breaking the news to many of those closest to the victims, their cold-hearted and ghoulish fascination with our grief can only be compared to a form of sadistic voyeurism; their preoccupation with every gory detail, the true pornography. In a wild attempt to rake up even the tiniest scrap of dirt, the behaviour of journalists degenerated to that of savages.

What really angers me is that all this is justified under an umbrella of approval, from which newspapers pretend to take a moral standpoint. Many would argue that this was impossible, because the press have no morals and are therefore incapable of making such judgements; the only morality they present is by implication and it is in fact the public who make the moral judgement. The press print a collection of short statements and 'facts', not necessarily true or even connected, and allow readers to draw their own conclusions – to do the sums, as it were – but I would disagree with the argument and say they are fully aware of the perverse morality they are selling, and knowingly lead their readers to the conclusions they want.

A particularly damaging example of this, leaving little to the imagination, appeared in an issue of the *Daily Mail*, on 12 September 1985, just after Jeremy's first arrest:

As officers broadened their enquiries to include known drug dealers in Britain and Holland, Essex police refused to say why 32-year-old Colin Caffell was interviewed.

Fortunately, I am now able to defend myself – at the time, I wasn't – but for Bambs, as the victim of much more than a vicious murder, this can only be done on her behalf. Even very recently, late in 1993, some newspapers were publishing extremely misleading, uncorroborated articles about yet another Jeremy Bamber appeal attempt, thereby continuing to violate Bambs's reputation as both a woman and a very gentle, loving mother; stories based largely upon the lies of a convicted murderer. To the *Guardian's* credit, they at least printed my two-thousand-word letter of response two weeks later, in full.

When newspapers tried to fit theories and explanations to the facts, the stories of what happened became extremely far-fetched. Like all of us, they were trying to piece together a picture created out of garbled snippets from various police officials – who shouldn't have been talking to them anyway – and other newspaper stories equally based on spurious rumours and misinformation. The same has been the case with nearly every book and report on the subject since the trial; there have been many.

Some weeks after Jeremy's first arrest and with the truth now screaming in their faces, many papers continued to defend their original theories. With almost grim determination, some showed great reluctance in admitting they had been wrong. For example, the *Daily Express* on 12 September said:

A contract killer may have executed four of the five victims . . . it was revealed last night. The new theory came after it was revealed that model Sheila 'Bambi' Caffell was the tragic go-between in a terrifying drugs war. Detectives believe she became a blackmail target for high-society gangs keen to widen their evil sphere outside London . . . Police think she was ruthlessly exploited by racketeers cashing in on her plight after she fell on hard times . . .

They still believe Sheila turned the gun on herself but are keeping an 'entirely open mind' on who shot the four other victims.

Who's trying to fool who?

At around the same time, other newspapers followed a rapid conspiracy to cover up and lump all the blame for their own gullibility back on to the police. In a report which disclosed the existence of the silencer and the discovery of a pattern of torches in a field, the *Daily Mirror* said under the front-page headline, **'SECRET MURDER CLUE TO BAMBI KILLINGS':**

The fresh evidence known to the police but exposed for the first time today by the *Mirror*, puts renewed pressure on the police and raised grave doubts about their handling of the case.

Despite the initial gross incompetence of Essex Police − for which they have since suffered considerable embarrassment and internal investigation − they were well on top of things long before the press, who constantly violate any sanctity of human fallibility by deliberately amplifying or distorting something way past its limit, simply for profit. The sin is not in making mistakes, but in knowingly perpetuating the same. In the case of the *Sun*, they were still blackening Bambs's name with some particularly malicious *post-trial* coverage, fifteen months later! They wrote:

Wild Bambi's life of shame.

The free-and-easy sex life of Bambi Caffell drove her adoptive mother June to a nervous breakdown.

Lustful Bambi had an abortion when she was 15 after becoming pregnant through a one-night stand at a village dance.

Two years later June caught her making love with a farm worker in a field.

The deeply religious mother branded her the Devil's

**child – sparking Bambi's plunge into an obsessive belief
that she was possessed by evil . . .**

**And her appetite for men, her broken marriage and
drug addiction continued to drive staid June and her
ex-World War Two fighter pilot husband to distraction.**

Bambs was not having flings with farm workers or one-night stands
at village hops, but was sunbathing in the field with me, her regular
boyfriend – two days after her only abortion. I would also like to
point out, once and for all, that Bambs was not a drug addict and
never had been. Like many of our generation, she smoked a bit of pot
and experimented occasionally with other drugs, but rarely found the
desire to repeat those experiences.

Her brother, on the other hand, has almost been idolised by the
press as a frequent drug user, with stories about trips to Amsterdam to
buy himself marijuana, sampling different brands in a café for quality
– yet they have never once referred to him as a drug addict. Once
again, it all seems to come down to the question of gender: one set of
rules for the boys and another for the girls.

In contrast to this savage and inexcusable attack, other post-trial
coverage further built up a romantic and almost acceptably roguish
image of Jeremy as the high-living but murderous Romeo. References
were made to the 'handsome womaniser', 'ploughboy turned playboy' and to the police investigating him in connection with ' "Raffles
style" country-house burglaries'. What had been contemptible for
Bambs, as a young mother – leading 'a double life' – was almost
commendable for Jeremy.

The press told us, **'Women drooled over his dark, charming
good looks'.** Headlines included things like: **'Bamber is cool right
to the end'; 'MY SEXY SPREE WITH BAMBER – He made
passionate love to a rich Swiss girl'; 'WOMAN LAWYER
PAID BAMBER FOR SEX'.**

His boasts of having committed the 'perfect murder' and the
immortalisation of statements like, 'I am evil. I just can't stop having
evil thoughts,' caused numerous extremely attractive women to leave
amorous propositions at the courtroom for him – in case he was let
off. Somehow, being allowed to read them, after the verdict, seems a

most fitting part of his punishment – to know he will never be allowed to enjoy their fruits.

In the hope of discovering a den of psychopaths, several newspapers spent a lot of time and money tracing both Bambs and Jeremy's natural families, but they found only respectable people of senior church and military backgrounds. This didn't seem to deter them, however, and in the resulting coverage, they even managed to drag both the Queen and an Archbishop of Canterbury into the headlines:

> **'BAMBI SCANDAL AT ARCHBISHOP'S PALACE – She was given away to avoid Church scandal and ended obsessed with the Devil'; 'THE SECRET OF BAMBI'S BIRTH'; 'AGONY OF BAMBER'S PALACE PARENTS – The shame's not ours says Queen aide'; 'Queen backs Bambi beast's father'.**

To make final comment on what was, without a doubt, some of the most destructive, so-called investigative reporting, I would like to quote from a reader's letter published in the *Today* newspaper on 7 November 1986. Although they were not directly responsible for this exposé, *Today* still followed other newspapers in reporting it:

> Your front-page article, 'Palace aide is Bamber's real father' has blatantly caused great pain to [Jeremy's birth parents] . . . Your article stated: 'Major . . . and his wife . . . claimed they were unaware of any connection between themselves and Jeremy Bamber.' I strongly feel that is how it should have remained. What right have you to play God and inform these unsuspecting people that they have given birth to a son who is now a convicted murderer? Any guilt they had felt about having their son adopted at birth is nothing to what they will now feel for the rest of their days. Your article has breached the confidential rights adoptees, birth parents and adoptive parents deserve.

On 18 June 1987, the newspapers responsible for this received their perfunctory slap on the wrist from the Press Council. In a ruling which followed three complaints from NORCAP (the National

Organisation for the Counselling of Adoptees and Parents), Mrs Lynne Cowley, press officer of NORCAP, said that 'adoption information is confidential, but the press had conducted a wanton witch hunt in this case. It was unreasonable to identify or name either set of parents as some sections of the community might attempt to hold them responsible for their offspring's actions.'

Each newspaper – the *Sun*, the *Daily Mirror* and *Daily Mail* – was required to publish the full contents of a Press Council ruling against them, but in the case of the *Sun*, they appeared to flaunt the impotence of the Council's authority by making further good copy with: **'BAMBI AND THE PRESS COUNCIL'**. They were the only newspaper not to give the names of the other papers affected by the ruling and seemed almost proud of their censure.

What I fail to understand is the fact that any complaints concerning the grandparents, also identified at the same time, were not upheld by the Council. In addition, the ruling did not account for these unfortunate people suddenly being 'door-stepped', as we had been. Tim Miles, the *Daily Mail's* chief reporter, actually travelled all the way to Canada and harassed Bambs's natural grandparents, causing untold distress to a very elderly couple. In some ways, they were fortunate in having had only one reporter at their door – they usually attack in packs. The intimidation and victimisation of those too old, weak or vulnerable to defend themselves seems to be a reporter's favourite tactic. The prey is far less likely to bite back.

For example, back on the first day after the murders, at Vaulty Manor Farm, where June's ninety-five-year-old mother was still living, there occurred one of the first 'door-steppings' and a prime example of the appalling behaviour of reporters coming dangerously close to killing a very weak old lady.

Being very ill and bedridden, the family were keen to keep the news from her until she was stronger. The press, however, had other ideas. Fortunately, it was one of those rare occasions that Gran was particularly sleepy and didn't hear the awful commotion outside her bedroom window. Normally she was quick to hear any arrival and ask who it was.

The housekeeper, Reg, another elderly lady and ex-matron, told me that although there had been a number of visits by the local press that first afternoon, there was no trouble until about 8 p.m. when the nationals started arriving. Fortunately, they didn't stay long and by nine they had all cleared off again. But it was too good to be true: at 7 a.m. the next morning they returned in force and didn't leave again till about 9 p.m. that night.

When I asked about their behaviour, she said, 'They were all over the place; standing in the front garden, shouting, and on the porch, ringing and banging the door. If it wasn't the front door it was the back.' She asked them to be quiet, explaining that Gran had not yet been told, so they raised their voices even more and began 'screaming about drugs'; did she know how many shipments there had been? 'It was a most terrifying experience,' she said, 'and a miracle Gran didn't wake up!'

At one point, this kind of banging and screaming at the front turned out to be a tactical distraction, because at that moment she noticed, through a side window, someone heading for the back of the house. By the time she got back to the kitchen, a young man was on his way through the scullery with a tape recorder in his hand. She'd had enough and dismissed him very quickly, locking the door behind him. But there was more to come.

Early the next morning, another reporter tried to take advantage of the fact that Gran had a large family of regular visitors, not all known to her, and pretended to be one of them.

'Good morning,' said the smart, well-spoken young man with the beard, stepping into the hallway as one familiar with the place, 'I've come to see Auntie Mabel.' Reg went to let him through, but at the last second, alarm bells started ringing in her head – so she blocked him and very politely asked for some identification. At this point, he hesitated and, as Reg walked towards him, stumbled backwards into the rosebushes from where he said, 'Ah, well, perhaps I should have said that I'm from the *Sunday Express*.'

'Yes, I think you should,' said Reg, who then 'read him the riot act' and insisted he tell the other reporters, who were just arriving, to go away and not come back.

I shudder to think what might have happened had that man, in his irresponsible quest for a story, conned his way past her. Apart from the absolute violation of privacy, he could have been up those stairs and talking to Gran within seconds – breaking the news to her and further adding to the tragedy.

Who the hell is responsible for all this? Is it purely down to the business of selling more newspapers than the competition, by out-sensationalising each other, or is it the product of a sick society that demands it? A society that is so terrified of and out of touch with its own pain, that it needs to gloat at other people's misfortune? Who are the real voyeurs? The newspapers and their staff? Or the public who read and believe what they write?

CHAPTER TWENTY-THREE

To a Murderer

In memory of Sheila, Daniel and Nicholas Caffell,
June and Nevill Bamber, shot 6–7 August 1985

A sunflower strains to heaven, then hangs its head.
In summer's last, belated blaze of light
The morning glories trumpet till they fade . . .
You have denied them this: denied them day and night.

Schoolchildren fool and chatter in the park,
Grown-ups remind themselves that life goes on
In spite of everything: but in what dark
And unimaginable undertaking have they gone?

A fox howls near my door, then slinks off, stunned.
Worms rot the grounded apples to their core.
Anger burns coldly and consumes the mind;
Existence shrinks to hollow places, nothing more.

Sooner or later we must all be dead.
But morning glories rise along the wall
When their time comes, and sunflowers have their head . . .
Know that the dead are praying, murderer, on your soul.

Peter Jay, October 1985

I HAVE SPOKEN A great deal, in various parts of the book, about the appropriate expression of feelings and what can happen when they are continually bottled up and not allowed to come out. 'To a Murderer' is a beautiful example of how we can express or give form to feelings in an appropriate way. Painting or making sculpture, me writing this book, are all examples of the same thing: activities we can all do in some form.

It is a sad fact that creativity is a grossly undervalued commodity in modern society. It sits way too far down on our list of social, economic and technological priorities; something exclusive to a select few – when it really should be accessible to everyone. This is not the fault of individuals but of our education systems, representing society, that want people to fit in rather than be different. Much of our natural creativity, our individuality, is stifled at an early age by grown-ups – our teachers – forcing us into little boxes representing how *they* think we should draw or paint, think, play or behave, rather than allowing our natural expression of how *we* perceive the world.

Creativity also walks hand in hand with our spiritual life and hence, our relationship with what we call God, something, as I said before, most organised religions would not have us do. To have a direct experience of God, outside a suitable container – such as the Church or a strong healthy ego – can be dangerous; one can get burnt out or go crazy, as Van Gogh did. Unfortunately, our churches, in fear, it would seem, of any religious experience that might challenge their established dogma, and hence their right to be, have done every-thing they can to destroy genuine spirituality.

It was also inevitable then, that Western society would eventually swing towards its opposite; to the realm of the intellect and extreme rationality with all its technological advances. But with that also comes the death of religion as we know it, the death of God, which in turn has given rise to a fundamentalism harking back to the medieval atti-tudes that supported witch-burnings, as a last-ditch attempt to save it.

By trying to destroy or deny what we most fear or simply do not understand, we ultimately destroy ourselves.

There is a quote from the Gospel of Thomas – an apocryphal Gnostic writing, outlawed by the early Church fathers – in which Jesus said:

If you bring forth what is within you, what you bring forth will save you.
If you do not bring forth what is within you, what you do not bring forth
  will destroy you.

Which brings us right back to my growing fascination with what I earlier described as the 'Shadow'; the unlit parts of our conscious personality that have been relegated to the unconscious.

Chetwynd's *Dictionary of Symbols* tells us that, 'Much of it can never be transformed. It is part of the data of living which cannot be ignored either; we have to adapt ourselves around it. The malice that is always there, generation after generation, unalterable, ineradicable, was the side consigned to unquenchable hellfire in traditional Christian symbolism.' He then reminds us of another more positive aspect, which poet Robert Bly has reintroduced to general awareness in his book *Iron John*; an aspect which is vital, fierce and primitive, full of vigour: instinctive qualities that connect us with the very roots of mankind; what Bly refers to as the Wild Man or Wild Woman.

A few weeks after the trial – and long before I ever began reading about these darker aspects of human nature – I had the following dream. A dream which, in consequence, played a major part in directing my inner quest over the coming years. I must also add that I have never in my life had such a full and tactile experience in my inner world. So much so, I even wonder if, on some *other* level, it *was* real.

For reasons that will quickly become apparent, I have called it 'The Graveyard Dream':

I was on a journey by plane, destination unknown, that was broken at Heathrow for several hours. My travelling companion was male and, as far as I am able to remember, an old college friend some of the time and, at others, Jeremy. In the dream it appeared that the twins had been buried in a small country graveyard near Southampton and my companion – at this point the potter friend – reckoned there was plenty of time to get there and back to the airport in time for the connecting flight. It was afternoon, lunchtime possibly, but by the time we had reached the churchyard, it was dark.

I was worried about the time but, more than anything, glad we had made it there. The sky was clear, stars were out and the moon was full.

I was now on my own – the friend had gone to the village for a drink. It was a typical rural churchyard with old lichen-covered, dry-stone walls and a squeaking rusty gate – a perfect scene for a 'Hammer Horror' movie.

As I surveyed the scene by the grave, I became aware that the moon was emitting tremendous heat, like the sun, but it was still night-time. My throat became extremely dry, so I decided to walk the half-mile to the village to have a cold glass of beer. This 'hot moon' made me feel very uncomfortable. I could actually feel the heat on my face.

I had not gone more than a few yards down the lane, away from the cemetery, when all of a sudden, the moon 'went out'; there was suddenly no light – as if it had been switched off. I was in total, utter darkness! In fear I dropped to the ground and felt my way back to the graveyard – my only point of reference – and I realised that, as well as feeling temperature (the hot moon), I was feeling everything through my fingers, the textures. I had never had a tactile dream before and this was incredibly tactile! I could feel every detail of the road, the hedge, the stone wall and the first stone steps leading to the gate.

On touching that cold, rusty gate the moon came back on. I obviously wasn't meant to leave even though it had previously made it very uncomfortable to remain. This time, however, the moon was cool, as normal. But in the cold I shivered and my skin crept with highly charged sensitivity. The air seemed full of expectant static electricity, my whole body was gooseflesh – every hair was erect.

As I stood there, I noticed that just behind the twins' grave there was another with Jeremy's name on, which I found odd but even so I accepted it. It seemed to me that there were two of him; one alive and menacing, and the other, completely dead. I felt sad for the dead part – 1 felt there was good in it.

Just then, with my skin still crawling, Nevill sat up in the grave, followed by the twins, who were behind him. It was like they were a pack of cards that had fitted close to each other but now they were solid and real. Nevill smiled and told me he was 'jolly thirsty after such a long time in the ground', so he got up and went off to make himself a cup of tea. The twins leapt up and ran to hug me. We sat on a nearby bench and hugged and talked and kissed for several minutes. I felt so happy to be with them.

Just then my travelling companion (now Jeremy) returned and told me we had to hurry because we would miss the plane; it was already 9.15 and the flight was at 9.30. I got angry with him for not telling me sooner what the time was. He just said it would be OK. I then joined a queue from the graveyard to the check-in desk which was now outside the church at another gate. Unfortunately, the queue wasn't moving – everybody was dark, grey and solemn.

I was now in a real panic that I would miss the plane, but just then the companion (again Jeremy) returned. He told me there was a quicker way and led me into the church, into a side chapel with no glass in the Gothic windows. It was very bare and cold, but as I was noticing where I was – and that there was no exit – large unseen hands lifted me high into the air. The floor below me opened like a trap door through which I was dropped into the 'fires of hell'.

As I fell into the bottomless pit, I let out a yelp of excitement that I was at last going to have some real fun. I woke up shivering, sweaty and panting. The dream was so alive and so real, it took quite some time to completely come out of it and I kept slipping back into the memory of it. I felt like I had travelled to a very real place.

Looking back, it was both a terrifying and wonderful experience that I will never forget. I feel that what we call nightmares are an incredible gift from God, from that wise part that we all have inside; and they often show us exactly where our 'gold' is hidden. Something deep inside me was suggesting that I wasn't owning, or even acknowledging, my own dark side. It was also telling me that I was ready to face it. The unseen hands that lifted me up would represent that wise inner being who only has our best interests at heart; our Higher or God Self.

My thought, now, is that the moon often symbolises the 'Trickster', an archetype I mentioned earlier, which, in this case, would seem to fit, in that it pretended to be the sun and switched itself off and on. I also understand that, in general, when a figure appears in a dream in double form (in this case Jeremy as dead and alive), it means that whatever is being represented, symbolically, is approaching the threshold of consciousness. In some cases, according to Jungian psychologist Marie-Louise Von Franz, when that same character has brutish or criminal associations in one's mind, it can also represent 'the Shadow' in that it has a double aspect: a dangerous one and a positive one; regressive and progressive.

This would fit in very well with the feeling of sadness I had for the 'dead' part of Jeremy. It also supported that strange feeling of connectedness I had been experiencing all those months.

The dream confirms that this is about my own Shadow, in that the 'travelling companion', as the college friend, is a disguised representation of me that changes into Jeremy. In real life this young man not only studied ceramics at the same college as me, but we also went to the same school before that. This is one of the ways in which 'disguising' works in dreams; it presented somebody who was sufficiently like me, to make the suggestion.

We all know what it's like to be given insights into our character when we haven't asked. To be suddenly told directly that we have something equally murderous, judgemental, cruel or whatever inside of us, is bound to cause nothing less than severe resistance. We have to be told symbolically and then discover the real truth in our own time. It's only when we continually ignore the messages that these unlit parts of our psyche turn nasty and begin to be more direct. This dream was bordering on it.

Von Franz goes on to point out that 'criminal' images of the Shadow, of this kind, mean that both aspects, or possibilities, become locked into place. They can either blend with the dreamer and add to his consciousness, or remain outside and become projected.

In my own life, I had always avoided, and was fearful of, what my parents would call 'rough men' – in fact any men – as my father had. Their aggression frightened me, because I was afraid of my own unlived aggressive nature. Whenever I was ganged up on at school, I was terrified, not only of getting hurt, but also of the level of anger that was released in my attempts to defend myself. If I couldn't run away, I kicked and punched for all my life was worth, added to which I really didn't like or enjoy that feeling of rage that came up inside me. I couldn't own that aggression so I projected it, instead, on to other men who fitted that image.

I had begun to find, however, that the level of anger I now had inside me, after what had happened, could no longer be contained; it seemed to be leaking out, inappropriately, with people I cared about. I was also afraid that I might attack the next reporter stupid enough to overstep my boundaries, which, apart from giving me some satisfaction, would not otherwise serve any purpose bar getting me locked up for assault.

Another example might be the fact that I had unconsciously searched out girlfriends whose fathers had achieved in a way that my own father had not: I projected my need for a strong father on those men, in the hope that they might teach me what Dad was unable to do. But that didn't make any difference until I became conscious of it. Rather than find this power within my own psyche, they carried it for me. Or rather, I projected it on them. Ultimately, I needed to realise that I had the potential to become all of those things that I either admired or despised; both possibilities were in me. For a long time, however, I swung like a pendulum – or maybe it was more like a hanged man – between these different extremes. In fact, I am still swinging, and occasionally touching those unlit parts of myself. It is a lifelong process.

The more I swung, the more I began to learn that I was none of these things; I was not a saint, martyr or murderer, Nevill or Jeremy, good man or bad, but had the potential to be any of these things if really pushed to it. To identify with one side, either good or bad, at the expense of the other, only brings about an angry 'other'. True healing only comes about when we can learn *not* to identify with those opposites but say, 'Yes, I have both within me'; then to push them as far apart as we can and live in that almost electric space between them; to recognise and own both possibilities but at the same time say, 'I am neither'.

This is the world of paradox. And wherever there is paradox, it seems to be accompanied by an incredible surge of energy. For example, when everything first happened, I described my experience as a 'fast-forward slow-motion blur' – that everything was so foggy yet at the same time remarkably clear. These were paradoxes, yet with them, something healing was happening.

Now I was faced with my own potentially destructive side, personified in Jeremy as everything I despised, but with it came the potential to heal; to move beyond the pain. But first I had to own the fact that I too was arrogant, vain, greedy, full of unexpressed rage; plus a whole lot more that was personified in other people who caused a reaction in me. The more I realised what was happening, the more determined I became to try and make peace with all those denied parts of myself. I didn't want to end up blowing a fuse and finding myself in the same position as Jeremy; I had to acknowledge those destructive parts before they destroyed me.

I also had to remember that there is tremendous good in those parts; that the dark side of humanity, as writer and explorer Laurens van der Post has said, 'is a valid part of the human spirit with its own immense energies available to the human spirit'. But if these energies, these resources, are allowed to accumulate, through not being used or given any conscious expression or say in our lives, then and only then, do they turn nasty; Hades, the God of the Underworld – often represented holding the richness of his domain, symbolised by the cornucopia spilling with fertile abundance – bursts out of the ground and rapes Persephone. Or, as van der Post puts its, referring to these energies: 'As we will not let them in by the front door, they break in at the back.' Just as Jeremy did in real life.

So how did I begin to find out about all this, apart from reading every book there was on dreams and emotional healing?

Well, that was *not* the answer, because whenever I actually went in search of something to read, I could never find what I wanted; I was, more often than not, overwhelmed by the sheer volume of printed matter available and left bookshops empty-handed and disillusioned. As with everything else on this strange journey, the books I needed were placed before me, when I was ready for them; just as Betty Shine had suggested they would be.

One of the first significant books presented in this way, although very much earlier, was *The Hitchhiker's Guide to the Galaxy* by Douglas Adams. Now this may seem extremely incongruous in relation to what had happened, but it turned out to be the perfect thing for me to read, especially after the funerals, during our trip to Norway – to get away from it all. That was exactly what the story did: it took me away from it all but, at the same time, prepared my mind for what was yet to come.

I also found in it some very silly but valuable common ground to stand on: like the main character, Arthur Dent, my world had been completely destroyed – in his case, the earth itself – and nothing could have prepared either of us for the mind-boggling experiences we were each to encounter on our journeys; it felt, half the time, that I too was living in an alien universe where nobody understood my needs. In a way, the story both parodied and questioned every aspect of not only reality but all the experiences I have had, keeping me in touch, most of all, with my sense of humour. It was, however, only possible to see the importance of it to my healing once I had reached, as one friend put it, 'the laugh on the other side of the experience'. There was also one very important piece of advice printed on the *Guide*'s cover. It said, 'DON'T PANIC!'

Another book Betty Shine actually gave to me herself when, nearly a year after the trial, I told her of my failure to find anything that really helped.

'Try this one,' she said, as she fished a book from her own shelves. 'I haven't read it yet, so I don't know what it's like. Somebody sent it to me for my opinion.' The book was called *I Fly Out with Bright Feathers: The Quest of a Novice Healer* by Allegra Taylor. Chapter Two described the author's experience of an Elisabeth Kübler-Ross 'Life, Death and Transition' workshop; a workshop in which people with every imaginable experience of life could explore and express all their pent-up negativity in a safe and non-judgemental environment.

Some of the methods sounded a bit crazy – in that people who needed to express their anger, for example, were encouraged to smash up old telephone directories with a length of reinforced rubber hose – but I no longer cared what people might think. This finally sounded like what I needed – what I had been looking for. I couldn't put the book down and kept reading that chapter over and over.

During this time I had also joined what I would describe as the most exclusive club in Great Britain. So exclusive, none of its rapidly increasing list of members ever wanted to join. It was called 'Parents of Murdered Children'. But even that didn't have what I was looking for. It was helpful to share stories with people who had been through similar experiences, but the level of pain in the room was so great – and so frightening for many of us to really talk about in a way that might be cathartic – that having tea and discussing fund-raising always took precedent. Nobody there was really equipped to deal with such human suffering, but it was clear that some form of help was needed. I thought I had some of the answers, but quickly realised that I had to look after my own needs first. Taking care of others was not the way to do that.

Within weeks of reading Allegra Taylor's book, I found myself staying with someone who had a video of a programme the BBC had made all about Dr Kübler-Ross. When I saw her face and heard that thick Swiss accent and her captivating rhetoric, everything I had felt from the book was confirmed. I had to meet her. But it took nearly another year before I did. When I wrote for information, the only workshop she was doing in Great Britain, in fact in Ireland – and supposedly her last before retirement – coincided, exactly, with another workshop on 'healing the cause', which I had already booked and paid for. I would have cancelled this had there not been such a powerful collection of synchronistic events leading up to that booking, so Jill went to the Kübler-Ross workshop instead.

By this time, Jill and I had rekindled our teenage love affair and were more or less living together. The relationship with Heather, like many that go through such difficult external crises, had floundered within months of Jeremy's arrest. This is a matter of personal private regret, but I'm glad to say we're now friends again.

Jill and I met up in Scotland, after our respective workshops, and went to spend a week on a very small, very remote island off the Scottish coast, where we immediately ran into Ruth Oliver, the frail old lady who organises the Kübler-Ross workshops in England. Although Jill had not met her before, I had; it just so happened that she had also arrived that afternoon, from London!

In a subsequent conversation, we discovered that Ruth also organised the Gregg Furth workshops on interpretation of drawings that I spoke about earlier and Jill had heard about on her own workshop. Jill wanted a place, but she later had to cancel the booking and I ended up with her place instead.

It was at this workshop that Gregg Furth looked at all the pictures I had collected by Bambs and the boys and gave me many of the insights I now have. I knew then I was ready for Kübler-Ross. Her workshops were still going even if she had retired, but there was not one in England for another six months! I couldn't wait that long. I was desperate, but I couldn't afford both the workshop and a trip to the States, which was the other option.

So Ruth suggested I write to the Center in Virginia and ask for a bursary. She also suggested that I offer a copy of a sculpture *she* had commissioned me to make, for auction at the end of the workshop, as a part payment. The reply came back: I had a place with a reduced fee of '$200, plus a work of art' – the normal fee was then $550. The only workshop they could fit me into that year was near Washington DC, six weeks later.

My next problem was to find the money; I was still unemployed and very broke. Within two days, a man knocked on my door and asked if I wanted to sell my Volkswagen Camper that was now rusting outside in the road. I hadn't really driven it since the boys had died, so I thought maybe it was time. We haggled over a price and agreed on a sum which turned out to be exactly what I needed for the trip – with a few dollars spare for spending. When I asked his name, for the registration documents, he told me he was called Washington – the name of the city I had to fly to. I was speechless.

The sculpture, called 'Chrysalid', later sold for $1,000! It not only paid for my bursary, it also paid for two others. And they say there is no such thing as magic in this world.

I think I have now reached the point in my life when, like Carl Jung, I can say with all honesty that I don't believe in God, I know it! I don't know what it is – or really care for that matter – but I am now totally in awe of it.

I once heard somebody say: 'Coincidence is God's way of remaining anonymous.' I like that idea.

CHAPTER TWENTY-FOUR

To laugh is to risk appearing the fool.
To weep is to risk appearing sentimental.
To reach out for another is to risk involvement.
To expose feelings is to risk exposing your true self.
To place your ideas, your dreams before the crowd is to risk their loss.
To love is to risk not being loved in return.
To live is to risk dying.
To hope is to risk despair.
To try is to risk failure.
But risks must be taken because the greatest hazard in life is to risk
*   nothing.*
The person who risks nothing, does nothing, has nothing and is
*   nothing . . .*
He simply cannot learn, feel, change, grow, love and live.
Chained by his certitudes, he is a slave.
He has forfeited his freedom.
Only a person who risks . . . is FREE!

Anon

MUCH AS ALL the curious coincidences eventually led me to the point of flying to a Kübler-Ross workshop, everything went wrong with the actual journey to Virginia. There were even moments when I didn't think I was ever going to get there.

My flight, the day before the workshop, was cancelled due to fog at Heathrow. Thousands of people crowded the terminal on what had been expected to be a quiet day. Luckily, Jill managed to get me a cabin crew jump-seat on a later flight to Philadelphia, the next nearest destination her airline flew to. Problem solved. I could hire a car and drive the one hundred and fifty or so miles to the hotel near Washington DC where I had a room booked, and still get a good night's sleep. What could go wrong? Well . . .

This flight was also running several hours behind schedule, so US Immigration asked that everyone, including the crew, disembark at Boston and clear Immigration and Customs. This is where I discovered that my suitcase, in which I had packed everything I needed for the workshop, had gone on its own little holiday. All I had was my carry-on, which contained the sculpture and my camera. Nothing else.

'Report it in Philadelphia,' I was told. I also had the feeling that the man at Immigration had heard of Kübler-Ross, because when I stated 'purpose of visit', I have never seen – either before or since – immigration documents being stamped and cleared so quickly! I think he was afraid I might start crying or something.

By the time we finally landed in Philadelphia – even later than expected when we first took off from London – I was getting very tired. But by the time I had reported and described my missing suitcase, *and* discovered that I couldn't hire a car without a credit card – regardless of how many American Express traveller's cheques I had – I was not only exhausted but beginning to get frightened. As well as being my first visit to the States, it was also my first proper trip *anywhere* on my own.

When I was then advised to get a train or cab downtown to 30th Street Station, where I could catch the Amtrak 'Night Owl' service to DC, it struck the fear of God into me: memories of Jill once telling me that 'the last place in the world you ever want to get stuck in the middle of the night is downtown Philadelphia' began to fill my mind. With images of America coloured by TV and tales of armed muggings in dark alleyways, I hoped I would get there in time. All I could think about was the safety of my bed at the Dulles International Airport Holiday Inn, in Virginia. I couldn't even consider booking into another hotel where I was, because I would never meet the coach that was coming to collect participants from the one in Dulles in the morning . . .

The airport station in Philadelphia looked very dark and deserted, so I decided to take a cab into town. At this point a big black guy loomed out of the darkness and started shouting and swearing at me. I don't know why. I might have got in the wrong cab or something. My heart was racing by the time I was pushed into another much more tatty one. Was it even a cab, I thought as we hit the freeway? It didn't seem to have any sign up to say so, but the driver appeared friendly enough, so I sat back and watched the city as it got closer. In my exhaustion, I was becoming very paranoid.

Eventually we arrived outside this huge, deserted art-deco railway station – that looked like something out of Batman's Gotham City – only to find I had missed the train by just ten minutes. My imagined nightmare was becoming a reality. There wouldn't be another train until 5.45 a.m. – nearly six hours away! With time now to look at the place, it was even bigger and more oppressive than I first took it to be. An enormous 'heroic' statue stood at one end, and in the middle, facing it, a small information desk. There was someone there. Then I noticed a policeman – someone else I could talk to. And then finally, glowing red and yellow and bright in the corner of this vast and colourless place, my saving grace: an all-night McDonald's! I never thought I would be so glad to see one.

By the time I was speeding towards Washington DC, at daybreak, I had consumed three plates of scrambled eggs and told several people the story of my journey. Most of them looked sympathetic but a little confused. I think this was because I spoke English rather than American, which I have since discovered are vastly different languages. My somewhat unsuccessful attempts at sleep, on a station bench, had been hindered mainly by the fact that my bag, containing camera and sculpture, made an extremely poor pillow, although with the police officer around, safety had not been an issue.

When I finally got to the Holiday Inn, at 9 a.m., the combined costs of the food, two cabs and a train fare had come to more than my room and car hire would have done. My reward for surviving the ordeal was the hospitality and generosity that is typical of America. Another participant, whom I ran into at the hotel reception, gave me the key to her room – so I could catch an hour's sleep before the coach came. Although I needed a great deal more, it was heaven! It was now two o'clock in the afternoon, English time, of the day after

I had left home; and the workshop didn't start for another three hours.

This sort of experience, this seemingly systematic demolition of inner defences, is common amongst people who, like myself, keep their real feelings locked in a box. It's part of what I have since come to know as 'the workshop magic'.

As I said much earlier, I came from a family where feelings were never openly expressed, especially by my parents. As in many families, strong emotions were considered a source of embarrassment; shameful and destructive. So I had built a wall around my own – a huge wall of twenty-foot-thick reinforced concrete – like a dam. I knew what it felt like inside that wall – inside me: I felt both murderous and terrified. But of course I couldn't acknowledge the first part, even to myself. I was a nice guy, gentle; I shouldn't have feelings like that. But *I* knew they were there. Where I was heading that day, in November 1988, sounded like the only place on earth I might be able to safely let it all out *without hurting anybody*.

So what happened? How did Elisabeth's staff enable me to do this? I say staff, because she was not there for the first three days of the workshop. She *had* retired from that part of the process. But it didn't make any difference. It was not a process that relied on the presence of a charismatic teacher, but more on the fact that her training brings out those same qualities in all her staff. Elisabeth makes a unique contribution, which cannot be duplicated, but it is not essential. There were in fact nearly eighty people there, plus a staff of eight, who made it clear, during introductions, that they too had all been through the process; through all their own pain at some time in the past.

When we first gathered, they talked about the absolute sacredness of confidentiality; that what is shared by other people at the workshop stays at the workshop. Many would be sharing things with the group that they may never have shared with another human being before; things that make them feel shameful; how they might, for example, feel tremendous rage towards their dying child for being so sick – things that sound terrible in the saying, but are very real in a person's feelings and need to be not only respected but kept private. It is a very small world, as I have since discovered, and it is very easy to identify your own story – no matter how much it has been disguised in the telling.

We were also encouraged to listen with our hearts rather than our ears, and to make a mental note of what triggers our feelings. This, they said, was because everything that makes us feel – both in a positive and in a negative way – is directly or symbolically connected to our own 'unfinished business'. This could be caused by somebody else's story – which may be very different to what we think we have come to work on – or it might be a particular song or an old movie. They are all keys that unlock those doors.

On hearing this I caught my breath, because the only movies that ever brought tears to my eyes were those that ended with a scene in which lovers, who had been parted by death, were reunited as ghosts; *Wuthering Heights* with Merle Oberon and Laurence Olivier being a prime example. Now that may seem an obvious trigger for me in the circumstances, but I had been like that with those particular movies for as long as I could remember. What part of me knew, all those years before, that this would be one of the major experiences of my life? I was quite shaken.

As people began to introduce themselves, I began to realise that the room was full of people in as much pain as I was. Some had life-threatening illnesses, many were bereaved in some way and others were healthcare professionals who were looking for better ways to help their dying patients, but were also hurting in their own right. There is no hierarchy of pain.

One man in particular caught my eye and in an exchange of glances we both knew, instinctively, that we each had something for the other. He turned out to be a Vietnam veteran who, because of a sudden posting, had been unable to bring his old command of a hundred combat soldiers, his 'buddies', out of a major siege; he could only sit there listening to the body counts on the field radio. His story touched me deeply. But when he later screamed out, 'I should have been there, I could have saved them!' the concrete around my heart started to crack. They were *my* words.

This level of assault on my emotions continued, almost without let-up, until halfway through the third day when the dam finally broke. The flood was sudden and unstoppable. I had watched a continuous stream of participants, many of them bereaved mothers, crying for their babies, supported lovingly by members of the workshop team as their own individual dams broke. I had also watched those same people coming through at the other end of their 'work', shining and elated. That in itself made me feel safe enough to have my own feelings.

It was also to do with the anonymity found within a crowd. As I had travelled that far, I was able to share my story with people who had no preconceived ideas about me or my family, who had not read my story in a newspaper and were not likely to discuss my story outside our group, because they also valued, and had been provided with, the safe space in which to share their own.

As it turned out, I hardly used 'the hose' at that workshop – except on some particularly upsetting front pages from the *Sun* newspaper, the remains of which were ritually burnt at a fire ceremony on the last evening. I spent most of the time crying, not only for my sons and their mother, but also for the loss of my own life that would have been. I need not have been concerned about getting up in front of the whole group, because when I was ready, *nothing* was going to stop me. Unfortunately, at the point I finally threw myself on to the mattress, already howling, Jack, the facilitator leading the session, looked at his watch and called the break for lunch.

'Aarrgh!!!'

Luckily one of the other staff helped me to the backroom to work through the break in private. With all the grieving I did, there was little energy left to express any anger. That would have to come later.

When I finally got to the canteen, everybody cheered and applauded: my suitcase containing not only my clothes but all my 'props' had finally arrived. Now I could tell my story and *show* people what it was like to be hounded and to have the ones you love be victimised by the press, to go through such an experience. So, after lunch, that's exactly what I did.

There is much one can say about Elisabeth Kübler-Ross, but I can only speak here about what was relevant to me then. It was, for me, like the meeting of a kindred spirit, an old friend. Of course I cannot speak for Elisabeth. But what most impressed me was the fact that although many people, including myself, were in awe of her, she was very ordinary, a 'practical Swiss with a sceptical, scientific mind'. It was as if the guru status imposed on her was of no interest; she happily sat and talked about the pain in her own life – the 'wind-storms' – as a way of illustrating what she had to teach.

That was the style adopted by all her staff; that one cannot accompany another person into those dark places in their lives if we have never explored and dealt with the similar ones in our own. If ever our own unfinished business is not dealt with, either the process itself or a member of staff will soon bring it to our attention. This is a philosophy that none of us are excluded from – including Elisabeth; she is just as human as the rest of us, as I have found more and more as I have come to know her.

But that day, I was in awe.

She spoke about the 'inner Hitler' that we all have inside, and that when we get in touch with that part of ourselves – and allow it to scream and rage – we will also begin to find our 'Mother Teresa', the part of us that is totally compassionate and capable of 'Unconditional Love'. What most impressed me, however, was how she and her staff spoke a lot of basic psychological truths, but in a language that even a child could understand; that we have purposeful natural emotions, 'God-given gifts' that get distorted by our upbringing and past hurts.

When we are not allowed to grieve, for example, to cry and talk about what happened to us, we end up with a reservoir of repressed tears and self-pity; feeling as if we are a victim and blaming everybody else for all our hurts. Depression also lives here. Self-styled martyrdom was another distortion: trying to make others feel as though we ourselves are blameless; my God, that one touched a raw nerve. And finally, shame: when we believe it really *is* our fault, that, in some way, we ourselves really *are* to blame. And below distorted grief there is often anger: anger that we have not been allowed to express ourselves or grieve properly; that we have not had our needs met and maybe never have.

In every workshop, according to Elisabeth, there is always at least one potential mass murderer waiting to explode. But once the unique sound of that rage has come out, the danger will have passed for good. 'It's like Mozart to my ears!' she said enthusiastically.

I was beginning to crumble by this point, realising I had far more to do than I was prepared to admit. Would I survive the lecture without crawling under the floorboards? I then noticed that others were suffering just as much as I was. This was raw stuff indeed, but worth listening to.

Jealousy was the 'natural emotion' I had the most trouble with –. and it took a long time before I even began to get a handle on it. Much to my surprise, it has also turned out to be one of the most important: like many before me, I really couldn't understand how it could ever be regarded as a positive emotion. To me, it was an adolescent condition that ruled and destroyed my relationships well into my early thirties – whereas all the others felt more like adult emotions. But if we look at the purpose of jealousy, it is possible to see why it deserves a place.

The purpose of jealousy is **to identify what we want.** It is a stimulus to identify what is missing in our lives. Another quality of it might be admiration – the desire to emulate. It is how we learn.

Often we may be jealous of a person because they have skills, perhaps material things or qualities that we'd like, and this can be very useful as a way to identify them. Sometimes, early on in our lives, we have teachers as mentors, or people we admire – and there is some jealousy there. We would like to be a teacher, just like them. We would like to have their qualities. In my own case, for example, I had a lot of admiration for both Herbie and Nevill, because they were successful self-made men who were not afraid to stand up and be counted; not afraid to play the clown and appear foolish in public. These were qualities I admired – was jealous of. Whether these men were driven by courage or by fear is quite irrelevant here – it is the qualities or skills that really matter.

On the other hand, if we get into the distortions, we are judging or envying them. And because of that we are also being critical of ourselves. It is a distortion of jealousy to lose our self-esteem, to have no self-esteem at all. We find ourselves competing and comparing – judging ourselves – and through that we always end up losing in some way.

I put these men on a pedestal, but in doing that I also put myself down below them; I didn't think I could ever achieve the same stature. They ceased to be human beings and became icons of my aspirations. Comparing and judging myself, I was beaten before I began; old messages ever flooding my mind: you're too shy; you haven't got the guts; you've got no sense of humour; you're just an ordinary person; you're too nice (that was a really hard one for me); you're just like your father, and so on.

During the coming years, as I continued on my journey, I slowly began to realise that I didn't have to be everything Herbie and Nevill were. In a way, they personified some of the more positive aspects of my Shadow. By looking back at them, at their individual qualities, I could begin to learn from or call upon each of those qualities, one at a time – as and when I needed to. I would imagine how *they* might deal with a certain situation and emulate them until I found my own style, my own way which is inherently me.

Very briefly, there are only two natural fears: falling and loud noises. The rest are given to us by grown-ups. Some are useful, but in their distorted forms, they become all our phobias, panics and anxiety attacks.

The last natural emotion was love; what many would call the 'Divine Principle'. It's that part of us that tells the whole world who we are from the very centre of our being. It's all about nurturing and relating, giving and receiving unconditionally, without any strings attached – something I have already talked about at length; the kind of love we need and should get simply because we are alive. The love that can also say, No!

'But LOVE,' said Elisabeth in her inimitable Swiss–German accent, 'is also our biggest problem!'

She talked about how we 'prostitute' ourselves. A really strong word, but if you think about it, it's the way in which we bargain away bits and pieces of ourselves and are then left with very little. We give away so much of ourselves – pretending in order to receive love – that we don't know who we are any more. Pretending we don't feel something when we really do. If we do that year after year, as many of us do, there is hardly anything authentic left. In my life, I began to recognise it in many forms: being a good boy and not throwing tantrums in order to keep my parents' love is one example of where it started.

Other distortions Elisabeth mentioned were: possessiveness, which is also a distortion of jealousy; an insatiable need for love and affirmation; clinging; expectations and, with that, disappointment; manipulation and controlling; poor boundaries, and, of course, conditional love – where we hear things that sound like, 'I'll love you IF . . .' For example, when we are children we get messages from our parents, either actual verbal or subtle non-verbal ones, like: 'I'll love you if you do well in your exams.' Or, 'I'll love you if you don't get angry.' Or, 'I'll love you if I can say my son or daughter the doctor, the successful businessman or the famous artist . . .'

There is also another version which the child *really* hears when we say such things and that is: 'I will *not* love you *if* you don't behave yourself,' or, 'I will *not* love you *if* you keep hitting your sister.' Then comes the pay-off or bribe: 'I'll buy you some sweets if you do,' or something like that. How many of us know that one? Later in life it became for me: 'If you get married, we'll buy you a nice flat wherever you like.' And then – to put the lid on it – came the guilt trip: 'We're not doing it for you, we're doing it for the child.'

Which brings us right back to prostitution. It took a long time before I began to recognise and accept *that* pattern in my life. But when I first heard all this, I sat there squirming. In my arrogance (a side of myself I have also only just begun to recognise), I thought I had already come so far. But that illusion was rapidly fading.

Elisabeth spoke about many things that afternoon, most of which can be found in her numerous inspiring books: care of the dying; the death experience, based on extensive research into 'near death experiences', and also her own evidence of life after death. Much of this was connected to her work with terminally ill children and the evidence they left behind in the pictures they made shortly before death. Having read so much about her work with children's drawings, this was in fact my main reason for wanting to meet her.

Over the years, Elisabeth had looked at literally thousands of pictures, concluding that, on some intuitive level, the children not only knew how they were going to die (depicting exactly where the illness occurred in their bodies), but also how long they had left to live. So much so, their own unconscious prognosis was usually far more accurate than their physician's.

Drawing on the extensive research by Dr Susan Bach, an ex-student of Carl Jung's living in London, this had been assessed by learning to read various symbolic indicators that perennially occur in drawings. But what most intrigued me was the fact that, through using these indicators, Elisabeth had also seen many examples of drawings which predicted the issue of sudden or accidental death. My earlier conversations with Gregg Furth about the twins' drawings had suggested this, but Elisabeth's discussion that afternoon confirmed it for me.

Daniel and Nicholas left me with many pictures but two in particular, by Nicholas, have become very special treasures indeed. One – made the day of our house-warming party, four days before he was killed, depicted the three of us at the party. The other – rediscovered some time after I decided on the title of this book – depicted a beautiful rainbow beneath which a number of ladybirds were climbing a tree towards it. The trunk of the tree in this picture (the 'tree' motif is in both) is dissected immediately above the sixth pair of branches by a blue line representing the sky.

When Gregg saw this, he pointed out that when a line cuts across what he described as a 'Tree of Life', it is usually significant. But when that line also represents the sky, this may well be to do with a movement or transition between heaven and earth – from life to death. He then asked how old the twins were. When I told him they were six years old, he pointed out that two of the ladybirds – who were climbing the tree way ahead of all the others – were literally crossing the blue line above the sixth pair of branches.

In drawing such a bright rainbow, Nicholas also knew that everything on the other side of that line, in heaven, was good. Finally, there is a bright yellow sun (with six rays) just under the end of the rainbow on the right-hand side or east (sunrise), which often denotes the future.

As in Daniel's drawings, there were a lot of other indicators which, without verification of specific information, cannot be used as evidence. But it is interesting to note that the total number of ladybirds in the picture is twenty-eight, the age at which their mother also died. If objects are repeated in a picture, the number of repeated objects can be an indicator of units of time (past, present and future) or age. This is usually how terminally ill children have shown how much time they have left.

In the other drawing, of the party, the tree motif is this time dissected just above the fourth pair of branches by a large table filling the width of the picture. Gregg described this as an altar. The floor below it is blood-red – like it would be after a sacrifice. Nicholas has drawn me in front of the table, with no arms and my feet firmly on the ground, but he and Daniel (one of whom is wearing a dress!) are separated from me, behind it. What first grabbed my attention, however, was the fact that *their* feet were no longer touching the ground; they had already left, so to speak.

Another similarity between the two pictures is that the only use of purple (often considered the colour of spirituality) is immediately above the central Tree of Life motif in the image of a large balloon. There are many balloons in this picture, five of which are attached to red streamers coming from the top of the page, from heaven (significant in itself, in that there were five victims), but only one balloon is purple.

Again, like all the other pictures, there is a great deal more information within it than is relevant to the point I want to make, which is: that, on some unconscious or intuitive level, those two little boys knew exactly what was going to happen to them, and when.

As a final note on drawing interpretation, Elisabeth said that we must NEVER go home and start trying to analyse our own family's drawings. It not only takes years to learn, but to do so would be an invasion of privacy, and abusive: 'I will haunt anybody who does this!'

With dead children's drawing, one can perhaps be excused, but it is important to be aware that such an exploration might uncover things about which we really don't want to know – as I found with Daniel's book. Fortunately, by the time I began to realise the potential significance of those drawings, I was better equipped to deal with the pain.

* * *

I left the workshop both lighter and heavier. The greater adventure, to face my own inner demons, had really begun. As an unexpected bonus, I was invited to New York for the weekend, before I flew home. In learning to say 'No!' I was also learning to say 'Yes! I am going to have some fun! I am going to take some risks! It is good to be alive!'

CHAPTER TWENTY-FIVE

How little a person knows what is in himself. To see all the fissures and fractures, to throw light into the dark cavities, to see the landscape of a mind and recognise no part of it but know that it is yours is a fearful and disturbing thing.

Brian Keenan, Beirut hostage

Don't turn your head.
Keep looking at the bandaged place.
That's where the light enters you.

Rumi

M Y 'WORK' AT that first workshop was only the tip of the iceberg, in that the dam of grief had burst, but the waters of that flood, having washed clean the open wounds, now settled into an enormous lake in which all sorts of terrible monsters lurked unseen. Monsters that were a part of me.

It was not until my third workshop that I finally experienced that dark, destructive, murderous part of myself that I had refused to acknowledge until then – or rather, it burst out of me in what I now know to be a 'homicidal rage' that scared the living daylights out of me. But in that moment of total darkness, I also knew and began to understand the mind of a murderer and got a sense of what was going on inside him or her; all the ugly, brutal, vengeful feelings that had been lurking inside me for God knows how long.

I can't remember who I 'killed' – in the symbolic sense – but something really huge had shifted in me. It was as if, in releasing that part of me, in giving it a voice and physical expression, the rest of my anger became far more manageable; it no longer had a terrifying tail on it. And the more I did this, the more I became able to express myself fully without fear of going over the top.

But the best part, that afternoon, was when I came out at the other end of it. I saw the most amazing sight. Rather than opening my eyes to find frightened people hiding or turning away in disgust, I found the whole group gathered around me; watching and smiling and loving me, all there giving love and support. I had let the beast out and survived.

From then on, I made a personal commitment to learning more about the whole process and found myself drawn to others with similar experiences – especially to the Vietnam veterans, who had been branded by the American public as 'child murderers'. I have since spoken to many.

Something in me needed to look into the eyes of people who had taken the lives of other human beings – in the same way that they possibly needed to look into the eyes of a murder victim's parent; to see our own reflections. And through that I began to recognise all the different faces of *my* Shadow in my projections and judgement of others.

Before I came to that place, however, and the decision to undergo Elisabeth's training, a great deal more than I have yet mentioned had already happened. By then, I thought I had all the answers, but I still wanted to know more about Jeremy, as a person. In my arrogance and naïvety, I also thought he might be willing to talk to me about his childhood and life.

It was almost as if he wasn't real to me any more and I needed to get him back into a human frame. Through looking at Jeremy as a personification of my own darkness, I had dehumanised him in much the same way as his family had: Uncle Bobby, for example, only ever refers to him now as 'Prisoner L12373'. In the press, such dehumanisation takes the form of descriptions like, 'This evil monster'.

Such projection, and hence denial, of our own negativity on others – or in my own case, immersion in it – effectively takes us away from reality, from the truth. I may have begun to learn a lot about myself, but I still knew very little about Jeremy. In trying to understand him as a human being, through owning my own Shadow, I was still caught up in the duality of shame and blame.

It was really my unnatural responses that first made me apportion blame – as a way of avoiding my own conditioned shame – and the fact that, on some level, I believed it really must be my fault. My initial blaming was a way of avoiding that fact. It had seemed to me that I had only two options: either to beat myself up, or to point my finger at somebody else who fitted that image. Another option, which was not then apparent to me, was to step outside of it altogether and tell myself that I don't have to identify with either. That's not easy.

There are also times we have very good reason to blame or feel shame: my handling of our marriage breakdown would be a perfect example – and there would be occasions that it would bubble to the surface again, as I was soon to discover. But how I deal with it within myself is what changes.

Anyway, I decided to write to Jeremy at Wormwood Scrubs, where he had been imprisoned since the trial, in the hope that he might furnish me with some of the last pieces of the jigsaw puzzle – and in a sense he did – but I was far from prepared for his response. It brought me back to reality with a jolt. It was written on 16 August 1988:

DEAR COLIN

I READ THE ARTICLE IN YESTERDAY'S INDEPENDENT WITH MUCH SADNESS, THE SAME SADNESS I ALWAYS FEEL WHEN I READ ABOUT YOU AND WHAT YOU'VE BEEN THROUGH IN THE LAST THREE YEARS.

YOUR LETTER TODAY, COLIN, WAS I'M AFRAID A TOUCH PREMATURE. YOUR WRITING TO ME HOPING, I GUESS, FOR THE LAST FEW PIECES OF THE JIGSAW SO THAT YOU MAY HOLD THE PICTURE OF WHAT HAPPENED IS NOT POSSIBLE.

The rest of the letter, continuing in the same block capital style for another two pages or so, was an assertion – at times seemingly taunting – that his appeal would be successful and that he would prove his innocence, even suggesting that I should doubt the media reports about him in the same way I questioned the tabloid smears about

Sheila. I had almost forgotten how convincing and seductive Jeremy could be. His directness and almost sickly sincerity shocked me. He even signed off the letter with:

LOVE JEREMY
P.S. I TRULY WISH I COULD HELP YOU.

Initially, I almost began to believe him, to believe that he was innocent, and I quickly had to remind myself of all the evidence: that, regardless of her heavily tranquillised state, Bambs had never used a gun and could never have fired so many bullets so accurately – especially with her parents as moving targets. There has to be tremendous naïvety or an ulterior motive in anybody who wants to believe she could.

I also couldn't help but notice that the entire letter – in fact nearly all of his letters that have appeared in the tabloid press over the years – have been written in block capitals. I know nothing about graphology, but the use of such handwriting very much seems to represent Jeremy's need to be believed; that if he says something both clearly visible and plain enough, he *will* be believed.

Not long after this, and shortly before I went to America for the workshop, I was introduced to a BBC television producer, who planned to make an *Everyman* programme on the subject of forgiveness. This meeting came about through my contact with the National Association of Victim Support Schemes, with whom I was guest speaker on volunteer training days of the Home Office-backed 'Families of Murder Victims Project'.

It was a question that often came up, especially since I had spoken on a *Kilroy* programme *against* the reinstatement of capital punishment about to be debated in Parliament: could I ever forgive Jeremy? And what would that mean to me?

After several lengthy discussions, I agreed to take part and the film was made within weeks of my return. It consisted of my own story and three others and was a great success. I won't go into the discussion here, because there is no total answer. I can conceive of the possibility of forgiveness, as an attainable ideal, but it is not something that is possible until we have faced and dealt with all our emotional unfinished business connected with the hurts and violations that have been inflicted upon us.

If and when forgiveness happens, it happens spontaneously, not because the Church has told us to. The Christian philosophy, that we *must* forgive, is a terrible and almost impossible burden for any of us. In a double-page interview in the *Radio Times*, shortly before the programme was screened, I described forgiveness as having 'given up my claim on revenge'.

This printed report alone brought a very sudden response. The next day another letter arrived from Jeremy, a very angry letter in which he touched every doubt and raw nerve in my body; one that was so painful to read, I couldn't show it to anyone until very recently. Having been brought up in such a similar emotional climate, Jeremy's ability to shame me was quite horrifying. Those who have been shamed are usually the greatest shamers:

SCRUBS PRISON, WEDNESDAY [2 FEBRUARY 1989]

DEAR COLIN,
    SO YOU DECIDED NOT TO REPLY TO MY LETTER. I WONDER WHY? MAYBE IT'S BECAUSE YOU CAN'T FACE THE TRUTH THAT I DID NOT KILL YOUR CHILDREN OR SHEILA OR MUM OR DAD. HOW SAD, COLIN, THAT YOU CAN'T DISTINGUISH REALITY FROM MEDIA HYPE.

The letter continued in this vein for several paragraphs, accusing me of having made myself *'A COG IN THE MEDIA WHEEL'* – *'POURING OUT* (my) *GRIEF TO ANY FILM CREW'* and intimating that the timing was almost a deliberate attempt to confound his appeal. That first part of the letter didn't cause me too much pain. I could bear the criticism. But what followed cut me to the bone.

His voice and that of the judging, criticising part of me became one. But underneath that, it was also the voice of not only his mother, but every judging, controlling woman I had ever met – my own internalised negative female. The part of me that I could not defend myself against or say 'No' to.

It reminds me very much of that part in the Grail legend when the Hideous Damsel, having ridden into the celebration of Parsifal's greatest triumph – in my own case, feeling I had completed my journey and hence the book – then recites all of his sins and their consequences, in detail:

> GO AND ENJOY YOUR CELEBRITY STATUS. MAYBE YOU'LL BE ON WOGAN NEXT AND CAN ADVERTISE YOUR BOOK AND SCULPTURES THAT WAY – HOW YOU CAN CHEAPEN DANIEL AND NICHOLAS AND THEIR TRAGIC DEATH I JUST DON'T KNOW . . .

In his opinion – and those of many others, I am sure – I was using the shootings for my own ends: 'PRETENDING ITS GRIEF COUNSELLING'. Intensifying his savage character assassination, he went on to say, 'I HOPE YOU LOVE YOURSELF, IN FACT I BET YOU DO', and then suggested that it was my fault that Bambs 'WENT MAD AND KILLED EVERYONE.

> YOU KNEW SHE WOULD BREAK UNDER THE STRAIN OF BRINGING UP A FAMILY ON HER OWN – YOU DIDN'T CARE FOR YOUR CHILDREN EVEN IN THE WOMB . . .

And so he continued for another page or so. The only thing that made it bearable to read was the fact that, in his damning accusations – the truth of which I would eventually have to face and deal with within myself – he was also giving a very good description of his own attitudes and desires. One might never find a better example of the Shadow being projected on to another person. The hardest part has been to type it up. I could still feel the venom coming off the pages.

Again, he has written in block capitals but apparently very fast, which is actually very hard to do. He concluded:

> YOU'VE DONE ME MUCH HARM WITH YOUR SELFISH USE OF THE MEDIA SO I'D USE THE SAME TO GET MY OWN BACK. LOOK FORWARD TO AN ARTICLE SOON

COLIN MAY IT PRICK YOUR CONSCIENCE IF YOU HAVE ONE, YOUR NOTHING BUT A LEACH JUST THINK WHAT YOUR FEEDING OFF
WITH VERY MUCH SADNESS
JEREMY

The full impact of the letters and their subtle nuances that give a rare insight into the nature of Jeremy Bamber's character cannot be easily described here without quoting the text of the letters in their entirety, which space and other considerations preclude me from doing here.

Suffice to say, however, their effect on me was profound, and it is only as I write this piece, more than four and a half years later, that I am only just beginning to realise that I have finally reached the point where I can say, with all honesty, 'I have dealt with those accusations.' Or at least those that truly applied. Writing it here has been the final catharsis. Had I not faced them, I could never get the book out in this form, nor do the work I am now doing.

Much as Parsifal had to accept the Hideous Damsel's quest to set his sins to right and rediscover the Grail castle, I had to participate in Jeremy's challenge and go back to face all those denied shadowy parts of myself. Back then, however, I did not want to look behind me, but I could feel the ground begin to crack and open . . .

Clasp hand in hand, keep face to face,
Whilst here below
The bridge formed by our arms embrace
The waters of our longing pass.
Night may come and clock may sound,
Within your shadow I am bound.
And like this bridge our passions flow,
Our love goes by;
The violence hope dare not show
Follows time's beat which now falls slow.
Night may come and clock may sound,
Within your shadow I am bound.

From 'The Mirabeau Bridge'
by Apollinaire

CHAPTER TWENTY-SIX

A DREAMED SEQUENCE WRITTEN on BA flight 145 to Bombay, 22 February 1989:

A blinding flash briefly interrupted a playful dream and found two small points of light becoming aware of each other. They were floating somewhere near the ceiling of a tiny room. It was dark. There were several more loud cracks, like those that had accompanied the flash, and then silence.

The shadow of a man slipped quietly out of the room.

As was so often the case they had been out playing with each other in their dreams but now there was an odd feeling of detachment, an expansive feeling that somehow felt different to the dream. Two small boys lay sleeping below them.

Out of curiosity they followed the shadow – dancing and teasing around each other – out through the door, along the narrow hallway past the dark well of the stairs and into the main bedroom . . .

At the speed of a single thought images of brutality were lost in the comforting glow of loved ones, angels and three more points of light, spinning in silent confusion. A father cried in his girlfriend's arms, sunflowers swayed in the warm night air and friends slept peacefully in the safety of their own beds.

All was seen by the unseen.

Nothing was missed in the darkless . . .

Within a week or so of receiving Jeremy's letter, Jill and I decided to get away for a while. I had not told her of the letter or its contents, so she had no idea that in my sudden desire to visit India, part of me was running from what I knew I had to face.

This was to be one of many outward journeys embarked upon spontaneously as a way of easing my inner conflicts. But each time it always brought me closer to the next piece; towards a greater under-standing of myself and my relationship to the world. It was as if, in having made that commitment to myself to face my fears, I couldn't run away, even if I tried; there was no getting off the plane until the end of the journey – until the end of the quest, whenever that happens to be. To do so, symbolically speaking, would mean certain death.

So what was I looking for?

Peace? It certainly wasn't death, in the literal sense. I had been exploring that for the last three and a half years and would continue to do so, as a way of gaining a greater understanding about life. If anything, I was looking for a way back into life. So was it courage? The strength to stand up and be seen as I am – warts and all. Was it recognition, respect? I knew I would have to earn those. Was it even the Grail itself, the crock of gold at the end of the rainbow? And what does that mean? Are they the same thing? In the legend according to Chrétien de Troyes – which is the earliest known written-down version, the story ends before the Grail is found. It is left for each of us to find and define for ourselves.

My reason for choosing the 'Rainbow' title goes back to my second session with Betty, a few months after the trial; a session in which Bambs came through with some very intimate and personal messages. The communication ended with a request for me to put a rainbow in my book.

'She is giving me a rainbow,' said Betty, 'and she's saying something about the pot of gold at the rainbow's end. This seems to be nothing to do with the twins, but to do with you two. I can see it so clearly, it's brilliant and beautiful – almost as though, at the end of that . . . that's where all the secrets are. And now she's saying to you, "Do have a rainbow in your book, do have a rainbow . . ."'

So what else could be driving me? Because that's how it felt some of the time.

Fear. Such a small word, but even alone it can begin to agitate the breathing and set the heart pumping faster. Added to other words, of our own choosing, it can become totally debilitating: fear of rejec-tion, of not being loved or of falling in love; fear of abandonment; fear of responsibility, success or failure; fear of not being rich or attractive; fear of spiders, rats or snakes; fear of the unknown; fear of being overwhelmed by all the other natural emotions – anger, grief, jealousy and love; fear of fear.

Desperate attempts to control others' actions are all born out of fear, *and* we do everything we can to avoid facing them. I couldn't help but notice how quickly I passed over the subject earlier in the book. Some part of me needed to prove I was fearless, not just to the world outside but to myself. Fear underlies all. It influences, to some degree, nearly every decision we have to make in life and most of those fears we learn at a very early age. As the mechanism which controls our fight or flee responses, some fears are useful, most are not.

I was to have a number of very powerful dreams during this time; dreams that stretched and opened me up to the greater possibilities, and to my own fears. One in particular, a few days before our trip to India, began in a classroom . . .

The purpose of the class was to learn about the needs of the whole person: body, mind and spirit. The scene changed . . .

Underwater, diving in tropical seas with Nick Flowers and one other male. Very deep water – over a hundred feet – many large colourful fish, exquisite. Rising past an underwater cliff, looking in holes, I saw, to my horror, the large severed hand of a Negro. I was very distressed by this and swam rapidly to the surface, where I found myself back in the classroom. Still shaking with fear, I quickly tore off the wetsuit, wrapped myself in a large towel and went to the changing room, where I met a very beautiful woman: brunette, very stunning and not unlike Bambs.

I was given the insight that she had a strong distrust of men and that she believed she had destroyed the part she didn't like, forever. I had another insight that she had failed in this because she had only hidden it away. I then realised that the changing room was only a façade and that it hid another one, behind the badly hung wallpaper. I tore that down to find the entrance to another changing room. I knew, then, that whatever she thought she had destroyed was still alive in there. That room, I then realised, concealed another identical one, and so on for seven changing rooms.

When I eventually broke through the final wall, I found a small boy in a red dressing-gown, pyjamas and slippers, who I recognised as part of myself. He was about eight years old. I hugged him and the dream ended.

I realise now that this dream had to have some connection with my family's slave origins – or at least, how I perceived them; the severed hand and frantic removal of my wetsuit, which was like a black skin, carrying most of the psychic energy. But this wasn't fully understood until much later, when I was reminded of the biblical reference to the sins of the fathers being visited upon seven generations. The seven changing rooms then began to tie in, but the beautiful woman remained an enigma until a few months later, when I made my first ever visit to the National Portrait Gallery in London.

At the far end of one of the rooms was a painting of a very beautiful young woman; dark and seductive. I was captivated by her eyes, she had the look of many of my girlfriends, especially Bambs and Jan. The woman's name, on close inspection, was Lady Colin Campbell, a descendant of my ancestor's keeper.

Seeing her really unnerved me. I began to wonder how many attitudes, beliefs and standards we pass on from generation to generation, our desires – even between servants and their masters – and how each generation tries to either complement or compensate for the last. I finally began to see and understand all the fears I had acquired from my childhood, but to accept that the essence of those influences, filtered through from more distant ancestors, was beyond my imagination. But it also made sense; how we are unconsciously drawn to people who, as lovers, friends and colleagues, help us to maintain and reinforce those influences.

Was the lady in the painting, who I have come to know as 'The Woman in Black', typical of the type of woman admired in the line of Sir Colin Campbell? Living between 1858 and 1911, she was the wife of a later Colin Campbell. And if that is so, could one of my own beshackled ancestors have admired or idolised a similar beautiful woman of the Campbell family? I know, when I brought Bambs home to meet my parents, I also brought home my father's 'fairy-tale princess'. He has grieved her loss even more than me.

⋆　　⋆　　⋆

During the months following the *Everyman* programme, I was approached by a literary agent and an art dealer with whom my dealings were premature in both cases. Neither my book nor the sculptural work was ready for the commercial world, but that didn't stop me from trying. A part of me was enjoying the attention and potential celebrity status implicit in our dealings. Jeremy had not been far wrong. I was still relying on my old ways of getting my needs met, which were a form of prostitution. Getting love and affection, attention, through other people's interest in my story. Sympathy. The realisation, when it came, turned my stomach over.

I suppose this was really hammered home when I was invited to join Jill at a wedding reception in May that year. She had given me an address in Holland Park, but when I drove into the car park, I suddenly realised that I had not only been there before – only once – but it had been the very evening I first met the Flowers family: Herbie's record company had organised a reception to celebrate the end of Sky's first tour after their concert at the Royal Albert Hall. I had been given the invitation by *Billboard* magazine, which I worked for then, and had met Jan for the first time only a day or two earlier.

That in itself might not seem unusual, but by the time I'd found Jill (at the wedding reception), I had also worked out that it was ten years almost exactly to the day!

I felt that crack in the ground behind me suddenly yawn into a great chasm that represented all those years and found myself teetering on the edge, desperately trying not to fall back in – back into the abyss. It was as if some part of me had reached up out of the ground and dragged me down into it. But at least it was part of me this time. I also had a very strong lifeline: the workshops.

I was no fun to have at a party. I spent the rest of the evening in shock as every event from the day I met Jan passed through my mind's eye. All the joy and tears, the pain of partings, guilt, shame and the realisation that I'd relied on so many people to prop me up financially, or rescue me when I was quite capable of fending for myself – especially Herbie and my mother. I couldn't believe it was happening. It seemed I had no choice but to go back and look at how I had learned those ways to survive; who taught me these things and how? It was something I could no longer ignore. It was also time for me to do another workshop – in fact, several!

That next Kübler-Ross workshop, a three-day Intensive which happened to be in London, was the beginning of my exploration of more conventional issues common to therapy: grief over lost opportunities; anger at parents – at Mum for holding me too tight, for over-protecting me, and at Dad for not being strong enough to intervene on my behalf, so that I might get an occasional bloody nose from a fight. They had created what Robert Bly calls a 'New-Age wimp' – the kind of man who would always need strong women around to look after him – and I no longer felt good about that.

In time, however, I came to recognise that I had in fact been very lucky with my parents; that my father, especially, had given me everything he could. He had taught me everything he knew, but in my thirst for knowledge, which he also gave me, I was left wanting. Although I could not blame him for that, the feelings I had about it then were very real and had to be dealt with before I could see the truth. He is now a man I am once again very, very proud of. But it took me quite a while to get back to that.

My first thoughts about doing Elisabeth's training came about at that second workshop when Phyllida, one of the staff trainees, suggested I think about it. I was surprised, because I thought I needed to be qualified in some way but she said no, that it was Elisabeth's policy to recruit anyone who is willing to grow and face their own darkness. Those who are not up to it fall by the wayside fairly quickly. Elisabeth uses the analogy of a tumbling machine into which we are all put as rough stones. It is our own choice whether we come out 'crushed or polished'.

The training is therefore long, tough and experiential, but the most rewarding thing I have ever done. That commitment to your own process and work is essential and never-ending. The work would not be possible without it. And that's what makes it so special, in that the staff have all been into their own darkness time and time again and, in doing that, are able to symbolically hold another's hand as they explore theirs.

When Elisabeth later announced that she had found a prison in Scotland that was willing to host one of her workshops, I volunteered immediately. This was something else my father had never encouraged. As far as he was concerned, volunteering was risky business – but I was finding it very exciting. It was taking me into places I had never imagined, with people who could give me that part of my education that had always been missing. Rather than growing new pieces of myself, I was rediscovering bits that had been mislaid.

It was wonderful! I began to feel whole in a way that I'd never felt before. And it was all to do with trust and a real belief that anything was possible if I really put my mind to it. This kind of invincible thinking lined me up for what would become one of the major initiations of my training: six workshops in five weeks, back to back.

I went from staffing a three-day training in London to a five-day workshop in Scotland, which then led straight into another five days at Saughton Prison in Edinburgh. From there I flew to Texas, where I spent nine days in a psychiatric hospital (assisting, not recovering!) and then on to California, where I took part in a men's abuse workshop as a participant. This was led by Sharon Tobin, another of Elisabeth's staff with whom I had worked a number of times, and then, finally, straight into a women's abuse workshop – again as a staff trainee.

Out of thirty participants on that last workshop, roughly one-third of them were survivors of satanic cult and ritual abuse – my first real experience of this. If anything, that workshop was harder than the prison, but ultimately very rewarding. It would be difficult to weigh against any other experience the satisfaction of seeing horribly victimised people begin to regain their power over the terror of brainwashing, torture, human sacrifice and enforced cannibalism; activities forced upon them as small children by powerful and so-called respectable people.

I do not have concrete evidence of this as such, but to have witnessed the violent body memories and level of terror in these people, I have no doubts whatsoever that they believe it exists and that they were victimised as a result of it. Whether this dark ritual magic works or not, I have no idea, but a belief that it does fuels these terrible sadistic practices and that has to stop!

Sad to say, these activities are not limited to the United States, I have no more illusions about that. Whatever the truth of these allegations, the undeniable truth is that children are being harmed all over the world, all the time, and need our love and protection, not abuse in any form.

CHAPTER TWENTY-SEVEN

In Memoriam
Heidi Koseda

It wasn't our fault, it wasn't theirs,
so nobody was to blame;
but the banner headlines screamed aloud
to expose the fearful shame.
And the public thrilled vicariously
to the evil in this world,
and they poured out their shocked pity
for the sake of one poor girl.
And they vilified the monster,
not part of the human race;
but they never stopped to think how
it could have taken place.

And the girl who had died so wretchedly
has failed to make them see
that the monster that they hate so much
could have been you . . . or me?

George Smith

*Heidi's stepfather was convicted of killing her the same day as George was
given a life sentence for murder. He wrote this poem two years later in an
attempt to recapture his own feelings that day, when Heidi's story filled the
headlines.*

I DIDN'T KNOW WHAT to expect when we arrived at Saughton Prison, yet it was everything I imagined it would be: cold, harsh, grey and Victorian on the outside, razor-sharp barbed wire everywhere, and stiflingly hot on the inside; bars on all the windows. I had many fears inside my body and a need to do some of my own work before we met the participants the next morning. But I knew I was meant to be there; of that I had no doubts.

During the previous workshop, I had come to love and deeply respect one of the female staff that I had never met before. She was a small, grey-haired woman with a beauty that heralded the Cherokee blood which made up an essential and sacred part of her ancestry. There was something of the shaman in her. In time, Bobbi was to become another of my 'Sisters' in the very deep spiritual sense that I would not even attempt to explain here. I've met several on the journey. Right then, however, I just felt she was the best person for what I needed to do.

We had tried to make some time before we left the previous workshop, but that didn't work out, so we had to set things up for a session during the prison briefing. To Elisabeth's mind, my personal 'mattress work' was far more important: 'It is mandatory!'

As ever in this process, we always get what we need at the right time, because the piece of work Bobbi pushed me through – 'push' being the operative word because it was a fight from start to finish – was all to do with what I would call my own 'inner prisoner'. That part of me that had kept me locked into all the old dysfunctional ways that no longer served me – a side that was actually making Bobbi feel sick! The weak, publicity-seeking part of me I still hadn't fully recognised: the 'prostitute'. My God, did she lean heavily on me!

She said that while I still held that in front of me, inside me (there were actually some press clippings on the mattress), I would always dance to other people's tunes: the tunes of the media, the influential and all those I have believed better than me; I would never dance to my own tune!

At that moment, looking at the bars in the windows and all the barbed wire outside, something changed in me and the rage finally broke from my throat. But it was not *my* voice that came out of my mouth. It seemed to be the voice of a slave – perhaps my ancestor from all those generations back. Who can say?

'I'll not dance to any white man's fucking tune any more!' he boomed, and the rage just poured out. When it was all over, Bobbi and I looked at each other, stunned. In myself, I felt that something had shifted for my entire family; that we no longer had to be the underdog, which was an attitude I had grown up with. But it also released a new level of compassion in me – for underdogs, victims and perpetrators alike. Now I was ready for the workshop.

When the group gathered the next morning, it was hard to tell, especially with the men, who were inmates and who were prison staff. There were no uniforms, no key chains or marks of office, just forty-one human beings sitting on the floor in front of us. Half of the group were inmates – many serving life for sex offences or murder, others with life-threatening illnesses. The rest of the group was made up of prison officers, social workers, chaplains, psychologists and a governor.

Elisabeth had insisted that a cross-section of the entire prison community was represented, because the work is not about fixing 'sick' or criminally violent people, but recognising that we all have wounds that are potentially destructive. There is no us or them. Our main aim was to demolish some of those barriers that keep us all separate.

The philosophy of confidentiality and respect applied to this workshop just as much as any other, so outside of my own experiences, I cannot say any more about what happened than the participants themselves have offered to share. Naturally, in the prison environment, where raw emotions are so near the surface but even less safe to bring out than in the outside world – and hence locked down tight – things got very hairy at times.

Dealing with that level of anger, that strength of feeling, a lot of buttons got pushed but slowly, very slowly, the common ground was established. For me, the scariest part of the whole workshop was not in having to facilitate the 'mattress work' of a killer, which might understandably press a few of my buttons, but to give Elisabeth's 'Drawings' talk in front of her!

I also had the gift of really appreciating, at first hand, what Elisabeth means when she says, 'In every Hitler there is a Mother Teresa, and in every Mother Teresa, a Hitler. We all have both within us.' I had understood it on an intellectual level, but had never fully experienced it outside of me, in others before. The most frequent phrase I heard from the mouths of prison officers, that also found its echo in me, was: 'There but for the Grace of God go I.'

What I saw in that room, as I do in every workshop, was a group of human beings in tremendous pain. Many of them were men like me: quiet, well-mannered and gentle. People who find it difficult to show their so-called negative feelings and always have; those who were pushed once too often by someone who had power over them (i.e. wife, neighbour, mother-in-law, boss) and snapped! A lifetime of bottled-up rage poured out of them in one terrible moment; a moment of overwhelming fear and anger: the pain of being left, bullied, laughed at, sacked or whatever.

Some grew up in violent ghetto environments, others didn't. But what they all needed, prison staff and inmate alike, was a safe and acceptable way to deal with the pain. We are all prisoners of our wounds and past hurts, the conditioning of our lives, and we all need ways in which to deal with them.

This pain will never justify the violence, never justify the crime – on that I have no reservations – but if we can begin to understand and deal with how it lives in each one of us, then there has to be a reduction in the likelihood of it recurring.

When we see television news coverage of prisoners rioting and smashing up their environment, they are showing us what they need, showing us their rage and frustration at the depravity of an environment where there is often little respect or understanding. When I see such images, I can envisage those very same people kneeling on a mattress with a length of rubber hose in their hands, screaming and smashing up old telephone directories.

Which is cheaper? A pile of old phone books or a new prison roof? Because that's what it ultimately comes down to. As things stand, there is no appropriate way for people in that environment to really process all the pain and grief of their incarceration.

Some would ask why on earth workshops like this happen at all in prison; why should offenders get therapeutic help when their victims and, in the case of murder, the victims' families get very little? I would agree, there should be more help for victims – but not at the expense of the work in prisons. It should be happening right across the board.

Like everybody else, I want the world to be a safer place in which to live, so I would much rather see violent offenders deal with all their pent-up negativity before they are released than see them leave prison carrying even more than they went in with.

It was clearly indicated by John Pearce, the prison's governor at the time, that, as a result of the workshop, he was 'acutely aware of substantial growth in a number of participants, staff and prisoners. A common perception was of people having become more assured and at peace, with a marked reduction in tendencies to get things out of proportion or to overreact. There is the potential for such workshops to be extremely valuable, both for violence in the prison setting and in the community thereafter.'

To put it another way: with that release of emotion, that finding of the common ground, comes a new level of respect, compassion, inner security and inner authority, making almost redundant much of the need for external authority and constraints. *That* is the 'magic' of workshops of this kind: they don't hide, bury or attempt to transform feelings, but deal with them directly.

To quote one participant: '. . . the rubber hose and telephone book seemed nonsense, it didn't make sense, hitting a book, yet people looked better afterwards. What really threw me was seeing a governor on the mattress . . . I respected her for the courage she had in showing her feelings, especially in front of prisoners.'

Later in the same letter, the writer said, 'I spilled my violence, my revenge, on to the telephone books and actually felt years of frustrations pouring out of my system. Images and memories were battered until there was nothing left.'

There was a moment during the later Follow-Up Intensive that I will never forget; a moment of 'holding' the group, but also having the feeling of being held; of fully realising that the dark side of a villain or murderer (the side that is not and never has been safe for them to bring out) is often tender and gentle and nurturing. These hard and often violent men (both inmates and staff) began to realise that the hard-man mask they had hidden behind all their lives doesn't have to remain nailed on; that there were others within that environment to whom they could reach out a hand for support and comfort.

It was an unbelievably moving experience made possible by the simple fact that we had provided a safe space for everyone present to express, without fear of judgement or reprisal, all their pent-up negativity – all the anger, frustration, hatred, fear and grief. As one inmate said in a letter to me: 'I cried out for all the years and years of loneliness and woke to the realisation that I was no longer alone.'

At the end of that second workshop – our third visit to Saughton – the workshop leader said that she had never in her life felt so safe in a room full of men. I can only add that I have often felt far less safe in a room full of so-called pacifists. It is only when we can find the courage to step out from behind our 'masks', our roles in society – whether that be the clergyman from behind his theology, the therapist from behind his therapeutic jargon, the reporter from behind his notepad and tape recorder or, in my own case, as a victim, from behind the tragedy – that things really begin to change. With that, almost anything is possible.

There are perennial endeavours in Parliament to reinstate capital punishment as the only effective deterrent to certain crimes. But after what happened at Jeremy's trial, with the jury reaching only a majority rather than a unanimous decision, I can only see it as an effective deterrent to jurors. People who, by law, are dumped in the unenviable position of having to decide a person's future and, if there was capital punishment, having to return a verdict which could end a defendant's life.

Police officers with vast experience of serious or violent crimes trials have described to me the regular sigh of relief that runs through a jury when, having returned a guilty verdict, the judge reads out a list of previous convictions, thereby letting them off the hook as far as their consciences are concerned. In the case of murder, it is usually the first offence and there are no previous convictions – the jury are not let off the hook so easily.

If juries are so afraid of returning a verdict which may allow a judge to pass a heavy sentence, what are they going to be like if that sentence could actually mean execution?

Had there been the death sentence, I suspect that Jeremy might have been let off, because people cannot understand how 'a nice-looking young man like him' could 'do something like that!' Even though we can see from the evidence how dangerous he is, Jeremy doesn't fit the stereotype image of a desperate killer: he is good-looking and charismatic, a character with charm, a good education and everything to live for; a man who could, and almost did, sway the hearts of the jury; a man who could easily kill again.

There is also a psychological view in that, if and when we accept the return of capital punishment, we not only further brutalise our society, but we ask one individual – the public executioner – not only to kill the convicted murderer, but also to kill the Shadow for us.

Unfortunately, that doesn't solve the problem, because until we have each dealt with the one inside – have killed or tamed it ourselves, thus breaking its spell – we will always pull that shadow energy back towards us. Not only that, but each time we ignore or try to destroy it without dealing with the internal one, it only comes back bigger and angrier than it was before. Just look at the soaring American crime rate to see what I mean.

The death sentence will never be a deterrent to a disturbed or desperate mind. If a person is pathologically dangerous – as I suspect Jeremy is – then the life sentence should mean life and nothing less.

Now that may offend some of my new friends in prisons, but a sentence has to be what it says it is, otherwise it has no meaning. What might have greater meaning, however – and thereby give meaning and purpose to the whole experience of long-term incarceration – is to begin training inmates in the same skills I have acquired, so that they can begin to help each other in a positive and purposeful way. *They* are the people who are best equipped to help others coming into the system – not social workers and psychologists (although they do serve a vital purpose) but other 'cons'.

As a final thought about Jeremy, I suspect his pain is far more complex, more convoluted than anything I experienced at Saughton. He didn't snap suddenly, nor was he driven by an uncontrollable compulsion, like many of the sex offenders. But instead, without any compunction, affect or emotion, any real sense of guilt or remorse, he planned and schemed and waited for the right moment – when he could kill everybody!

In that sense, I can see now, he really is 'evil beyond belief' and there we depart from any common ground. I am *nothing* like him and never will be. Jeremy simply served as a conduit through which I could access and begin to understand my own negative or destructive impulses.

In his book *Inside Time*, author Ken Smith described Jeremy as 'a resident monster of the public imagination, dragged out into the tabloids to rattle at the public from time to time', and as such, 'occupies a strange corner in the human psyche'.

Yes, Jeremy Bamber touches the imagination – and it's a role he carries very well for us – but let's not forget that he is also very real and very dangerous. Can we ever really risk letting him out of that role, out of prison? I very much doubt it.

PART FOUR

Coming Home

CHAPTER TWENTY-EIGHT

Way into Life

I do not doubt my strength,
It is not fear lingers me upon the beach
I know my goal at length.

You who would tempt me out at your own whim,
In vain, you waste your speech;
I am no slave, nor is my purpose dim.

Some day you'll wake and falter, unprepared,
Finding me gone whose heart you never knew,
On quests you might have shared.

So do swallows when their call is heard
Drop southward in the blue;
Marvel, complain: my heart is like a bird

Stanley Richardson

THERE CAME A time when past, present and future began to merge in my life, when the ancient archetypal world of myth, fairy tale and legend began to blend with the experience we call reality. Inner and outer were no longer so distant.

I can't really say where or how it began or even explain it in concrete terms, but there was an awareness – or rather, inner knowing – that something quite magical had been happening. That with the opening up of my world of grief and feelings – with its buried history of dreams and disappointment – I had begun to sense something 'other' in my life, something far greater; a sense of purpose that rang with clear sounds which resonated through a history of great quests and challenges. I had taken the path of initiation and survived. I also knew to the minute when that journey had ended; a powerful, almost synchronistic moment, as I wrote the final paragraphs of the last chapter; when, once again, inner and outer became one.

It was as if something had shifted, psychologically, and I no longer felt 'tied' – either to Jeremy or to the journey; as if something in me had said, 'You can go home now. The journey is over.' It seemed as if I had finally killed the dragon inside – or, at least, severed my relationship with it, because it had nothing more to teach me. I was free.

It is easy to see that, in linear time, there was nearly a year and a half between that second prison workshop and me making that final connection about Jeremy. Or rather, my disconnection with him. The decision to start on the book again was also part of that realisation, that I was indeed on my way home. It is clear, too, that a lot more happened during that time, to make that final conclusion possible. There were many more challenges to meet on the way, but this time I had the inner, psychological resources to face them.

This also didn't mean I had finished questing, but having forged my own sword and used it for its rightful purpose, I could safely put it away for a while and think of other things – other journeys that needed different, more creative tools. This 'killing' was also nothing to do with Jeremy, the press, June Bamber or anybody else that had hurt or angered me over the years. The dragon was my attachment to all my own negativity that I had been carrying around, like useless rusty armour, for so long: all the blame, judgement, shame and self-pity – even the desire for revenge.

Another clue that the journey was nearing its end came some months earlier, when I found myself watching *Conan the Barbarian* – a typically violent Arnold Schwarzenegger film – on television one evening. Now this was not the kind of movie I would normally watch, but something in the mythological theme caught me. And I am glad it did, because I found a very important piece of my own picture in it.

The story begins with the hero, as a boy, witnessing the brutal massacre of his entire family and then being sold into slavery, where he is trained as a gladiator. He eventually becomes very powerful, the best, and in winning his freedom, sets off in search of revenge.

After numerous adventures he finally catches up with the villain, an evil wizard, and is about to kill him when the wizard says something like: 'You can't kill *me* because I am your father now; I have fathered the hatred that has made you the man you are. Without me, you would never have become such a great warrior . . .' And so he goes on . . . but the hero kills him anyway – not so much out of revenge now, but out of a need to break the enchantment that the dragon/shadow holds.

Similarly, the real connection for me was that Jeremy, and what he did to my family, has made *me* the man I am now. Without that terrible event, I may never have left the safety of my extended; overprotected childhood and become the man I am. For that, I could almost *thank* Jeremy; but I would prefer not to. I also no longer feel the need to destroy him or reap any revenge, but hope that one day he too might be given the opportunity to take part in the kind of process I have had to go through. Jeremy is currently seeking leave to appeal his case.

I have also realised that in the sense of what I have gained, especially for my future wife and children, Bambs and the boys did not die in vain. It will always be a terrible loss to me, but I have not let it lie without giving the whole experience – their senseless sacrifice – some meaning. Making it count for something. That will never, on the other hand, make it all right.

There is a tremendous amount of grief in coming to the end of a journey, of closing one door in order to open another – standing on the threshold of a new adventure and looking back at what was . . . Much of those last weeks of writing was spent rediscovering relics of time gone by: photographs, letters, a tattered copy of an Al Stewart songbook; the words of 'Old Compton Street Blues' and 'Swiss Cottage Manoeuvres' reaching deeper into my soul than they ever did when I first heard them as a teenager.

During the weekend following my completion of the last chapter, I also finally found the time to read a book by Jungian analyst Jean Shinoda Bolen called *Ring of Power*. In it she explores the mythology behind the four operas which make up Wagner's 'Ring' cycle, as a metaphor for the entire dysfunction in modern Western civilisation; a dysfunction that centres around the quest for power as a substitute for love.

I was not at all surprised to see how much of the drama I had outlined in *this* book was laid out before me, like an ancient tapestry, in hers. There were so many parallels, not only with my own images of Jeremy – as the abandoned, loveless child, who sought power as compensation for something of which he had no psychological concept (that being love) – but also for me: in having awakened the 'heroic' part of myself, I had also left myself open to its numerous pitfalls.

The danger that, in having learned to fight my own battles and find success – in whatever form that might take – I might also, like Siegfried, lose sight of the people, places and events that made it all possible. Having spent so long in the battlefield, centuries, it is also very hard for us to put away our swords and risk, again, being vulnerable; that has been the terrible plight of many war veterans, as it certainly has been for me.

The status of hero can be very attractive, socially – *is* very attractive socially! But it can also blind us to other more creative possibilities. I could no more identify with the hero than I had previously done with my more negative traits. In order to really heal, I had to go back to being just Colin Caffell again – living in that 'space between the opposites'. Not trying to *be* one of them. And *that's* where my grief lay. I could no more be the hero than the villain.

It was also another paradox because, with publishing this book, I would be thrust further into the world of what I see as the extraordinary; life would never be the same again, nor did I want it to be. I felt I had learned something worth sharing, that regardless of what many 'caring professionals' might think, it *is* possible to get beyond the effects of the sort of nightmare I have been through *and* find genuine peace. If nothing else, I am setting a new target on the path.

Those of us who have been thrown into the category of victim, for whatever reason that might be, do not have to carry that label any longer than we want to. We can take steps to change our lot and say, 'No! This is not acceptable to me any more.' The same goes for religious abuse, as so much evil is done in the name of some god or another. As Phyllida Templeton, a dear friend and colleague of mine, who happens to be an ex-nun, says: 'Religious abuse legitimises other abuses.'

Her catalogue of thoughts on this is extensive, but at the bottom line, any subjugation of other human beings – adults or children – for whatever reason, is always to do with abuse of power. It is only when we learn to say 'No!' – as people like Mahatma Gandhi have shown us on a larger scale – that things really begin to change. The power structure crumbles.

When I had finished reading *Ring of Power*, I dug out the tape of 'Siegfried's Funeral Music', taken from the second act of *Götterdämmerung* (The Twilight of the Gods), the final opera of the 'Ring' cycle. It had been a long time since I last played that piece and, as before, I found myself racked with tears as I listened to it. I was overcome with grief.

But this time the music had also become a 'positive anchor' for me in that, before, it was an indulgence in melancholy, a 'negative anchor' – as it is for many who can only associate Wagner's music with Hitler and the Nazis – but now, in my own life, it had become a celebration, signifying the end of one very painful journey and the beginning of a new one that is, hopefully, far less painful.

It may sound like the whole saga has been put into a neat little package, with all the pains and hurts of my past dealt with and tidied away. But that's not the way it works. I have only touched upon some fairly basic psychological principles in order to push a few buttons and begin to destigmatise the whole idea of therapy being only for sick people.

True, there are many chronic, pathological cases where the wounding has been so bad it has become diseased. Bambs may have come into that category, but I suspect that this was not the case. Without seeing her clinical notes, however, I cannot say for certain. Nor do I feel I have the right to look. No, I am referring more to the kind of psychological wounding we all receive in some form during the course of our lives.

When a person is physically injured – a gash, for example – we stitch up the wound and treat for possible infection. That person is not sick, they are wounded. They only become sick when the wound is left untended and open to infection. That's when disease sets in. But even then, with tender loving care, healing can happen. Wounds also leave scars – patterns on the body which never go away, but still serve to remind us of what happened. For myself, I have found it much harder to sort out and deal with the psychological patterning of my childhood, which had been left untended for more than thirty years, than I have to deal with the effects of a domestic mass murder.

I had nothing to lose then by following the little voice inside, because I had nothing left to lose. My own body and soul knew what I needed in order to recover from that. But when it came to sorting out the layer upon layer of old wounding, some of which was still hurting (although I was numb to it), *then* I needed professional help. Kübler-Ross worked well for me, but for those who are not so turned on by the prospect of beating the hell out of telephone directories, there are numerous other forms of therapy available. What I have described in this book has only been my own way of surviving – what worked well for me.

In 1952, on the Japanese island of Koshima, scientists observing the social habits of a particular species of monkey, *Mucaca fuscata*, were feeding them with raw sweet potatoes dropped in the sand. The monkeys liked the taste of the sweet potatoes, but found the dirt unpleasant. An eighteen-month-old female, named Imo, found she could solve this problem by washing the potatoes in a nearby stream or in the sea. She taught this trick to her mother. Her playmates also learned this new way and they taught their mothers too.

This innovation was gradually picked up by various monkeys before the eyes of the scientists. Between 1952 and 1958, all the young monkeys on the island learned to wash the potatoes to make them more palatable. Only the adults who imitated their children learned to do this. Other adults kept eating the dirty potatoes. Then, in the autumn of 1958, something startling took place. A certain number of the Koshima monkeys were washing their potatoes – the exact number is not known – when suddenly, in a matter of hours, nearly every monkey on the island was washing its potatoes. But even more remarkable was the fact that it was not long before other colonies of the same species, across the sea on other islands, also began washing their sweet potatoes!

It appeared that when a certain critical number achieves an awareness (an arbitrary figure of one hundred was used), this new awareness can be communicated, telepathically, from mind to mind across almost the entire race.

In our society, we have tended to have rather a fatalistic belief that no matter what we do, our own little contribution to change things won't make one iota of difference. But none of us know if we might *be* the 'hundredth monkey' for the human race. Nor does it matter if we are only the tenth or the eighty-seventh monkey. We all make a contribution to the whole. In fact, we actually experience this phenomenon all the time in our society – but in reverse, as we pass on all our fear and negativity, rather than our inspiration.

We can't change other people by telling them to change, by telling them what they are doing wrong, it only elicits some form of retaliation or defensive behaviour. But we *can* begin to change things by changing ourselves, by taking responsibility for, and dealing with, all the worn-out attitudes and beliefs that have driven us far longer than can be healthy. I have long realised that I could never change my own family, even if I wanted to, but the more I began to grow and change in my own life, the more I noticed that they were also changing.

To give a very simple example, which brings it right down from the global/cosmic level to the family: at thirty-five, when I finally began to refuse my mother's hand-outs of cash, she could begin to let go of being a mother and start living her own life again. She didn't have to look after her little boy any more. That doesn't mean to say she ever stopped being Mum to me, it simply changed our relationship, which in turn had its own knock-on effect.

A few years later, she told me that she was glad I had been able to push the money back into her purse – much as she hated it at the time – because she knew she could never have done it herself. Mum now has a gang of friends that she hangs out with and life is very full for her. She now touches other people with her kindness. Imagine what might happen if we all began to deal with those crippling, destructive sides of our relationships, rather than constantly blaming others for what is wrong with our lives. We might have a lot more energy for real caring, real life and real fun.

There also comes a point when we must forget about gods and archetypes and fairy tales, strange supernatural forces, and remember that this story is predominantly about flesh-and-blood people, a family that could not sit down round the dinner table and interact or make the occasional *faux pas*. Like the time Nicholas, keen to make his own contribution to a story I was telling the family, about some really bad weather we had experienced on a weekend away, squealed excitedly, 'Yes, it was pissing down!'

Almost before he'd finished saying it, he began to wish he hadn't: Bambs and her father, barely hiding their amusement, tried to look shocked. Jeremy nearly sprayed a mouthful of food across the table. Daniel looked out of the window, disowning the remark altogether, glad that *he* hadn't said it, while June looked stonily at Nicholas, Bambs and myself all at the same time.

Trying desperately to keep a straight face, I looked at Nicholas, who was sitting next to me, and thought, 'Beam me up, Scottie!' but actually said, 'Who taught you to say things like that?' Nicholas, who had never lost any of his childish innocence, just grinned up at me, then looked away. We both knew the answer.

Remembering episodes like this, it is very clear to me that I have never stopped being a father, and always will be. Daniel and Nicholas will always be my sons.

So what happened with my quest to find the 'crock of gold' – my personal Grail? As a metaphor, was it simply an illusion, or did I really discover what I was looking for? At some time or another we all dream of finding the pot of gold at the end of the rainbow, yet it always seems an impossible dream; one which is within walking distance of a solution, yet forever just over the hill. And that's where it's meant to be: just out of reach and forever urging us forward.

Bambs dreamed of wealth and a strong, creative husband to fulfil a life without worry but, like Psyche, her dream was clouded by her beauty. Jeremy also dreamed of riches, but impatient for luxury and fast living – power – it ate at his soul, turned to greed and became his captor. Now he is even further away from the love that he and Bambs so desperately needed in an environment even more severe than the boarding school he had resented so much. *That* is a tragedy.

A child's view of a rainbow will always have mysterious significance, for we may never know what they have not yet forgotten. Nicholas often included one in his pictures but was never, as far as I know, told of the crock of gold. And in Daniel's case the gold was already in his heart as love and compassion. For me, it will always be the hope that, one day, I will meet my loved ones once again and walk with them in the forest of many colours. I also began to realise that, with all my searching on the horizon, I had failed to look at the ground at my feet, or inside me.

A rainbow is light broken down into its component parts; making the invisible visible and projecting it on a screen, usually a dark sky. In my own case a dark experience. Finding the pot of gold is about bringing all those colours back together again, inside our own hearts.

The twins knew where to find it – that crock of gold. In fact Nicholas even showed me his rainbow picture, if I had cared to look properly. He had drawn a bright yellow sun – which, as I said earlier, can often represent the father, in both the literal and spiritual sense – just below the foot of the rainbow. He was saying, in simple symbolic language, that the pot of gold, for him, was in heaven, in God, in the spiritual side of father; that everything I really needed was already in my hands, nowhere else.

The journey took many more twists and turns, with travels through many other dark tunnels before I began to realise this. My continuing work as a sculptor also played a powerful role, in that each piece, an image from the heart, led me to other unlived parts of myself, each with its own story and a key to unlock the next mystery.

And so it goes on . . . The rainbow has many colours, but like a dream it is only around for fleeting moments, and no matter how much we run towards it, we never seem to get any closer. It simply fades away into memory. And, like God, it is not something we can ever hang on to. But to experience its presence, in all its pure, vibrant colours, will always fill our hearts with joy. And that's all we can really hope for.

We are here,
we are not wanting.

We can all now love,
and laugh
and share our thoughts.

We can forget pride,
and live,
Can't we?

Bambs,
14 February 1976
St Valentine's Day

PART FIVE

In the Shadow of Angels
2018

For Sally and Juliette

CHAPTER TWENTY-NINE

A FTER THIS BOOK was originally completed in 1994, I felt I had crossed a threshold. The extraordinary journey of my life continued, bringing numerous opportunities that I would continue to grasp with both hands. Having said this, I also yearned to be 'normal' again, to be ordinary, but that was never going to be possible. Even though I was now completely at peace with my losses, I had to accept that there was a dark back story to my life that I was destined to live in the shadow of. In the same way that one can never get close to the end of a rainbow, this shadow followed me wherever I went.

When I eventually remarried and began a new family, this became even more challenging, especially for them. Having an unusual surname didn't help. There were many times I considered changing it, but by so doing I would render myself untraceable to everyone including friends and acquaintances. This would also negate any history of my creative achievements.

It was inevitable that Jeremy's attempts to appeal against his conviction would regularly hit the news-stands but on the whole, I tended to turn a blind eye and get on with my life. As far as I was concerned, the conviction was safe and not worth thinking about.

Although I had moved on, it seemed that the rest of the world had not, and with this I continued to experience a real sense of loneliness born out of endless stereotypical projections of how people imagined I should be, once they realised who I was and what I had been through. Over the years it was clear from people's reactions that I would be forever seen as a 'victim' and had to fight to earn the more realistic epithet of 'triumphant survivor', as I was once described in *Good Housekeeping* magazine. I could understand that meeting me confronted many with their worst nightmare, especially if they had children themselves, but they often didn't stick around long enough to find out that I was actually human, with a very positive outlook on life.

About the time of the original book launch, I was also actively involved in launching a self-help group for families of murder victims. Although it fulfilled a valuable role, I quickly realised that I was surrounded by people, many of whom needed to fiercely defend their right to be seen as victims, and I was the complete opposite, so I knew I had to leave in order to not be seen as a victim myself. To my mind, one can be victimised by circumstance, by events beyond one's control, but the role of 'victim' is nearly always a choice.

I had by this time begun training analysis as a requirement of my formal psychotherapy training; something I had begun a year earlier with encouragement from my Kübler-Ross colleagues, some of whom were beginning to refer clients to me. I couldn't have found a better person to help me through this next phase. Nicholas Spicer, a Jungian analyst who'd undergone his own analysis with one of the co-founders of the Jung Institute in Zurich, was absolute gold dust!

Nicholas, like Elisabeth Kübler-Ross, was a little unconventional in his approach to psychotherapy – a bit of a maverick who was not on my training institute's 'approved' list, but they could find no fault in his credentials. Knowing of my connection to Elisabeth, they asked instead what it was about me and 'mavericks'.

He had been recommended by someone who knew I was looking for a strong father figure, who could give me the kind of guidance my own father was ill-equipped to do. I had already interviewed several others who, when asked to tell me something about themselves, hid behind the therapeutic concept of the *tabula rasa* – the blank screen – a philosophy that I don't personally hold with.

When I told Nicholas that I wasn't going to 'spill the beans' about myself until I knew something about him, I didn't get a word in for the next forty minutes, as he related his own fascinating journey to becoming a Jungian analyst. When I finally got to tell him something about myself, he assured me that within a few sentences I had given him everything he needed to know. By his openness, he had my immediate respect and I left with a strong feeling that I was being heard and held. Thus began a very rich, intense and fruitful relationship that helped me further on that journey to truly grow up and embrace my potential.

During the next five years, I never asked Nicholas another thing about his own life, but was intrigued by the photograph in his consulting room of his wedding to someone who looked vaguely familiar. It was only after I finished analysis that I discovered he was married to one of Jill's classmates from school. Another of those curious coincidences that continue to remind me of those unseen guardians at my shoulder.

A more recent example of this occurred when I had my first very reassuring meeting with New Pictures and discovered the very next day that they had just engaged the husband of an old friend of my second wife as producer for the series. I met his wife-to-be for the first time at our wedding, and I met him at the wedding of the friend who accompanied me to that first meeting with New Pictures. These synchronicities will forever continue to excite and reassure me that things are still on the right track.

Over the years, like many of Elisabeth's staff, I began running anger and grief workshops outside of her programme and giving talks on that work in anticipation of her inevitable retirement or demise. We all knew how important a contribution Elisabeth's approach had been in helping to heal the devastating effects of trauma and loss, including Post Traumatic Stress Disorder (PTSD), especially in war veterans and families of murder victims. We couldn't let that slip away.

After one such talk at St James's Church in London's Piccadilly, I was approached by Neda, a young Croatian woman who had been running a programme providing holidays for children traumatised by the war in former Yugoslavia. The first summer camp had already happened the previous year in England, as their country settled into an uneasy peace. The next would be in Croatia. Neda asked if I could come and do what I 'do' to help them. I was very concerned that this might be extremely difficult with a language that was completely alien to me. 'Don't worry,' she said. 'I will translate. Just come!' Thus began several years of very successful summer camps for these war-weary youngsters.

In a way, we were kindred spirits. When so many bodies and souls have been ripped apart by war, and so graphically portrayed in the world's media, it is hard to imagine an explosion of love and joy in a group of people who have come through that war. But that is exactly what I experienced with this group of young Bosnians and Croatians, and not an ounce of 'victim' amongst them.

Aged between eight and twenty-three, they had all seen terrible things, had all experienced terrible losses: mothers, fathers, siblings, friends, their homes, and more than anything, their youthful innocence. One seventeen-year-old, Marko, for example, was late meeting a group of friends to play basketball and arrived just in time to see them receive a direct hit from a Serbian mortar grenade fired indiscriminately from surrounding countryside. Of the ten waiting for him in the square, only two barely survived the carnage. Marko suffered terrible survivor guilt.

I didn't know about the two badly injured survivors, Iljo and Ivica, or their horrific experiences until, with the encouragement of Marko and some of the others, they came on the following year's summer camp, also in Croatia. That second holiday was an important opportunity for all three boys to spend quality time together and begin to heal some of the painful emotional wounds that still lay between them, and to speak some of the things that had been left unspoken.

This was just one of the many horrendous stories that the group slowly began to share with us as their trust developed. Many had experienced the deaths or found the remains of their closest loved ones, and others had the agony of still not knowing if a missing relative, a father for example, was alive or not. They had all seen a lot of death.

When I first met them in Zagreb, from where we travelled to the ancient island of Korcula, I was surprised to see how much like our own teenagers they were. Seeing them so trendy and well-dressed really brought home their plight. They were young people trying to have a normal childhood, but behind the bright smiles, humour and beautiful faces, there lay a mountain of unexpressed pain.

I also realised that Daniel and Nicholas would then have been a similar age to many of them, as I would also be in age to some of their lost fathers and uncles. This could have been a minefield for me had it not been for my training with Elisabeth but also, perhaps, a rare and profound opportunity for mutual healing and repair.

I decided that if we did nothing else with our time together, I could do something to establish some common ground and create an opening ritual that would first honour those we had lost, and with that give ourselves and each other permission to have a really good time in their memory. I knew this would be another minefield for us all, but also knew that if my limited time there was going to make any difference to them, I was going to have to act fast.

It was clear from the look of trepidation on their faces as they came in that they would rather be somewhere else. It was our first evening in Korcula and, having spent the day resting and sunbathing after a long overnight bus ride, the older ones were all dressed up and ready to go out. I had placed candles, one for each of us, in the middle of the floor around a ring of soft clay into which they could push their individual candles as they were lit.

With Neda's help, I drew attention to the fact that we had been brought together because we had each experienced at least one violent bereavement, and that it was important to acknowledge this and actively remember those we had lost. This would also set a trend for each one being truly heard by everyone else. I asked Pamela, as our youngest, to light a large central candle for Peace on Earth. I then asked that they each light a candle from the one she had just lit, naming those they had lost and how they had died. With Neda translating, I went first, to show them what I meant, naming those I had lost and how.

It was a very difficult and beautiful ceremony, which ended with a birthday cake blaze of candles in the middle of the floor. Our birthday cake! So I suggested we all get down on our knees and blow them out.

I will never forget that tight circle of glowing, tear-filled faces, or the burst of laughter as the last candle went out. Later, I was told that although none of them had wanted to come to the ritual, they were glad I had pushed them. The rest of the week was spent sunbathing, playing in the sea and eating lots of ice cream. We made masks on each other's faces which were then painted to represent the faces they didn't show to the world, and clay objects representing something unpleasant that they'd like to leave behind.

These clay things were later thrown into the sea in another candle-lit ceremony on the final evening. Everybody, this time, was a willing participant.

The idea for this ritual evolved a few years earlier, when I created a personal letting-go ceremony at a remote Cornish cove, where I swam to the bottom of a gully on the seabed with a unique clay sculpture of a child-like me with the twins and left it there to dissolve. When the piece of wood it was on floated to the surface, I knew it was complete. That same weekend, I also cast the twins' wicker crib and Sheila's modelling portfolio into the deep ocean near the mines at Land's End. With a close friend as silent witness, these rituals were both incredibly powerful for me.

If loving cohesiveness had marked the nature of that first group, with people remarking that there was something special in how we interacted with each other, the next much larger group from different communities was more like a controlled explosion. Our main task then was to make the container strong enough to hold those powerful energies, but loose enough to also live in the moment. It was those numerous 'moments' that grew to be our most treasured memories: animated sea battles on hired pedalos, cushion fights in the clubroom and curfew challenges that turned into candlelit sing-songs on the beach after midnight.

There were also quieter, more subtle 'moments'.

One afternoon I wandered into the clubroom to discover eleven-year-old Alen giving one of the fifteen-year-old girls a back massage, and Sanela, a seventeen-year-old who had lost her father, doing the same to Iljo's heavily scarred body. This had followed my expressed concerns that the group were tending to come to us to do things for them, when they needed to start turning to each other for support, because within a few days we would no longer be there.

For many, the need for safe, appropriate touch was essential to their emotional healing. This is where the mask-making and massage were so valuable, in that both required a deep level of trust and sensitivity. For Iljo and Ivica, two good-looking, once athletic teenagers who were now regarded by many of their peers as cripples, and hence a little untouchable, there had been little experience of caring touch since the grenade had left them with terribly mutilated limbs.

Iljo, especially, used every opportunity to be helped in this way, being one of the first to have a plaster mask made on his face and to receive massage. Not long after, we heard that he had regained his confidence so much that on a Zagreb hospital visit he had found a very beautiful girlfriend.

Nearly three years on, during a personal visit to their home town of Orasje on the banks of the River Sava, there were still many signs of the war as we crossed a temporary floating bridge from Croatia into Bosnia – the original having been destroyed in the conflict. We passed a burnt-out Serbian tank and buildings still pockmarked from gunfire and explosions. Ilija, another of the original group who had collected me from Zagreb airport, also took me to the graves of the eight basketball players who had been killed in the Serbian mortar attack. The date on each one shouted loud from the cold stone: 7th August 1995. Exactly ten years to the day from when Sheila and the twins had died. It was an unexpected but sobering moment for me.

Looking back, I think my relationship with those wonderful young people helped pave the way for the next stage of my life: becoming a husband and father again. I finally felt ready to settle down but as it turned out, not with Jill, the woman with whom I had spent a big part of my adult life.

Jill and I were together for the second time in our lives for about eight years. In many ways it was as if we *had* been married. Jill was a long-haul airline stewardess with a passion for literature and I was struggling to write this book and make some sense of the appalling tragedy that had befallen my family. It also felt safe because, like Heather and a few others, Jill knew the twins – and that was very important to me then.

If the truth be known, we were an ideal match during that period, because I needed the time and mental space to write and reflect on the journey of my life; she fulfilled her passion for travel and the time it gave her for reading. On her returns she would be my toughest critic, cross-examining every nuance of my thought processes, but when the book was finished, it left little to sustain the relationship. By the time it was published, although still good friends, we had parted again.

A few more years passed with one final attempt to make it work, but that also failed. Neither of us had ever felt completely settled together, but without Jill I may never have finished the book. I will always love her for the way she stuck by me through the most difficult times – a bit like a mother – and that, I suspect, is why things would never have worked. She gave me the world, literally, with her airline travel concessions, but knew I had to grow up and leave home.

CHAPTER THIRTY

I FIRST MET MY second wife, Sally, at the Findhorn Foundation in Scotland. I was one of a number of invited speakers at their 1998 Easter conference on the subject of 'Conscious Living and Conscious Dying'. I was also going to be giving a clay workshop as an experiential demonstration of one of the ways I worked with people in groups. Needless to say, I was feeling very nervous about speaking in front of over three hundred people, especially knowing that many were leading lights in the New Age movement.

Findhorn's co-founder, Eileen Caddy, came in one door to hear me. Phyllis Krystal, author of *Cutting the Ties That Bind*, through another. Jill, whom I hadn't seen since we finally split up six months earlier, was also there, having stayed on to help out after another workshop the previous week. Seeing all three come in, I reached for the hand of my friend Sarah Boyle (wife of ex-convict and sculptor, Jimmy Boyle), who was sitting next to me at the time. Then Sally walked in, looking more glamorous than was usual for Findhorn. She was there to cover the conference on behalf of *Positive News*, a journal that focused specifically on good news.

Sally introduced herself to me straight after the talk, saying that she had already put her name down for my workshop that afternoon. She had seen that the list was full, but added her name anyway. On hearing this, I pointed out that she could only take part if someone else dropped out. Luckily for her, and for me, someone did.

After the workshop, we agreed to meet at another activity that evening and discovered that we lived only a mile or so apart in the same area of London. Jill, seeing the obvious spark between us, left the following day.

Some months later, well into our relationship, Sally told me that when she first noticed me across the auditorium, she thought to herself, 'Oh, he looks nice,' at which point a voice in her head clearly said, 'That's the father of your child!' Surprised at this sudden intrusion, she did a double-take, saw me holding hands with the woman next to me and assumed I was already attached. It was only when I got up to give my talk that Sally realised I was running the clay workshop she had signed up for.

Years later, she told me that if that intuition hadn't happened, like others before her, she might never have entered the relationship once she'd heard about my past. It also came as quite a shock, because motherhood had not been part of her plan; she was a free-spirited, well-travelled journalist and music presenter on a national radio station. When we discovered Sally was pregnant a year later, we were even more surprised, because problems during an earlier operation had nearly resulted in a hysterectomy to save her life. Yehudi Gordon, the brilliant gynaecologist who had saved her womb, described the pregnancy and subsequent birth of our daughter as 'a miracle'.

Being a parent again was something I had thought long and hard about. There was always going to be a very real danger of idealised projection of the twins onto a new baby, not just from me but also from those who knew the boys well; for this beautiful new child to find herself in the shadow of little boys who were regarded by many as 'angels'. I had to be very sure in myself that she would not be an emotional replacement, but seen for her own unique qualities. It was therefore an enormous relief to find we had a daughter on the way, sparing her the risk of any potential comparisons had she been a boy.

We hadn't felt the need to get married, but one day in the early summer of 1999, Sally was in a local dress shop in Primrose Hill, trying on outfits to suit an expanding waistline, when I spotted a very simple full-length, white cotton dress. I asked her to try it on. She looked fantastic! Later that afternoon I went back to the shop and had it gift wrapped. Back at the flat I handed Sally the package and said, 'I don't want to see you in this until the day we get married.'

A few months later, wearing that same simple dress, with her hair garlanded in fresh flowers, we had a white wedding in the village church where she grew up. At seven months pregnant, Sally raised a few eyebrows but looked amazing, like one of the fair maidens in Botticelli's wonderful painting *Primavera*. Much to our surprise, a shaman from Indonesia, whom Sally had met in Australia the previous year, turned up quite unexpectedly that morning and drummed her into church as she stepped from a neighbour's 1950s Bentley.

It was a very happy day for everyone in all its spontaneity, but the memory is also tinged with some sadness. The last time I saw my father in health was at our reception, where I had the sudden urge to kiss him goodbye as we left. His surprised response was, 'Well, that's the first time in my life I have ever been kissed by a grown man!' At which point Dan, my best man, also kissed him and said with a big smile, 'Well, there's the second time, Reg!'

Sally and I drove off a few moments later with Dad looking kind of pleased, but also rather flustered. The next time I saw my father was less than a week later in a coma at University College Hospital in London. He'd had a massive stroke. Dad never regained consciousness and died within a few more days. I felt at the time that he couldn't face falling in love with another grandchild and decided to let go.

I sat with him for many hours during those last few days, holding his hand and speaking to him, completing any remaining 'unfinished business' between us as best I could. I had learned from Elisabeth that even though they cannot respond, those in a coma *can* hear (and possibly see) everything quite clearly. Before his funeral, I made a terracotta urn for his ashes, onto which my mother, sister, nieces and Sally inscribed special messages before it was fired. His remains were then buried in this at Highgate Cemetery with Sheila and the twins.

Two months later, our beautiful daughter Juliette was born. Once delivered, I would not let her out of my sight, following the nurses closely to where they performed a quick health check. I then carried our beautiful little girl to Sally's arms myself. Like my own father at my birth, I was almost Juliette's first physical contact with the world. I knew then that my greatest challenge would be to hold her safely in my care, but without being over-protective. Understandably, there are times this hasn't been easy.

Although I'd had the experience of being a parent before, the demands were still quite a shock for two people in their mid-forties.

Sally had managed to maintain her commitment to broadcasting, but motherhood was more important to her and she realised it was time to stop. I had also been maintaining my psychotherapy practice at my London flat, commuting three days a week, but that also began to split my emotional and mental resources, so I decided to wind down the practice as well.

Up to that point, press intrusion had been non-existent, because we had chosen to live in properties that were still in Sally's maiden name. That all changed when we combined our resources and found a larger detached house not far from her Berkshire cottage, where we were now spending most of our time. Dated and run-down, the new house in an acre of beech woodland needed a lot of work but we loved it. It was our dream home.

Unfortunately, I now became easy to find again. Before this, I had been able to reassure Sally that these activities in the press had been purely an attempt by Jeremy to remain in the public eye and not be forgotten. What I hadn't allowed for was the fact that there were plenty of ambitious lawyers out there, who would like nothing better than to overturn Jeremy's high-profile conviction and build their reputations on the back of it.

It was one morning when I was on the roof with the builders that we had our first visit from tabloid hacks. Fortunately, I looked like one of the workmen and the contractor dealt with them brilliantly, sending them on a wild-goose chase to a distant village on the other side of the River Thames. Unfortunately, it wasn't long before they found Sally at the cottage. Closing the door in someone's face without comment was not something Sally was able to do easily. Her polite middle-class upbringing precluded such rudeness. She believed she could convince reporters that what they were doing was wrong. She had a very rude awakening. Even after twenty years, and much coaching from me, she still struggles not to engage in such conversations.

Not long after this, two passenger jets were flown into the World Trade Center in New York as a heinous act of terrorism.

On that ghastly afternoon, the whole world changed.

This single event increased everyone's level of fear and keeping a toehold in London became less attractive for both of us. Visits from the press also increased along with Jeremy's determined efforts to curtail his prison career. After a series of well-documented legal challenges through the CCRC (Criminal Cases Review Commission), he finally won the right to a full appeal hearing against his conviction. This time it seemed his lawyers might just win the case on a point of law.

We had already been contacted with news of this by DC Terry Whitlock, our lovely family support officer from Essex Police, who generally kept us informed of new developments, but it still came as a shock when formally announced in the press.

Terry was like a guardian angel. He explained that within days we would be contacted by a newly appointed team of detectives from City of London Police, and that numerous visits would be likely. They would be spending the next six months sifting through every detail of the original investigation, in order to re-present evidence on behalf of the Crown and prove that the original conviction was safe. He also said they would try not to disrupt our family life any more than necessary.

Inevitably, with so much evidence to go over, they would invariably stay longer than planned and Juliette would often return from playgroup to be greeted by these big strangers with dark suits and grim faces. To give them their due, they made every effort to appear easygoing and relaxed in front of her, but it didn't really wash.

They explained to us that they had to go through everything with a fine-toothed comb and, it would seem, second-guess every possible avenue that Jeremy's lawyers might try to build a case on. The police could not present any fresh evidence, even if they had it, but did have the freedom to clarify and consolidate any of the existing evidence, including DNA testing of blood samples, which didn't exist at the time of the first investigation. They would need a mouth swab from me and would be having one sent from Christine, Sheila's biological mother in Canada. Did I by any chance have any locks of the twins' hair, or milk teeth?

I had three milk teeth that I kept in a special box.

They explained that to make the test, the sample would need to be ground to a fine powder. They would possibly need two teeth to be sure, but would return the remaining one if they could. I felt very upset, reluctant, but knew I had to agree.

It was clear that, like me, they had absolutely no doubts about Jeremy's guilt, but also accepted that very clever lawyers have liberated some very dangerous people in the past. When it gets to this level of advocacy, these appeals are rarely to do with justice.

I also became very concerned for our safety should he be released. Over the years, I had probably been the biggest thorn in Jeremy's side, repeatedly countering the many claims his supporters had made on his behalf that Sheila was the murderer. He could accuse all the other key witnesses of having an ulterior motive for testifying against him, but with me he couldn't. Jeremy knew that I would never stand to benefit from his conviction, thereby making my only motive to see justice done.

We were all very aware that Jeremy had already proved himself more than capable of diverting attention from himself in a major crime. He'd now had nearly twenty years in prison to plan similar revenges. The best way he could hurt any of us would be through our families.

Seeing my realistic concerns, our next visit was from a police security specialist to ensure that our doors and windows were completely secure, and advise us on keeping safe in and around our home. Living in a rather remote woodland location steadily felt less idyllic and we soon found ourselves looking for a bolthole where we couldn't be found, and could put it in Sally's name.

Fearing for Sally and Juliette's safety, I also began concocting spurious reasons to leave, to 'draw the fire' so to speak. But Sally was having none of it. She was in for the long haul.

By chance, shortly after Juliette's rather late christening, Sally found an ad in the *Henley Standard* for a last-minute holiday let in West Cornwall. She loved her first visit there and by the end of that week was looking in estate agent windows. I couldn't believe my luck. She was falling in love with a part of the world that was very dear to my own heart. Before long we found a charming cottage with a secluded private garden in the middle of the village. It was full of old-world features and we couldn't help but love our much-needed home from home. Juliette was about two years old by then and with her being of pre-school age, we spent quite a lot of time there, especially off season.

Little Juliette was very much a water baby, racing for the water's edge like a newly hatched turtle, no matter how big the waves. We couldn't risk taking our eyes off her for one second! More than anything, there was a real sense of security for her, because local residents would always keep an eye out for all the village children. Added to this, many of the other parents we met on the beach were also professional artists and quickly became good friends.

In December 2002, the appeal judges, having examined all the evidence and trial records that were presented to them, decreed that Jeremy's conviction was still safe. If anything, the trial jury's original verdict was made stronger by the review of the evidence that was being challenged.

Notwithstanding the fact that in 1994 the Home Office, prompted by the European Court of Human Rights, ruled that all prisoners who had been given a whole-life tariff over the stated twenty-five-year life tariff be informed of this. Jeremy was one of that select group. Up to that point, such disclosure was not a requirement in law but, if anything, that had made him feel all the more dangerous and this appeal process all the more stressful for us as a couple.

We were, of course, enormously relieved and could begin to sleep easily again, but our dream home was now somehow tainted by all this. We also knew that we would eventually have to tell Juliette about her half-brothers and the circumstances of their deaths. I knew from having worked with people who were left full of rage and an unbearable sense of betrayal, after not being informed of such events through reluctance on the part of their adult carers. We couldn't let that happen to Juliette.

It was terribly difficult, because the enormity of such information was almost too much for any adult to take in without some degree of shock. In dealing with a five-year-old who looks to her parents to always keep her safe, the implications were far more complicated in that, in a child's eyes, I, her father, would have already failed in that undertaking. She would need an enormous amount of reassurance from me.

We decided that Juliette was too young to know how the boys died, but it seemed important that she knew of their existence and that a tragic event had ended their lives. Even that was hard to tell her and fraught with uncertainty about how to answer any ensuing questions. It was also important that she understood that these were not Mummy's children and that Daddy had been married to another Mummy long before. At least Sally hadn't failed in her role of protector.

We spoke about the issue with the school and they arranged for a counsellor to advise us, but it quickly became clear that this woman was completely out of her depth and we would be much better dealing with it in our own way. I then remembered Nicholas Spicer once telling me that I was probably the most qualified therapist in Britain to help others with these issues. I had to trust this. As it turned out, the existence of the twins didn't come as too much of a surprise to Juliette, with her being familiar with the school photograph of them at Grandma's, so she seemed to also take the news of them being dead in her stride.

Up to that point she had just thought that these were two little boys that Grandma knew. She did, however, immediately ask how they had died. Fortunately, our suggestion that 'a very bad man killed them' seemed to satisfy her curiosity. It was only some years later that, thanks to Google, she got the whole ugly truth.

Juliette had been playing with some of her ten-year-old school friends at one of their houses, where children's access to the internet was more relaxed than in our own home. They decided to Google their names to see what would come up. When it came to Juliette's turn, they were confronted with a collection of Google images that included a brutally shocking photograph of Sheila's bloodstained corpse with the bullet wounds to her neck. Needless to say, it was a very difficult moment for her both emotionally and socially.

In my opinion, I think she is still dealing with the repercussions of that event, albeit unconsciously, as is often the case with childhood trauma. God knows what the implications might have been had we not told her when she was five. The puerile behaviour of Jeremy's supporters who made those social media posts is absolutely disgraceful. One wonders what they could possibly hope to achieve by it? Thankfully, this image now seems to have been removed.

Juliette has since developed into a very beautiful and very bright young woman, who has an exciting life of possibilities open to her. Like the majority of youngsters growing up in today's world, life has had its challenges. Despite these, it has been wonderful to watch our little bird learning to fly. With my full encouragement and blessing, she has also decided to drop my surname.

After a long search, and what seemed like hundreds of viewings in Devon and Cornwall, we eventually found the house we are now in, also with a large woodland garden, but right on the edge of the village in sight of the pub. Juliette was six years old by then.

Although we were very sad to leave Berkshire, for me this move would be another chance to start fresh. I would have the freedom to put away the past and immerse myself in a new community, who didn't associate me with a tragic back story. It would also enable Sally and Juliette to thrive without that burden. The far west of Cornwall has long been a hub for British modernist art, including the foundation of the studio pottery movement by Bernard Leach in the early 1920s – hence a Tate Gallery in the remote Cornish town of St Ives. I felt that here I could, with hard work, begin to establish myself in my own right solely as an artist.

It was also rather lovely, because the Cornish don't seem to be at all interested in who you were before you arrived. They only want to know what you are going to do once you are there. First off, I joined a male voice choir and began selling my work in a few local galleries. Sally got involved in helping to launch the local community radio station. Even though we still had our lovely holiday cottage, this alone was not going to provide sufficient income, so we also acquired a beautiful but rather unusual art gallery right by the Atlantic Ocean, selling exclusively Cornish art – something else that cemented our place in the community.

In time we got to know a number of the leading artists, some of whom we met because they were already with the gallery. Others came through our ever-increasing circle of new friends. The physical environment was also beginning to have a significant impact on my work, in particular my pottery. Watching the constantly changing colour, textures and atmosphere of the sea and cliffs from the gallery window stirred something in me: could I make my glazes, which were ostensibly chemical reactions, behave more like pigments in an abstract painterly way? This single question was the catalyst for a style of work that began to establish me as a serious artist in the area and continues to do so.

As a sculptor, I also eventually left a permanent mark on the Cornish landscape by creating a memorial to the hard rock miners of the coastal region, which consisted of a 4-metre-high figure set in a sub-tropical garden, which I also designed.

So why was I, a Londoner, chosen to do this?

It all goes back to the early 1970s, when I used to collect rocks and minerals as a hobby. During that time, I got to know many of the working miners drinking in the local pub. I was very keen to go underground and see for myself where the crystals came from and often mentioned this. One evening Jim Taylor, a mining contractor, offered to take me down on his night shift. An hour later, kitted up with helmet and lamp, I was being thrown from side to side as we hurtled down the Skip Shaft at Levant Mine in a four-man cage.

We went more than 1,400 feet underground to where Jim and his team were working. He also took me to the level just below the seabed, where one could hear rocks grinding away at the ocean floor only feet above our heads. It was a profound experience that I will never forget: the intense heat, the cramped, filthy working conditions, and more than anything the mischievous gallows humour of the men.

Nearly forty years later, shortly after our move to Cornwall, I noticed a heated debate in the local paper about the selected design for a proposed memorial statue. Most people didn't like it. Neither did I. The figure looked more like one of the Village People, a camp American pop group of the disco era. It was certainly nothing like any of the men that I remembered. I joined the debate, suggesting the design should be put out to tender to local sculptors and selected by the community, not a committee. I soon received a letter thanking me for my suggestion and inviting me to join other local artists in submitting a design to be chosen in a public vote.

The actual brief was for a 'modern miner with a rock drill', but something didn't feel right about that; it ran the risk of looking more like a soldier with an anti-aircraft gun, like a war memorial. Knowing the design would be chosen by the community, I dug into the emerging 'maverick' side of my own Shadow and decided to go against the brief.

Having spoken to local people, many of whom expressed a preference for a man with a pick, I realised that the miner's pick was a potent symbol that served to unite all Cornish miners through the centuries. It was also a fact that many of the underground fatalities were suffered by the 'diggers' in rock collapses. These were the men whose job it was to use a pick or drill steel to clean up the stope after blasting. My design won seventy-one per cent of the vote.

The finished figure was installed at the entrance to Geevor Mine in 2016 with a ceremonial unveiling by the Lord Lieutenant of Cornwall, Colonel Edward Bolitho. The positive feedback from ex-miners, not only from Cornwall, has been phenomenal. I feel humbled that it soon became a place of quiet reflection for mining families and visitors alike.

For many years I lived with the events of 1985 as a constant back story, from which I couldn't escape. Part of my reason for moving to Cornwall was to enter a new community that didn't know me for that episode. During the twelve years since the move, I have worked hard to make a name for myself here in my own right.

In successfully completing the miners' memorial and more recently being elected to membership of the prestigious Penwith Society, founded by Barbara Hepworth amongst others, I am now succeeding in that endeavour and feel free to be more open about my past, but more than anything, to feel openly proud of what I achieved on that dark journey that went before. I don't feel I have to hide it any more.

It is said that in every creative endeavour there is something of the artist's autobiography. It was only recently, long after the statue's unveiling, that I realised that as well as fulfilling its purpose as a memorial to the tough, hard-working miners of Cornwall, it also symbolically represented me and my own re-emergence into the light of day, from the shadow of a long and challenging journey in the underworld.

This insight, I think, gave me the courage and clarity to support the television dramatisation, ensuring as much as possible that the story was properly told and the salacious myths about my first wife, Sheila Caffell, were laid to rest once and for all.

As a final word, a robin flew into the gallery and perched on the desk in front of me as I finally completed these two new chapters. This kind of robin encounter had not happened to me in all the years since writing the original book. I don't know who or what I am thanking, but thank you.

Bibliography

Dr Susan Bach, *Life Paints Its Own Span: On the Significance of Spontaneous Pictures by Severely Ill Children,* Daimon Verlag, 1991.

Gregg M. Furth, *The Secret World of Drawings: A Jungian Approach to Healing Through Art,* Inner City Books (2nd ed.), 2002.

Elisabeth Kübler-Ross, *Living with Death and Dying,* Souvenir Press, 1982.

Acknowledgements

THERE ARE MANY heroes in this story; people who have made great contributions in a small way, quietly, and those who have made small contributions in a great way. I would love to sing their praises but out of respect for privacy, many will remain unnamed and largely unsung, but their stories, their presence and their love have all touched my life in some way. I would also like to give special thanks to those who have specifically allowed me to colour the telling of my own story with theirs. You all know who you are.

Then there are those I *can* name.

In the publishing field I would like to thank Humphrey Price, my original editor, who, because of common ground in life's experiences, was able to both accept and challenge me in a way other editors may not have been able to. Thank you for seeing the value of this book, for being part of its magic and patiently polishing the windows, like facets of a crystal, so that others might also see clearly inside.

Rowena Webb and Ian Wong, currently at Hodder, who have helped me condense the significant events of the last twenty-five years into two meaningful chapters, and Jasmine Marsh, my publicist.

At New Pictures, I would particularly like to thank Willow Grylls for steering the television project with such sensitivity, and for hiring a great team to bring it all together: Kris Mrksa (screenplay), Lee Thomas (producer) and Paul Whittington (director); actors Mark Stanley and Freddie Fox, who played me and Jeremy respectively, for using me as a sounding board in their character development; Mark Ezra for supporting me through that first meeting.

Cathryn Summerhayes, Luke Speed, Idina Imrik and Irene Magrelli at Curtis Brown for looking after all the contractual stuff in relation to both book and television production. I couldn't have done it without you.

I would like to give special thanks to my wife, Sally, for loving and supporting me through the unexpected ups and downs of the last twenty years. It takes enormous courage and fortitude to live with the repercussions of a tragedy that you were never part of, especially in relation to a husband's earlier love.

I would further like to thank Jill for not only keeping me alive and sane on the first part of the journey, but also for not killing me on the numerous occasions she may have felt like it; she has been not only a friend and travelling companion, but literary task master and bullshit detector; the battles, which I usually lost, were often fierce. In order to accompany me on that journey, she also had to find the courage to travel her own equally difficult course along that path.

Chris Precious, a friend of long standing, for being there in both the good and the bad times – for both Bambs and myself; for his patient guidance during my early attempts at writing, but most of all, for sitting through the whole trial and collating most of the gruesome bits for this book when I still couldn't look at them.

Mary Lewis, Yvonne Roberts and Peter Jay for their additional support and guidance with my early scribbles, and to Sandra Precious for typing it all up before I got the word processor.

Jan Flowers, for being everything she was to Daniel and Nicholas, and to me; her mother, Ann, for also being all those things and a friend; Nick for his love and gentleness; and Herbie for 'Tuba Smarties' in Dunstable.

Dan Doherty, one of my dearest friends, for his unwavering love, support and generosity of self.

And all those who also held us together when everything was falling apart, especially Bruce (for that long drive to Colchester and all the hot food when nobody else could cook); Salah, for holding me like he did; Patrick, for all the beautiful songs and a loving funeral service; Sandra, for the reading; Jim and Min in Cornwall, and Stella and Ole in Somerset, for giving me safe places to escape to when I most needed it; P.L-T. and Kathy at Sky's office; John, Steamy, Tristan, Kevin, Francis, Tony and Haydon, Mark and Steve, Big Jim, Ronnie, Paul and all the others, for the gift of music; and David

Bray, for miraculously getting the press off my doorstep after Jeremy's arrest.

All those who wrote to me when you did. Many thanks.

Michael Ainsley of Essex Police and Barry McKay of City of London Police, for managing the investigations properly; and Stan Jones, for sticking with it and surviving them.

All those who have helped to fill out the picture with their own stories and anecdotes, especially Pamela, Robert and David Boutflour, Ann and Peter Eaton, Jackie Wood, Anthony Pargeter, Barbara Wilson, Bambs's best friend, Tora, Caroline Salmon and all the others who have been lost in the blur of time.

Betty Shine and Michael Bentine, for first opening up the door to other realities, and Laurens van der Post, for inspiring the spirit of adventure and encouraging dear Nick Spicer to become a Jungian psychotherapist.

Elisabeth Kübler-Ross for all her love, encouragement and inspiration, but even more so to her workshop staff, who became my professional colleagues; especially those who have either pushed me through some of my greatest barriers, allowing me to fall apart safely, or have brought a smile to my face in those moments of great adversity: Sharon Tobin, Jacob Watson, Bobbi Leone, Phyllida Templeton, Eolath Magee, Megan Bronson, Dianne Arcangeli, Shannon Steck, David and Nancy Mullins and so on . . .

Sculptor and 'maverick' Tony Southwell VPRBA, for taking a special interest in my work and becoming a great friend and mentor.

Finally but not least: Mum, who is still going strong, for spirit and love of nature.

Dad, for giving me everything he possibly could.

Diane, my sister, for always being available but never imposing.

Juliette, Lucy and Abbi, Chantelle, Chloe, William, Janie, Laura and Miranda – the next generation – for being children when you were. This story is for you.

Many of those mentioned in the original acknowledgements, and others who played significant roles in my continuing journey, have since graduated from this life – with full honours! I miss every single one of you.

*   *   *

In addition to this, I would like to give special thanks to the following for kindly allowing me to reproduce their photographs: APA/SWpix. com, Harry Dempster/Daily Star/Express Syndication, Einer Borchgrevink, Robert Boutflour, Arthur Strutt, William Finnigan, Mike Newman and Christine, Bambs's mother, for the photograph of us all together.

Also to the following for kindly allowing me to reproduce their poems: Roger McGough, for 'Dreampoem', Olav Hauge, for 'Slowly the Truth Dawns', George Smith, for 'In Memoriam' and Peter Jay, for 'To a Murderer'.

'Slowly the Truth Dawns', translated by Robin Fulton, is from *Don't Give Me the Whole Truth* by Olav H. Hauge, published by Anvil Press Poetry in 1985.

'Dreampoem', reprinted by permission of the Peters, Fraser and Dunlop Group Limited.

Excerpt from 'East Coker', *Four Quartets* by T. S. Eliot reproduced with permission from Faber and Faber Ltd.

Bambs, June and Jeremy with Jasper the dog at the front of Whitehouse Farm.

June and Nevill with baby
Sheila at Whitehouse, 1957.

Bambs and Jeremy at Whitehouse.

Bambs at Vaulty Manor Farm, 1985.

June and Nevill outside the kitchen door at Whitehouse Farm.

Daniel (*left*) and Nicholas (*right*), 5 years old.

The funeral at Tolleshunt d'Arcy. From left to right in the foreground:
Julie Mugford, Jeremy, myself, my sister Diane and, behind me, my mother.
I never saw Jeremy's face close-up that day.

The twins' funeral, West Hampstead, London. From left to right:
My sister, Jan, myself, Heather and, behind me, my father.

Bambs the model.

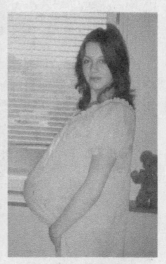

Two days till delivery.

And later, the newly elated mother.

Wedding day, 4½ months
pregnant and proud of it.

The only photograph of us all together, Easter weekend 1985. Nicholas has a new tooth coming through.

Story time at Whitehouse, Nevill and the twins.

Christmas at Whitehouse. Left to right: Nicholas, Jeremy, June, Daniel and Nevill.

Nicholas and Daniel's school photograph.

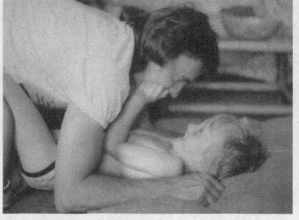

Me playing with Daniel at his Mum's.

The twins' 4th birthday party, with my mother, father and Herbie in the picture; Daniel is in the Superman outfit.

Patradonna (*bronze*), my first sculpture.

Drawing of Daniel, December 1985.

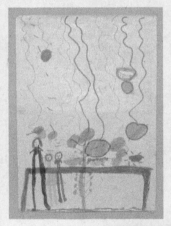

Nicholas's party picture, drawn 4 days before his death.

The author with the Tin Miners' Memorial in Cornwall, 2016.

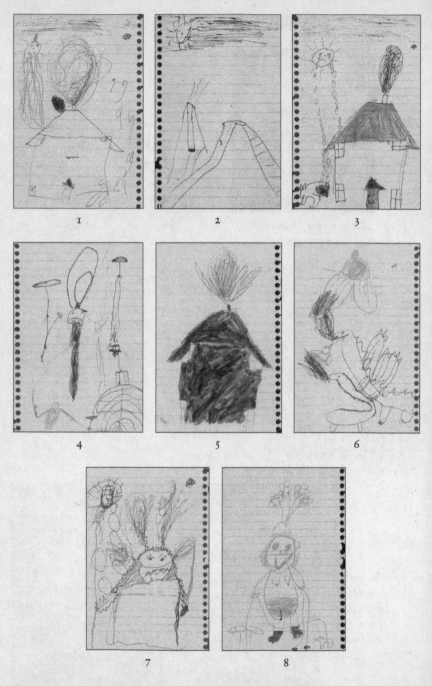

Daniel's 'Book', as described in Chapter 14.